Advantage Tennis

Advantage Tennis
racket work, tactics, and logic

Jack Barnaby

HARVARD UNIVERSITY

ALLYN AND BACON, INC.
boston london sydney

Photos on pages 1, 9, 105, 143, 175, 199, and 223
courtesy of the *Boston Globe*.

Copyright © 1975 by Allyn and Bacon, Inc.,
470 Atlantic Avenue, Boston, Massachusetts
02210

Portions of this book first appeared in
Racket Work: The Key to Tennis. Copyright ©
1969 by Allyn and Bacon, Inc.

Library of Congress Cataloging in Publication Data

Barnaby, John M
 Advantage tennis: racket work, tactics, and logic.

 Published in 1969 under title: Racket Work.
 Includes index.
 1. Tennis. I. Title.
GV995.B37   1975   796.34'22   74-22246

ISBN   0-205-04686-X

Contents

Contents

Contents

Foreword

THE ALLYN AND BACON
SPORTS EDUCATION SERIES
Arthur G. Miller,
Consulting Editor

Sports play a major role in the lives of practically everyone—the players, the coaches, the officials, and the spectators! Interest in sports is the result of several factors.

There is increased emphasis on *personal physical fitness*. Formal exercises or calisthenics, while worthwhile, are not as popular nor as motivating to the promotion of fitness as participation in sports. Through *sports participation*, children and adults gain fitness but also develop skills, group and personal satisfactions, and enjoyment.

Another factor in the growing interest in sports is the increase in television and radio broadcasts of sporting events. Team sports such as baseball, football, basketball, soccer, and hockey are seasonally covered by practically all channels. The lifetime sports including bowling, golf, tennis, and skiing are also receiving more air time. Activities such as gymnastics, swimming, and other aquatic sports have, and will continue to receive, more expanded coverage. The analysis of skills and strategy within each sport by knowledgeable commentators using instant video replay and stop-action techniques, makes the game or activity more interesting to the viewer.

The Allyn and Bacon Sports Education Series has been created to meet the need for players,

coaches, and spectators to be informed about the basic and advanced skills, techniques, tactics, and strategies of sports. Each book in the Series is designed to provide an in-depth treatment of a selected sport or activity. Players find the individual skills and accompanying picture sequences very valuable. Coaches gain basic and advanced knowledge of individual and team play along with techniques of coaching. Sports fans are provided information about the activities and are thus able to become more knowledgeable about and appreciative of the basic and finer aspects of sports.

The authors of the *Sports Education Series* have been carefully selected. They include experienced teachers, coaches, and managers of college and professional teams. Some books represent the combined effort of two or more authors, each with a different background and each contributing particular strengths to the text. For other books, a single author has been selected, whose background offers a breadth of knowledge and experience in the sport being covered.

Among the authors and titles of some of the team-sport books is George Allen, successful coach of the Washington Redskins, who collaborated with Don Weiskopf on the information book *Inside Football*. Weiskopf also wrote with Walter Alston, of the Los Angeles Dodgers, the *Complete Baseball Handbook;* and *The Baseball Handbook*. The book *Basketball—Concepts and Techniques*, by Bob Cousy and Frank Power, presents the game for men. *Women's Basketball*, by Mildred Barnes of Central Missouri State University, covers the "new" five-player game for girls and women. Dr. Barnes also wrote the book *Field Hockey. The Challenge of Soccer* is by Hubert Vogelsinger, coach of the Boston Minutemen, and the book *Winning Volleyball* was written by Allen Scates of UCLA. A group of authors including General Managers Jack Kelley of the New England Whalers and Milt Schmidt of the Washington Capitols collaborated on the book *Hockey—Bantam to Pro*.

Individual sports included in the series are: *Advantage Tennis: Racket Work, Tactics, and Logic* by Jack Barnaby of Harvard University, *Modern Track and Field for Girls and Women* by Donnis Thompson of the University of Hawaii, *Track and Field* by Jim Bush and Don Weiskopf, and *Women's Gymnastics* by Kitty Kjeldsen, formerly of the University of Massachusetts.

Dr. Thomas Tutko and Jack Richards collaborated on the meaningful book, *Psychology* *of Coaching*, and Patsy Neal of Brevard College also collaborated with Dr. Tutko on *Coaching Girls and Women: Psychological Perspectives*.

This Sports Series enables readers to experience the thrills of the sport from the point of view of participants and coaches, to learn some of the reasons for success and causes of failure, and to receive basic information about teaching and coaching techniques.

Each volume in the series reflects the philosophy of the authors, but a common theme runs through all: the desire to instill in the reader a knowledge and appreciation of sports and physical activity which will carry over throughout his life as a participant or a spectator. Pictures, drawings, and diagrams are used throughout each book to clarify and illustrate the discussion.

The reader, whether a beginner or one experienced in sports, will gain much from each book in this Allyn and Bacon Sports Education Series.

Arthur G. Miller
Chairman, Department of Human
    Movement and Health Education
Boston University

Preface

This book offers several special messages. One objective is to promote an ideal of teaching: we should so design our programs and progressions that they start from the bottom and move up, step by step, carrying all players to the peak of their potential or desire but not asking that they attempt to surpass themselves (the cause of much frustration). This book has made a contribution in this direction, and hopefully will continue to stimulate further progress.

Another aim of this book is to emphasize racket work. Teaching experience has indicated ever more clearly that the racket skills—as contrasted with footwork, moving well, power, tactics, strategy—require ten times the teaching emphasis needed for everything else put together. Doubtless this is an exaggeration resulting from a zealous attempt to make a point. So be it. Teaching by exaggeration, bending the stick the other way: these are tried and true methods of getting a concept across. However, even in this preface I would like to forestall a possible misunderstanding: it is not maintained that racket skills are ten times more *important* than other aspects combined; it is asserted that players, and therefore instructors, need to devote ninety percent of their *time* to these skills because they require endless repetition to become muscle knowledge. At any rate, it is suggested that all instructors, coaches, and players should give serious consideration to this approach, since it has been underemphasized for the most part in previous works.

Another special message is a plan for the entire game. This does not mean the book pretends to offer the pot of gold at the end of the rainbow—the one perfect way to play tennis. It does mean the game can be divided into areas of the court, each area presenting different tactical problems and therefore demanding altered techniques. The theory is advanced, and it is hoped justified, that racket technique changes as we move from the baseline to the halfcourt to the forecourt, and players and instructors should take this into account in their thinking. It is believed this area concept can be of substantial aid in giving coaches and players a complete and orderly picture of the game. It can be extremely helpful in coaching and teaching, and that is why it is singled out as one of the more important aspects of the book.

There will doubtless be a few surprises in the book for some, since an attempt is made to spike some prevalent misunderstandings about tennis technique: for example, the idea that to hit "flat" means "without spin," which it does not, or that "chopping" and "slicing" are evils to be avoided, which they are not. It is hoped the text justifies these views and helps to clarify current thinking about these technicalities.

The favorable response to the first edition, *Racket Work: The Key to Tennis*, has been gratifying, but it has not prevented me from seeing areas where improvements could be made. This revised edition contains new material that will better assist the tennis teacher or coach in the instruction of both small and large groups of players. The skill tests (Chapter 11), the suggested questions at the end of each chapter for written or oral testing, and some added drill suggestions are all calculated to aid the coach in insisting on application and thoroughness on the part of players. New sections have been added, such as "The Physiology of Grips," which should clarify areas where confusion and doubt sometimes occur. Diagrams are more numerous, captions are more thorough, and photographs have been improved. All the illustrations are larger. The content has been amplified and the format decisively improved. The book has been reorganized to make it more functional and to augment its service-ability for the participant, the instructor, the coach, and the spectator. The drills and skill tests should serve a dual purpose: (1) as a classification aid, to help beginning and advanced instructors evaluate their students, and (2) as a self-testing device, to enable players to assess their progress.

The main thrust of the book remains unchanged: to offer an in-depth, logically organized, and comprehensive treatment of the game calculated to help players at all levels and instructors in all situations.

Jack Barnaby

Advantage Tennis

I

Introduction

CHAPTER 1

Tennis in Society

THE BOOM IN SOCIAL TENNIS

Tennis is a game. Games are diversions, pursuits we take up for amusement, for healthy exercise, for sociability, or for all three. With the exception of professionals and a handful of professional amateurs—to coin a phrase—tennis, like all games, is not a primary occupation of the player. It is as a rule third: career and family take precedence with older people, and with students studies and friendships usually occupy the first two places in the protocol of life. Of course, tennis sometimes ranks higher—mainly with children—and often ranks far lower. The point to be made here is that it seldom ranks above third, and people should accept this status as a basic fact of tennis life, be they teachers or players.

The Need for a Selective Program

If tennis is then to be a minor occupation with a majority of those who take it up, this affects the program that should be offered to them—by teachers or authors or themselves. Instructors, of course, should know their subject with reasonable thoroughness. But should we attempt to impose this thoroughness on the hundreds of players who probably are never going to give it the necessary time to master a complete program? It would seem preferable to be realistic: judge with a cold and practical eye as to what the player will give to the game —and only then design the program. To pose the question another way, what will be most useful: an idealistic program that includes *everything* (so that no criticism as to omissions is possible) or a selective program that confines itself to the thorough inculcation of a few indispensable fundamentals—admittedly at the expense (by omission) of many of the finer points?

At first a reader may react adversely. This is compromise, this is taking the easy way, this is lowering the flag of excellence to which we all wish to subscribe. But think again. Which is easier: to write down everything with little emphasis on anything or to make the difficult decisions involved in a limited approach? And: what is our objective? Are we trying to serve tennis or society? If the former, then of course a complete treatment is desirable. If the latter, then is not the limited program more useful, more practical, even more idealistic, if you will?

Another objection may be that the duty of the teacher is to cover everything, leaving the selection or the matter of degree of progress to the player or reader. It would seem enough to state flatly that a beginning player has no knowledge on which to base such judgments.

Also, a leading function of any teacher is to guide one's efforts so they are as productive as possible. Clearly the acts of selection and emphasis are the teacher's jobs, not the player's. As will appear this is in fact a considerable part of effective teaching.

The current tennis boom has emphasized the need for a selective approach. Thousands of people of all ages are taking up the game, from children to busy adults at the clubs and parks to physical education majors and minors. A large proportion of these people cannot wedge enough time out of their schedules to undertake an exhaustive program of study in a difficult field: tennis technique. The proper function of the teacher is to adapt to the players' needs, and these in many cases indicate a limited program.

Progression Means Adaptability

Our emphasis on selection does not mean that a teacher should compromise the quality of instruction offered. Far from it. Good teaching consists in creating a ladder whereby, step by step—and no step hopelessly large—players can climb from nothing to something, or from less to more if they are not beginners. Any capable instructor has in mind a series of steps —a progression. Such a teacher will not move a player to step two until step one has been absorbed. This permits all players to progress in proper relationship to their ability, their available time, and their desire, ambition, and willingness to work. The quality and thoroughness of the instruction need suffer in no way, and the players as a rule are deeply grateful for this adaptation to their personal needs by a perceptive teacher. Take your own experience: how many times have you been mixed up by being told *too much* all at once—not just in tennis, but in any area involving technique? Don't do it to others!

The Hazard of Overteaching

The greatest fault of eager young teachers is overteaching. It is a source of frustration both to them and their players. It is usually out of line both with the players' desires and their available time. Social tennis is *big* these days. These people have no delusions about their talent or their future as threats on the big circuits. They want to get the ball in the court and have fun. They want to feel moderately competent in their own league. They want no more, have time for no more, and may not have talent for much more. Such players constitute the vast majority of people taking lessons today. This majority is the real "tennis in society." The top players are, each of them, one in a thousand. It is our job as teachers to meet the majority half way, to be willing (and happy) to give them basic tennis, with no delusions that it can approach Stan Smith tennis or Billie Jean King tennis except in those rare cases where we find desire, persistence, time, and talent.

Thus we arrive at a set of important assumptions. For most people tennis is a game, not a profession; it ranks third or lower in most players' lives. This is right, reasonable, and a fact of life we should use as a guide to policy, which means we should temper the idealism of the conscientious instructor with realism, judgment, and adaptability.

RACKET WORK

No Carryover

Everyone who has ever tried it knows tennis is a very difficult game. Topnotch play requires agility, quickness, stamina (both mental and physical), touch, quarterbacking under pressure (with all the resourcefulness and adaptability this implies), strength without weight, and a versatile technique with a strange thing we call a racket. In all, a great tennis champion needs to be generously endowed with just about every attribute desirable in athletes. Such paragons are rare, and this explains why a truly great player in tennis appears only at intervals.

Some of these skills are natural in the sense

that they are activities we perform in all games involving motion: crouching, staying on the balls of one's feet, balance, moving neatly, running, turning, twisting—these are common to just about all active sports. But the use of the racket is a completely new experience for anyone who takes up tennis. Beginners will tend to employ at once whatever agility and poise they have acquired in various other physical pursuits such as playing tag or running to school. They may move quite well if at all endowed athletically, but their racket work will be truly awful until they have worked on it over quite a period of time. Why? Because it is one hundred percent strange; they are really starting from zero. A similar situation obtains in hockey: what good is the finest athlete if he has never been on skates? And what good is a figure skater who has never handled a stick or experienced a body check?

If this be true, it dictates where the greatest emphasis should be placed by both instructor and player. Running, footwork, agility, balance—all the aspects of technique involving handling *the player* should be subordinated to a major effort to achieve skill with the racket. Like anything else this can be carried too far, but until the racket skill has overtaken the physical skill of the player, it would seem inadvisable to spend time widening a gap that is apparent from the start. And since, as has already been pointed out, most players are going to give the game only limited attention, then to emphasize racket work as a basic policy would seem wise.

Quite often fine players will remark, "This game is all footwork." It is—for them. They have long since acquired the racket work, so the only question is whether they arrive in time, get set, get leg drive and body turn for good power. But of what avail is it to instruct a beginner in all this if he cannot control even a small part of all this power?

Skill Versus Power

Obviously what we want is *balance:* a knowledge of how to get strength into the ball and how to control it. The beginner is always tremendously unbalanced in favor of the physical skills, which produce the power, and has no skill at all with the racket, which produces the control. When the control catches up, then of course more stress must be placed on other facets of technique, but this usually takes a long time and a lot of work.

A tennis ball is extremely lively. A slight tap will make it travel the length of the court. It is a cinch to hit it clean over the fence—as all beginners soon discover to their chagrin when they have to chase it. So power is nothing; every beginner is loaded with it. Control is what the beginning player lacks. The ball goes all right; in fact, it flies all over the place. And that is the beginner's frustration: not being able to make it go *in*. Watch youngsters: they all whale the first serve with impressive power but seldom get it in. Then they strive—on the second ball—for control, and what do we see? They ease way down and "poop" the ball in. This is a visible confession that they can control only a fraction of the power they already have. And what distinguishes the more accomplished players who can get a more forceful ball into the court? Do they have more power? No, they have control, and they get it by means of spin, and spinning the ball is entirely a matter of expert racket work.

Interdependence

One other approach to this concept has real importance. Bad racket work can force a player to have poor poise, balance, and footwork, whereas good racket work allows good balance and use of weight, as shown in Figure 1–1. Figure 1–2 gives an example of how poor racket work can have catastrophic effects on how well or badly one appears to handle one's self on a tennis court. All the apparent awkwardness is due to the very closed face of the racket, which necessitates pulling up violently to avoid hitting the ball into the ground. It is quite funny to watch someone play (or struggle?) with a stroke like this. If it happens to be yourself it isn't so comical. But the point is that

Figure 1–1. Good racket work makes good balance possible. The racket face is correctly positioned. No awkwardness is needed to clear the net. Good balance and use of weight are possible and natural, instead of impossible (as in Figure 1–2).

Figure 1–2. Bad racket work can ruin balance. An extremely closed racket face forces the player to pull up violently to clear the net, causing him to tip his shoulders the wrong way and move his weight back instead of forward. In sum, everything goes wrong because the racket is incorrectly prepared to begin with.

all the leaning backwards, bad balance, etc., are unavoidable if the racket is improperly handled to this degree. Figure 1–1 corrects Figure 1–2.

Extremes are usually absurd. Pressing for more emphasis on racket work does not mean that when teaching we ignore footwork, moving properly, or power. Quite the contrary. They are, of course, indispensable. But they can be learned—and taught—in one-tenth the time needed to develop decent skill in the matters of grips, changing grips, topspin, slice, spin on service, the idea of stroking as contrasted with hitting, etc.—in a word, the essentials of racket work. And if we add the aforementioned

fact that racket work is as a rule the one completely new thing to a person taking up the game, then the apparently rash statement that racket skill is ninety percent of the teaching problem becomes a sober and reasonable estimate.

Observing Racket Work: The "Catch"

Certainly all teachers are anxious to get down to the fundamentals. They watch the best players, and they teach what they see. This is the catch: much of racket work, like the tricks of a magician, tends to escape the eye. The fast footwork, the crouching, the timing, the application of weight, the sound of the impact, the tactics—all these are easily perceived, exciting, even thrilling at times. Moreover, they draw the eye so it tends to miss other aspects of what is going on. How many observers watch the racket leave the ball? Very few. They all watch the ball leave the racket. But only by watching the racket *exclusively* can one really see what the racket is doing from start to finish. And how the racket leaves the ball determines the spin, which controls the flight and drastically affects the bounce. Thus racket work tends to hide itself and to pass unobserved while other facets of technique force themselves upon us. It is therefore not remarkable that racket work is seldom overdone and often underdone in teaching programs. Of course, the exact degree of emphasis is a matter for personal preference, and the only dogmatic assertion to be made is that it is a major

ingredient of technique and merits serious attention, careful observation, and a lot of thought by all players and teachers.

QUESTIONS

1. How difficult is tennis?

2. What most limits the skill of most players? Why?

3. How important is footwork in playing tennis? In teaching tennis?

4. Comment on this: It is of prime importance to teach beginners how to get power into their shots.

5. Why do some good athletes look awkward playing tennis?

6. What is most difficult to observe accurately in a player?

II

Technique

CHAPTER 2

The Grips

THREE BASIC TYPES OF GRIPS

There are three basic grips used for holding a tennis forehand: the Continental forehand grip, which turns the face somewhat up in relation to the palm; the Western forehand grip, which turns the face somewhat down; and the Eastern forehand grip, which puts the face of the racket in the same plane as the palm of the hand. The three backhand grips likewise tend to turn the racket over, under, or to a more or less neutral position. All grips fall into one of these categories, so that while many variations are possible, the racket must be either even, over, or under in relation to the palm.

The Continental Grip

The Continental grip originated and still predominates in England and on the Continent,

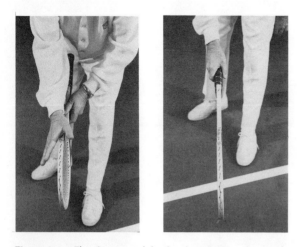

Figure 2–1. The Continental forehand grip. Note the hand turned somewhat over the top of the handle, which will tend to open the face of the racket when the palm is perpendicular to the ground.

Figure 2–2. The Continental backhand grip. Note that with the hand in its natural position, the racket face is open.

where heavy grass and slow composition courts tend to produce many low bounces, which can best be handled with an open face to lift the ball. Because the racket tends to go under the ball a little (i.e., slice), this grip is effective for slicing, chopping, and hitting low volleys. (See Figures 2–1 and 2–2.)

The one-grip system is nothing more nor less than the Continental grip. It is good for the backhand and good for the service. It is second rate for the forehand drive and the forehand volley. It is an oversimplification that retains popularity because it makes everything seem so easy; just grab the racket like this and make every shot without any change ever. It sounds lovely, but as one might suspect, there is a fly in the ointment.

The Continental grip gets the hand too much on top of the racket, thereby failing to get the hand behind the racket. The forehand shot tends to be pulled rather than pushed; and a shot that is pushed is far superior in strength, security, and control. The ball cannot be taken out in front, for the Continental grip opens the face too much, and it can be closed only by taking the ball late. Try it. Because the ball must be taken late, the wrist must often be snapped to keep the ball in the court. Thus Continental forehands tend to be late, too wristy, and lacking the power and length that characterize a good Eastern forehand. Only the best athletes with unusually powerful wrists, extraordinary timing and reflexes, and extremely fine eyes are able to make the Continental grip into a successful weapon. By contrast, any average player can have a good forehand using an Eastern grip.

Surely someone will point out that the Australians favor the one-grip system and they are very good. However, it does not follow that because they are excellent overall they are the best in every particular. Moreover, the big-time game stresses the net to such an extent that very few exchanges of ground strokes occur. The proportion of all tennis players who can thus get along without relying heavily on baseline technique is very small indeed—surely far below five percent, probably below one or

two percent. Add to this the fact that the big-time circuit has been on grass, where a low bounce favors the open-faced Continental style, and again we see it can work for the top-flight players but is nevertheless inadvisable for the rest of us. These are some of the reasons why a heavy majority of teaching pros of real repute advocate the Eastern forehand grip, not the Continental, for all teaching programs.

The Western Grip

The Western grip used to be popular in the West, where hard courts and high bounding balls tended to predominate; a closed face was desirable to cover a high ball. (See Figures 2–3 and 2–4.) A Western grip is good for high shots only, when a more closed racket face is desirable and sometimes necessary. For other shots, however, the Eastern grips are more effective. The physiological basis for this statement is discussed later in this chapter.

The Eastern Grip

The Eastern grip was adopted in the Eastern part of the United States, where clay courts

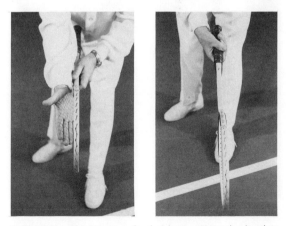

Figure 2–3. The Western forehand grip. Note the hand is somewhat under the handle, so the racket face will be closed when the palm is perpendicular to the ground.

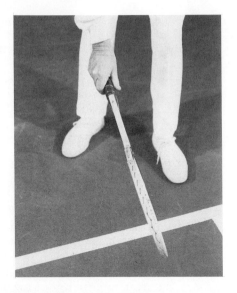

Figure 2–4. The Western backhand grip. Note that with the hand normal, the racket face is closed.

were in the majority and were neither as high bounding as Western facilities nor as slow as Continental and English courts; a middle ground grip was needed.

Experience has led to the general conclusion that the Eastern grip represents the closest

possible approach to the happy medium, and most professionals start beginners with this grip. The Eastern grip is the most "natural": the forehand is a perfect continuation of the palm, and the backhand, with the wrist in its most comfortably cocked position, will automatically produce a nice solid flat backhand contact. (See Figures 2–5 and 2–6.) As will be pointed out later, many good players vary their grip slightly to slice, but we are here faced with choosing not a complete technique but a starting point. The Eastern grip is generally accepted as best for this purpose, since it is as near as one can get to dead center in this business of over and under and flat.

ALLOWING FOR NONCONFORMITY

What of the many thousands who are already committed to Western or Continental grips? Should they give up and start over again? Hardly. They need merely realize that their grip tends to help them in some ways and not in others. For example, players with a Western

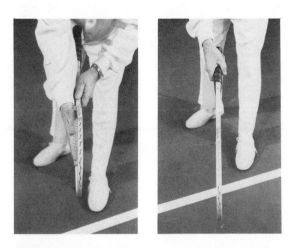

Figure 2–5. The Eastern forehand grip. Note that the hand is in the same plane as the face of the racket, so that when the palm is perpendicular to the ground, the racket face will also be perpendicular.

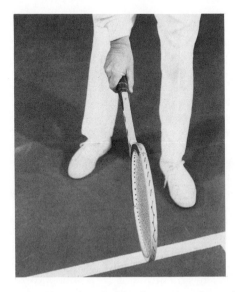

Figure 2–6. The Eastern backhand grip. Note that with the hand in its natural position, the racket face is perpendicular to the ground or flat.

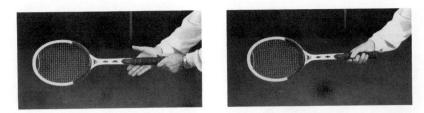

Figure 2–7. Forehand feel. These pictures show a racket held skillfully—that is, diagonally.

forehand will tend to hit low balls into the net because of the closed face. They should first try not to let the ball get very low, and if it does, they should slice under it some to make sure they don't net the ball. In sharp contrast are players who use the Continental forehand, who should consciously allow the ball to drop low; if forced to take a ball high, they should use a full arm chop rather than a flat or top-spin stroke. In these ways those whose grips are a trifle off the so-called perfect center can get along quite nicely and by clever play can even exaggerate the benefits of their grip and effectively cover its weaknesses. However, if a grip is far off the happy mean—as an exaggerated Western backhand—then it is just plain wrong, and a change is in order. Last, in spite of these apologies for the Western and Continental, the accepted consensus is that the Easterns are to be preferred.

WHY GRIPS ARE CRUCIAL

Your grip affects every shot you will ever make for the rest of your life. Once you get used to grip, change is not easy; it is an extremely disruptive process and causes much unhappiness. One sort of gets married to a grip and often just cannot switch. Therefore it is worth a lot of trouble to get it right the first time.

There are certain things about grips that need to be pointed out. Your grip must give "feel." Your feel is in your fingers in considerable part. Therefore, hold the racket *diagonally* so that the butt part of it is way up in your palm and the more forward part is down on your fingers. To hold the racket at a right

Figure 2–8. A racket jammed way up into the palm. This is called "clubbing" the racket, and does not give a skillful feel. It makes one clumsy.

angle to the hand so it is entirely across the palm and not at all in the fingers is called "clubbing" the racket. See Figures 2–7 and 2–8. It is clumsy and does not give feel. Many teachers like to advocate separating the forefinger from the others a little to achieve a greater spread on the handle, thus reducing leverage and increasing control. But the true feel of an Eastern forehand comes when you feel the back of the handle with your palm: the back of the handle being in the same plane as the face of the racket, you can feel *exactly* how your racket is slanted without looking at it. You also feel that a forehand shot becomes what the word means: you are playing the ball with the forepart of your hand—the racket being merely an extension of your palm. Thus you achieve that most desirable feel of all— that the racket is part of you.

The backhand feel is different. Again the racket should be placed diagonally in the hand, but we do not hit a backhand with the back of the hand. We hit it with the edge of the hand, as in karate. We get the feel of the face of the

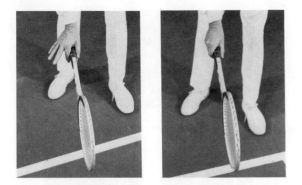

Figure 2–9. Feeling the backhand grip. Carefully note the thumb. It is half-turned behind the handle and is placed diagonally behind the handle. The top joint of the forefinger is against the front face of the handle. The butt of the handle is well in under the palm toward the little finger. A good way to get "feel" is to hold the racket as shown (in two fingers only) and slap the net flat with the face of the racket. This gives the feel of putting the racket face solidly onto the ball.

Figure 2–10. A less desirable backhand grip. Contrast this with Figure 2–9. Note that the butt is NOT as far under the hand, that the racket is now a straight continuation of the arm. A player with this grip will be forced to take the ball later (to avoid hitting too much to the right) and will be forced to slice rather than drive, because when the wrist is cocked in its strong position, the racket is quite open. Advanced players should learn this grip as a variation: ideal for digging up low balls, carving high bounding serves back crosscourt, and playing shots at full reach. But it is not the best basic grip for beginners.

racket first with our thumb, the side of which presses against the back flatness of the handle that is in the same plane as the face, and second with the top joint of the index finger, which presses the front flatness of the handle that is in the same plane as the face. Thus again the key feel is that which establishes rapport with the strings—with the racket face. See Figures 2–9 and 2–10.

On both forehand and backhand the test is to hold the racket out to the side and *don't look at it.* Can you tell—feel—exactly how the face is slanted? Now swing it, looking forward at an imaginary ball. Can you bring the face to the ball and put it on it nice and solidly? Can you *feel* that this is going to happen? A good grip, forehand or backhand, makes things easy. A bad grip makes things nearly impossible—the ball pops up, pops down, goes all over the place—because your grip isn't telling you what the face will do when it gets to the ball. Fiddle around on a bangboard, use your fingers, try to get this "touch." It is the key to feeling skillful.

Probably the illustrations herewith are worth more than all the foregoing words about grips, provided you study them with care and with the realization that what you are trying to do is to establish rapport between you and the face of the racket (since that is what plays the ball). Avoid systems such as "Put the knuckle of the index finger over the front edge of the handle" and similar landmarks that are unrelated to getting the feel of the flatnesses that are your means of identifying with the face of the racket—the strings. If you are a teacher, fuss repeatedly over your players' grips; their importance cannot be overstressed.

THE PHYSIOLOGY OF GRIPS

Players and teachers are constantly seeking out and trying out ideas on grips. The tendency is to base acceptance on the authority of the individual who advances or practices the theory. We would be better advised to eliminate all name considerations and base our conclu-

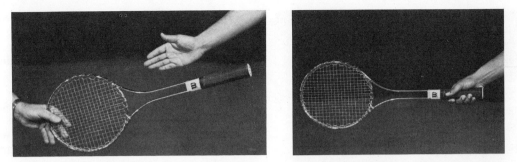

Figure 2–11. Forehand physiology. An aid holds the racket with the face slanted correctly for a drive. The right arm and hand simulate a solid flat blow with the front side (palm) of the hand. Put them together: the Eastern grip results.

sions strictly on reason. The question is not "What does the current winner do?" but "What is the most physiologically sound way to use the hand, the arm, and the body in order to achieve the desired result?"

Forehand

The most natural and physiologically sound method of dealing a flat forehand blow is with the palm. When we use the palm, we can meet the object to be struck a little in front of us and bring our weight in behind the blow, thus increasing its force quite markedly without putting great strain on the wrist, because the weight backs up the blow. The Eastern forehand grip makes the face of the racket a continuation of the palm in the same plane, thus allowing us to play a tennis ball exactly in this most sound and strongest manner. See Figure 2–11.

Now consider a Continental grip. If we make the same sound swing with our arm, hand, and body, and play the ball a little in front so as to get weight behind it, the shot will go too high, because the face of the racket is tipped back when the palm is perpendicular. To keep the racket perpendicular we must take the ball farther back—considerably later. See Figure 2–12. Now we no longer can bring our weight in behind the blow. We must pull or haul the ball, and a great deal more strain is placed on the wrist. This can be done, and

Figure 2–12. The Continental grip. This opens the face decisively if the ball is taken well forward to get weight into the shot. The shot will obviously go too high unless the wrist is snapped over at impact—undesirable, inconsistent, weaker, good on low balls only. To close the face the ball must be taken later as in the second photograph, which means a player cannot get weight behind the shot. Only players with the strongest wrists and arms can achieve success in this manner, and sometimes they have trouble.

15

Figure 2–13. The Western grip. This facilitates taking the ball out front to get weight behind the shot, but closes the face too much. It can and does produce devastating topspin power on high shots, but is otherwise less desirable. Note the discomfort approaching contortion to open the face enough to clear the net on a low ball (second photograph).

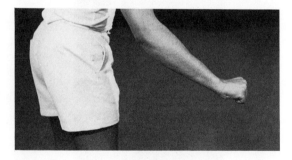

Figure 2–14. Backhand physiology. In dealing a backhanded blow, as shown, note that the heel, or edge, of the hand takes the impact, NOT the back of the hand. Note that the wrist is comfortably cocked.

many fine players do it, but it *demands* extra wrist strength and deftness to keep control, and many average players just don't have these physical attributes. Thus fine athletes can and do play the forehand with a Continental grip, but every average or mediocre athlete *always* has trouble if he relies on this grip.

Is that last statement an exaggeration? It is not. A short time after the Australians began to dominate international tennis, under that conditioning genius, Harry Hopman, the author, as a teaching pro, began to have a steady stream of customers with forehand

trouble. They were imitating the Australian one-grip system, and everything worked . . . except their forehands. The problem became so prevalent that whenever anyone said, "I need forehand help," I would respond, "No doubt you use one grip for both strokes" and the player was always amazed that this diagnosis was correct—made while we were still walking out to the court. Actually, there was a ninety percent probability that the diagnosis would be correct, and the problem still occurs frequently although the Australian prominence is not nearly so marked as it once was. These players did not realize that the Australians we saw and admired were sufficiently gifted to do what most of us find impossible. Perhaps it should be added that throughout the "Australian era" there were very few super forehands, while super backhands abounded. Thus, even with the most gifted players the Eastern grip produces better results.

For obvious physiological reasons the Western grip is not as sound as the Eastern. A natural swing of the arm and palm does not meet the ball squarely: the face of the racket is now too closed and the ball tends to go down. See Figure 2–13. It is awkward, physically, to open the face of the racket to get a low ball up over the net. One can, by endless practice, accustom oneself to play the ball this way, even as one can learn to walk duckfooted with enough practice, but it doesn't make sense. The Western grip is effective for high shots, as mentioned previously, but it is inferior to the Eastern grip for other shots.

Backhand

The most natural "backhanded" blow is *not* dealt with the back of the hand, but with the edge of the hand as in karate. The strongest position of the hand is with the wrist comfortably cocked, that is, with a little valley where the hand and arm join. See Figure 2–14. If the racket is held with the left hand so that the face is slanted correctly to produce a reasonable shot (just slightly open faced), the right hand is put above it in this sound position

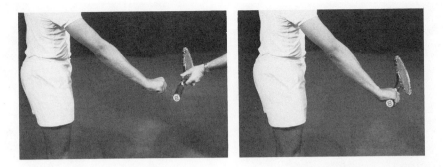

Figure 2–15. Hand and racket correct. Put them together: an Eastern grip results.

(wrist comfortably but not excessively cocked), and the two are then joined, the result is an Eastern backhand grip. See Figure 2–15. It is the most natural junction of the racket right with the hand right. Any variation tends to introduce difficulty for the player. Again, variation is possible and one *can* play the ball some other way, but it is less natural and therefore takes longer to learn because of the unnatural adjustments that must be made. The learning process is slowed and the final result less than ideal as a rule.

For the reasons just outlined, the marked preference of established teaching professionals in the United States for Eastern grips is no accident. It is based on sound reason and sound physiological analysis. It is not a matter of somebody's opinion, or a matter of what is done by a current winner, or the theory of someone who is looked upon as an "authority." It makes sense, so it is right. Reason is the true final arbiter.

Continental Grip for Slice

The preceding discussion deals with grips for basic solid topspin drives. But many times we do not wish to make a topspin or flat shot. Quite often the situation calls for a slice. In such cases, particularly if the ball is low, a Continental grip is the most natural, since it opens the face of the racket and thus facilitates slicing, as pointed out earlier in this chapter. See Figure 2–16.

Figure 2–16. The Continental: good for slicing and low volleys. Note it is the same for forehand and backhand, and that in each case the lower edge of the racket is advanced when the hand is held naturally. Thus the racket will "want" to slice the ball; i.e., the bottom edge wants to lead off the ball. Upper intermediate to advanced players should learn this.

Figure 2–17. A wristy get: forehand. This is an extreme example of the total NECESSITY of being able to change the grip. How could the player get around and under this ball, except by a drastic change to a grip that is close to an Eastern backhand?

Physiology Forces Variety

Surely many will urge that we can hold one grip and merely change the position of the racket by manipulating the hand one way or the other. This won't quite work. An extreme example of how the anatomy of the arm and wrist *forces* us to change the racket (i.e., the grip) occurs frequently when a ball gets somewhat past a good player. The player will snap around it with the wrist to bring it back into court, and will cut under the very bottom of the ball to get it high in the air as a defensive lob. What grip does the player use? On both forehand and backhand the player will use a super-extreme Continental, so that the racket is flat open. For the forehand the grip will be over the top of the racket perhaps even farther than a standard Eastern backhand grip. For the backhand the face will be so open it will closely resemble an Eastern forehand grip. *Every* player does this (including all those who say, "I never change my grip") because it is the *only* way to get the racket under the ball on this retrieve and lob play. Try it yourself. It is anatomically impossible to make the shot any other way. See Figures 2–17 through 2–20.

The basic principle is that the hand, wrist, and arm are built in a certain way, and operate

Figure 2–18. A wristy get: backhand. Here the player has changed from a backhand all the way to a Western forehand. Why? Because there is no other way to do the job.

in a certain way. You can change them some by manipulation but not very much. By contrast the racket can be changed all you want, by changing the grip. If the grip is correct for slicing, it is easy to slice; in fact, it is difficult and a bit awkward to avoid slicing. If the grip is set for driving, it is awkward to slice. And as was just pointed out, if the grip is set to play comparatively flat, it is *impossible* to get completely under the ball: your hand *cannot* do it.

Advanced players make these manipulations of the racket (as contrasted with the hand) in offensive as well as defensive situations. Very sharply angled volleys made at close range are facilitated by grip changes that get the racket far around the side of the ball to increase the angle. The thumb is put a little more behind the racket at times on the backhand to get extreme topspin on a backhand angled passing shot. The same swing is made but the grip is altered to get a different effect on the ball, in this case a more closed face so the racket

Figure 2–19. Eastern backhand for forehand volley. Why? Because the player is late and reaching, and this is the only way to get around the ball to make the sharp cross-court angle that will win.

Figure 2–20. Eastern forehand for backhand volley. Why? Because the player is reaching for the ball, and can make the desired angle in no other way. It is the only way to get around the ball.

brushes up over the top of the back of the ball instead of meeting the ball solidly. See Figure 2–21.

All this presents us with an unacceptable complexity, from the point of view of instructors and average players. We can resolve it by returning to the two basic skills—top and slice. *All* players who move beyond the intermediate stage should have a grip that makes driving (flat with a bit of top) comfortable, and should be taught a slight alteration (toward the Continental) that makes cut shots comfortable. Only if they become definitely advanced should they go in for the trickier variations that are at the command of the top tournament players.

Net Play

The same problem arises at net. The one grip (the Continental) will work well on a series of low fast volleys because the Continental gives a slightly open face on both sides. But when the ball pops up and a good chance occurs to hit down, a shift to the Eastern on either side is very desirable to close the face. See Figure 2–22. The modern concept of one grip all the time at net—based on the idea that there is no time to change—is true *only* when the exchange is fast and low. When a ball pops up, if it is going that fast it will go out; no volley is

Figure 2–21. Westernized backhand—useful at times. To get brushy heavy topspin on a dipping, sharply angled shot, some players will put the flat ball of their thumb behind the handle to close the face. Ordinarily this is considered "bad" just because it gives these effects: too much spin, no depth, a less than solid impact. But when these are the DESIRED effects, it is good.

needed. If it is slow enough to be a fair ball, or if it is coming from the baseline (far away) and is high, there is both need and adequate time to close the face *before* the shot is played. Otherwise a turning over of the wrist *as* the ball is played is necessary and leads to errors.

If the racket is held at the throat by the fingers of the left hand, it can be turned over a little, thus changing the grip, as the racket is lifted to play the ball. This, with a little practice, can be done as quickly as one can lift the racket to play. It requires *zero* increase in the time required to play the ball. This is true on both forehand and backhand.

Conclusion: Volleying requires the use of *both* the open and closed face. The needed changes *cannot* be executed by merely changing the aspect of the arm and wrist unless the ball is taken late on high shots. Try it. It is physically scarcely possible. The *racket* must

be changed in the hand to meet the ball out front (very desirable) and still have a closed face on a high ball. See Figures 2–22 through 2–25.

Check advanced players. If they have an extreme Continental at net (nearer an Eastern backhand), they will handle all volleys well except high forehand opportunities. If they have a slight Continental (nearer an Eastern forehand), they will handle all volleys well except high backhands. The author, as a col-

Figure 2–22. Forehand high volley—Eastern is best. Note how comfortable and natural it is to close the face with an Eastern grip.

Figure 2–24. Backhand high volley—Eastern is best. The face is closed with no strain.

Figure 2–23. Forehand high volley—Continental is inferior. The face of the racket is open: undesirable on a high volley. The ball will pop up and perhaps go out.

Figure 2–25. Backhand high volley—Continental is inferior. The face is now open: how does one keep the ball down and kill it? The answer is: one doesn't.

lege coach, has a steady stream of advanced players coming to him from secondary schools. Most of them have adopted the modern idea that one grip only is advisable (necessary) at net. Invariably they are prone to make errors on one side or the other. These are not just intermittent errors that might be attributed to concentration, overhitting, aiming too fine, etc.; they perform, *consistently*, much better on one side than on the other. The answer, as usual, is racket work, and because of the current prejudice in favor of one grip it is often very difficult to persuade them even to try changing. Once they open their minds, the job is three-quarters done, improvement is rapid, and soon they do it "instinctively"—i.e., from habit, without thought.

The most important principle for a teacher to realize and recognize is that there is no such thing as "one grip for every shot," because it is a physical impossibility. Straitjacket teaching with no flexibility is an attempt at oversimplification; it doesn't work. Skillful racket work involves manipulating the hand *and* adapting the racket (i.e., the grip) to the job to be done. It is hoped a close look at the accompanying illustrations will help make this clear, showing the different preparations that facilitate leading with the top or bottom edge of the racket.

CHANGING GRIPS: TECHNIQUE

The most important habit to form in changing grips is to use two hands. That is why we should always cradle the racket at the throat with our left hand while awaiting service and between shots. If supported in this manner the racket is held up by the left hand, and the right can let go and shift about without allowing the racket to drop. The left hand can help in another way, too: it can move the racket into position to play the ball and can arrange the slant of the face at the desired angle for whatever shot is about to be executed. See Figure 2–26.

It is clear that tennis is a two-handed game,

Figure 2–26. Changing forehand to backhand grip. Note that the right hand does very little except to sit there loosely and allow the handle to swivel in under as the left hand does the work by pulling the racket head about ninety degrees to the left. In other words, we change the racket more than the right hand, which turns back over the top a little less than a quarter turn and that's all.

and it is important to get this across to all students at the start so they manipulate their racket with both hands right from the beginning. It should be pointed out that they will not be sufficiently quick on the trigger when the ball comes fast if they use only one hand. They must learn not only to play forehands and backhands correctly but also to switch almost instantaneously. To this end a good drill is to encourage them to rally in a V against a practice board so they play their forehand to their backhand to their forehand to their backhand, etc.—each stroke requiring changing the grip and incidentally the feet. Nothing will improve manipulative skill more effectively than work of this sort.

There is one aspect of changing grips that is misunderstood by an extraordinary number of competent people. This is that the racket changes its position in the hand rather than that the hand changes its position on the racket. What's the difference? The difference is very great, and crucial; it is awkward to change from a forehand to a backhand grip without moving the racket. It is unnatural and a strain. By contrast, if the racket is moved (by the left hand) ninety degrees from the forehand position, so it is parallel to the stomach instead of at right angles to it, the change can be much facilitated so it is easy, quick, and also includes a good bit of the backswing motion. Thus changing the grip and preparing to play become one operation, not two. To do this the left hand, which always cradles the racket at the throat between shots, pulls the head to the left while the right hand rolls over the handle a little and moves to the left to start the backswing. The butt of the racket swivels around under the hand until it bumps into the little finger. Study Figure 2–26 carefully and note that while the right hand is now in the karate position (ready to deal a blow with its edge) still the most drastic change is made by the racket, not the hand.

There are two things to mention in teaching this. One, tell the players to pull the head back until the racket parallels the body. Two, tell them to point the butt forward at the ball and

get their hand on top of it. Have them do this facing front at first so they think of nothing but the racket work. Later coordinate footwork with it so everything happens at once, and in one smooth move from the cradled waiting position they are ready to play a backhand.

THE TWO-HANDED GRIP

Here and there a top player appears who plays a two-handed forehand (Segura), or a two-handed backhand (Chris Evert and others). There is a great deal of discussion and even controversy about this. Actually it is nothing new; it has occurred many times over the years. What is at the bottom of it? Strength. A beginner who starts with an Eastern forehand grip and does not learn to change for the backhand will feel extremely weak on the backhand. The hand is in front of the racket, and there is nothing behind the racket except the five fingertips. In an endeavor to overcome this feeling of feebleness (which is very real— try it yourself), it is quite natural for a beginner to grab the racket with his other hand also, with a left-handed forehand Eastern grip, and play with two hands. This at once gives a sense of greater strength, compactness, solidity, and security. It is really a left-handed Eastern forehand helped a little by the right hand. The swing is necessarily restricted because the left arm cannot go through as far as the right arm. This means the player must use a greater proportion of body turn and weight transfer. This can be done.

Is there anything wrong with this? No—as Segura and Evert have clearly demonstrated on the court, where their two-handed strokes have proved solid, accurate, and dependable. But an important point must be made: their racket work is *excellent*. They both prepare the head and face of the racket just right (below the ball), and get good spin on their shots. Thus, if one has good racket work and gets strength behind it, one has the makings of a good stroke from the baseline. Are there drawbacks? Yes. One's reach is limited by an amount equal to the width of the shoulders, since the left arm, on a wide ball, holds back the reach of the right arm to this extent. Thus a two-handed player must develop superior speed of foot to cover this shortcoming. It may be argued that the width of the shoulders isn't much, and balls that are hard to reach are on points that are already substantially lost—and this is in good part true. Yet it is a limitation, however slight, and its real effect is much more obvious at net, where lack of reach is a crucial handicap. Many balls at net that can *barely* be reached can be put away for winners if one is in close. If one suggests the two-handed player should now use one hand, to gain this reach, then in order to have a solid volley, the player must learn to change the grip, since the Eastern forehand grip is totally hopeless for a backhand volley (try it).

Thus it can be said that two-handed strokes can be sound and serviceable from the baseline but overall are not to be preferred. The record bears this out: two-handed champions are rare, though prominent two-handed strokes (backhands particularly) keep appearing. For teachers it is probably the better part of wisdom to teach beginners to change their grip and use a one-handed backhand, but if con-

fronted with a well-developed two-handed stroke to avoid trying to change it.

QUESTIONS

1. Name the three accepted categories of grips.

2. Which grip is most open faced? Closed faced?

3. What is the justification for saying the Eastern grip is the "happy mean"?

4. Why should a racket he held diagonally across the palm?

5. Do you like the "one grip" concept? Why?

6. Do you strike a backhand with the back of your hand?

7. Why have the greatest strokes of all time been made with Eastern grips?

8. Is the left hand important in changing grips? Why?

9. What are the advantages of a two-handed stroke?

10. What are the disadvantages of a two-handed stroke?

CHAPTER 3

Racket Work

DYNAMICS OF RACKET WORK

Racket work means the action of the racket—that is, the strings—on the ball. The racket can go through the ball, across it, under it, over it, up it or down it, inside it or outside it, plus various combinations. Each of these actions has a decisive effect on the flight of the ball. Forward spin tends to make the ball go down. Backspin causes the ball to rise or hang in the air as the effect of the spin and gravity cancel each other out. Side spin causes the ball to curve and bounce to the side toward which the front of the ball is turning. Any combination results in a logically combined result: as side and forward will cause the ball to curve sideways and at the same time drop, and the bounce will tend to jump forward and sideways. These effects of spin are not open to argument since they are merely predictable physical reactions: when a ball in flight through a gas (air in our case) spins forward (topspin) the top of the ball is meeting more air than the bottom, which moves backward. More air resistance, or force, is exerted on the top of the ball than on the bottom. The ball is depressed and tends to drop. All other spins act the same way: one side of the ball is acted on by the air more vigorously than the other side, so the ball is pushed one way more than the other and curves instead of going straight.

To a beginner this may sound very complicated. It isn't. A good rule for a pupil puzzled with spin is that all side spin shots bounce the way the front of the ball is spinning as it approaches. If your opponent cuts across from his left to his right, the ball will bounce to your right (his left). A ball with backspin tends to skid if it has pace, and to stop dead and bounce straight up if it is soft (as in a drop shot). Intermediate players should experiment on the court until they learn to recognize the swing that produces each spin and the behavior of the ball when so played. The more we pass the strings across the ball in any direction when we play a shot, the more spin we will get. The more we take the racket straight through the ball, so the ball tends to remain at one spot on the strings while being propelled, the less spin we produce.

RIGHT AND WRONG

Many people are very opinionated about spin. They favor no spin or favor moderate topspin and abhor all cut shots as inferior, or even ignore spin as being a matter of minor consequence in tennis instruction. The fact is that spin is a useful and necessary (note that word) tool, and *all* spins are *good* when they help us to our objectives. Forward spin aids us by allowing us to aim higher over the net and still make the ball drop into the court, by making possible sharp angles, by helping us to get the ball to a player's feet, by enabling us to force the opponent to volley a dipping ball. Backspin and side spin enable us to make the ball bounce low and sideways when we go to net, and heavy backspin on a soft drop shot kills it right where it lands—it doesn't bounce forward at all.

It is really too bad that so much time is wasted arguing about what is the "best way," when there is no such thing; it is the pot of gold at the end of the rainbow, and one never quite reaches it. As with the open and closed stance question we are again in a position where no critical choice is possible until the objective is defined: topspin for hard drives; slice and top and side for service; backspin for volley and drop; side and a little under for approach shots off low balls; side and a little over for high forehand approaches; heavy topspin or soft slice for sharp angles; slice for high backhands; flat for smashing short lobs; some slice on deeper smashes. There may be more, and one player's preferences doubtless will differ in degree from another's, but the point should be made by now: no generalizations are possible as to right and wrong spins *except* as applied to individual shots. All players and instructors are urged to keep a completely open mind and to shun all persuasive-sounding theories that seek to establish a single aspect of spin as the one and only. There is good in most of these limited theories, and there is reason for the enthusiasm they create, but when they are advanced as the answer to any and all problems it is time to call a halt.

THE FLAT THEORY

Of all current fallacious tennis thinking, the idea of meeting the ball flat and going right through it with as little spin as possible is without doubt the most prevalent and the most damaging. It denies us the use of the physical laws that govern the flight of a ball through the atmosphere with the exception of gravity (and gravity alone is not enough to give control). It renders the word *stroke* meaningless and substitutes *hit* (a baseball term). It limits us to one way of playing just about every ball. Simplicity is desirable, but everyone knows that oversimplification means superficiality and mediocrity. It leads to nonpercentage tennis, frustration, inconsistency, and failure.

These are strong words and will doubtless shock a good many devotees of flat hitting. How can so many be so wrong? Because there is a lot of good in the flat theory: the idea of meeting the ball solidly, as contrasted with meeting it in a glancing manner, has obvious merit and appeal. Just about any instructor demands this from players when they drive the ball, and to this limited extent is a supporter of the flat idea. The quarrel comes when the flat theorist urges going right through the ball with little or no spin. The argument is not how we should come *to* the ball but how we should *leave* the ball. The fallacy is that many—a majority—of players, when told "hit flat," take this to mean "hit without spin." Thus in their honest endeavor to secure a firm impact and a solid powerful shot, they toss control (spin) right out the window.

STROKE VERSUS HIT

It is quite possible—in fact desirable, necessary, indispensable—to meet the ball with a flat approach, secure a solid impact, and put spin on the ball as the racket leaves it. A little lift at the end of the swing gives one some forward spin. A pull downwards off the ball puts some slice on a cannonball service or an overhead and aids immeasurably in getting them in. (As an aside, it may be mentioned that recent analysis through the use of high-speed modern cameras has resolved the argument "the best players spin—or don't spin—their flat serves": the camera demonstrates beyond dispute that they *do* spin them. So the matter is no longer open to debate.)

The word *stroke* does not mean hit, strike, slam, or anything else that is essentially instantaneous. It implies time duration—something that starts and keeps going for a while before it is finished. Stroke means wipe, caress, pass over, across, or under something—as when you stroke a dog's fur. You stay on the ball for quite a time, and drag seven or eight strings across it while you are on it. You never *hit*, you *wipe*. Is it by happenstance that we say a tennis player has good "strokes," while a baseball player is a good "hitter"? Too often tennis teachers say, "It's just like hitting a baseball." Actually it is fundamentally different. The baseball player's one objective is to get the ball out of the infield. If it goes over the fence he is a hero. The tennis player's first preoccupation is to make sure the ball stays *in* the infield (the baseline). The player must worry about limiting how far it goes before it bounces. Therefore, instead of just propelling it and letting it ride like a ball player, the tennis player rotates (strokes) the ball to influence its flight so it will stay in. The fact that tennis shots

must be limited as to distance is what makes the ability to stroke (as contrasted with hit) an absolute necessity.

THE TWO EDGES

One who thinks right will usually end up doing right. It is of the utmost importance for all instructors and players to think in terms of stroke, not in terms of hit, because you do what you think. It is a very good rule to say "*Never* hit a tennis ball"; press it, carry it, wipe it, work on it, guide it, restrain it, limit it, but never just plain hit it. If you do, you don't know how soon or where it will come down, and it doesn't take much hit to clear the other baseline: a tennis ball is *very* lively.

The head of the racket plays the ball. It has a top edge and a bottom edge. If the top edge leaves the ball first, forward spin results. If the bottom edge leads off the ball, backspin is produced. Dragging sideways across the ball from right to left (forehand) or left to right (backhand) produces side spin or slice spin.

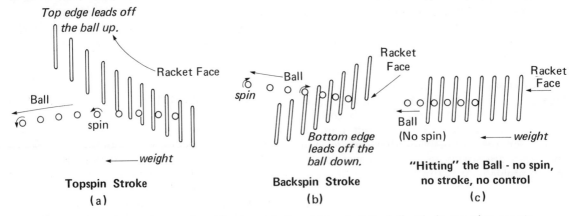

Top edge leads off the ball up.

Racket Face

Ball

spin

← weight

Topspin Stroke

(a)

Ball

spin

Racket Face

Bottom edge leads off the ball down.

Backspin Stroke

(b)

Racket Face

Ball
(No spin)   ← weight

"Hitting" the Ball - no spin, no stroke, no control

(c)

Diagram 3–1. The two basic racket skills: top and slice. (a) Lead off the ball with the top edge: topspin. (b) Lead off the ball with the bottom edge: backspin. If the motion of the racket is right to left (instead of vertical): forehand slice. Left to right: backhand slice. Note that the racket does NOT go through the ball, but goes OFF the ball. Only the weight stays with the ball, i.e., goes through it. Note that the racket plays the back of the ball, not the top or the bottom. The text points out that the racket moves almost at a right angle to the ball. This refers to the motion of the racket without the motion of the weight. Taken together, the two motions produce a composite effect that is about half a right angle. The contrast nonetheless remains sharp and valid. The above diagrams show a "stroke." When the motions of weight, racket, and ball coincide in direction, one has a "hit" (c), as in baseball.

Topspin (forward) and backspin can be mixed with side spin to produce combinations, but on *every* shot either the bottom or the top edge will lead through. This is the great fundamental of racket work: players who can make either edge lead at will as they play the ball have laid the groundwork for every shot they may wish to learn, no matter how good they become.

Thus, while racket work sounds complicated and "too much for me," it is not. There are only two basics: over and under, forward spin and backspin, top edge or bottom edge, follow-through high or low, lift up or pull down. The side spins (pull across or carve around) can be added later if a player becomes advanced.

Doubtless many readers have in their minds the question "Can this be taught to beginners?" Of course not if they are little children, and not at the very first even to college-age beginners. Good racket work is the *final objective*—what everything leads up to. And, above all, it should govern our thinking in everything we do: in our selection of grips, our preparation of the face of the racket for each shot, our plans for the follow-through. And as soon as a player is timing and meeting the ball at all consistently, the instructor should point out that how one leaves the ball is as important as how one comes to it—for example, if one accidentally goes even a little under the ball on a normal drive it will tend to sail and go far out.

With intermediate players and advanced players who complain of a "weakness"—that is, with all except rank beginners—a majority of problems derive from an incomplete or incorrect grasp of what the face of the racket should do while it is on the ball.

A FALLACY

Just about every beginner and a surprising number of more experienced players start with and retain one concept that is often at the bottom of most of their problems. They assume that the racket is what makes the ball go. This seems like a harmless and obviously true statement. It is not true. The weight makes the ball go, and the racket is merely the means of transferring weight into the ball. The big point is: it is *not* necessary to "swing through the ball" to get weight into it. If, instead of going through the ball and, as it were, coming out the other side, you wipe up the ball so the top edge leads off the ball, thus spinning it forward, the balls stays on the racket for a period of time as string after string strokes it. If, during this stroking interval, you press your weight forward, the ball gets a good solid forward push even though you did *not* go through it or even try to. The weight impels the ball, and the racket *spins* the ball and *controls* it.

To many this is a novel idea. The preceding paragraph may leave some readers with suspicion and doubt. For that reason it would seem desirable to say it in another way. Perhaps you have had the experience of slipping just as you attempt to make a drive. What is the result? Practically no shot at all emerges from the racket. Why? The weight did not move at all since the foot that was doing the shoving slipped, and no push was forthcoming. The racket met the ball, the arm swung; but without weight there is no shot. Of course, this is not one hundred percent true; some of the force comes from the swing of the arm. But it *is* true that the major force comes from the legs pushing against the ground and the turn of the body (shoulders and hips), not from lashing with the arm.

Those who *think* the racket makes the ball go naturally concentrate on making the face of the racket go through the ball with great velocity by flailing with their arm. They are inevitably wild and erratic and generally out of control. And, without knowing it, they throw their steering wheel (spin) right out the window, for if a racket goes flat through the ball little spin results, and the ball goes until gravity brings it down or the fence stops it. This, again, is hitting, not stroking. This is not a poor stroke; it is no stroke at all.

A very large number of average players perform beneath their potential ability because of this misconception: they think they must "hit" to make the ball go, so they hit and hit—and miss and miss. Now the racket cannot go right through the ball and also stroke up it or down it. It does one or the other. So long as one is a slave to the idea of hitting, it is not merely difficult, it is just about *impossible* to stroke the ball, to achieve any control of all this power we are generating. By contrast, once one realizes—and believes—that the racket can do what it wants so long as the weight of the player is pressing the ball while the racket strokes, then one's mind is free of this hit complex and can really learn to control the ball.

Another way of expressing this is to say that one cannot put the racket on the ball to stroke it without to some extent pressing, thereby making the ball go. Thus one should think only of stroking the ball: it will go by itself. Moreover, all players should strive to learn control first. It is easy to learn to lean harder, to apply more weight—to get more power. What good is power if the ball fails to stay in the court? And, as will be repeatedly stressed, it is easy to speed up a controlled stroke but very difficult to control a wild speedy stroke.

So *never hit through the ball.* This sounds like heresy. Could the time-honored cliché "Always hit through the ball" possibly be wrong? Yes, the way most people understand it, it is dead wrong. The majority think it means play through the ball *with the racket.* If this is accepted, then there can be no spin, and control is gone. The truth in the saying—the good in it—is that it makes us stay on the ball with our weight. We *should* hit through the ball with the weight but not with the racket. In order to produce spin, the racket must *leave* the ball (as contrasted with staying on it).

An analysis of any shot will show that the motion of the racket is almost at a right angle to the motion of the weight and the direction of the shot. For example, in the service the racket contacts the ball high and ends low on our left side—an essentially vertical motion. The turn of the shoulders and the bending of the back hurl our weight forward—a horizon-

tal effect. Take a topspin drive off a low ball: the racket comes from below the ball and finishes high—a vertical motion. The weight moves forward horizontally with the shot. If the weight goes up with the racket, a poor shot results. This is why the player is instructed to "Stay down." (But the racket does *not* stay down; it goes high.) Consider a backhand slice: the racket goes from the left to the right, cutting across. The weight goes forward with the shot. Take a volley: the racket cuts down or across, and the weight goes forward. Analysis of any other shot will reveal the same contrast: the racket goes *off* the ball nearly at a right angle to the weight, which goes *through* the ball. The fact that the racket goes off the ball is what produces the spin and also justifies the word "stroke"—just as if you stroked a cat. Your hand is the racket: if you follow through you will go right off the cat's back. While your hand does this, your weight applies a gentle pressure directly down onto the cat's back, i.e., at a right angle to the motion of your hand. Thus, on a tricky topspin angle we apply lots of "stroke" or "brush" to the ball, and very little weight, while on a deep drive from behind the baseline we apply a lot of "weight carry" to get depth and pace. But in *both* cases the racket goes off the ball, and the weight goes through it. It is merely the degree of emphasis that changes.

Perhaps some readers are in doubt, since this seems to contradict what is almost totally accepted. Check it out: watch good players, and *don't* watch the ball—watch their racket *all the way.* You will see the racket leave the ball and go high on drives, low on serves, across on slices. You will see the weight stay right with the shot. You will see the sharp contrast between the movement of the racket, which is stroking, and the weight, which is pressing with the shot.

Failure to understand the difference between the use of the weight and the use of the racket causes many people to "hit" a tennis ball and have little "feel" to their shots. The importance of this distinction cannot be exaggerated, since it is the basis of good stroking and good "touch." Many teachers do not incorporate this into their instruction of intermediate and advanced players, with the result that their players look good on the court but are very erratic in competitive play.

Why should playing a tennis ball be so different from propelling a baseball or a hockey puck? The answer is that in hitting a baseball or shooting a puck you do not have to worry about length. A puck must go straight and have the correct height, but the player is not concerned with how far it goes. In tennis this "third aim" is of crucial importance. The control of length is achieved by spin, and spin is created by stroking, which involves going off the ball in one direction or another with the racket, never through it.

A very good example of the difference between playing hockey and playing tennis occurred at Harvard. A star hockey player (one of the top three scorers in Harvard hockey annals), a top athlete with quick reflexes, definitely outstanding mobility and balance, and an eye like an eagle, decided to take up tennis. He looked very promising, but in his junior year he never even made the second six. Careful observation showed that his ball always went true in direction and height, but was forever going out. In other words, he aimed as he would if shooting a puck: for height and direction only. He had no sense of length whatever, and moreover was not aware that this was his trouble. When this was pointed out, he scored a phenomenal improvement, moved from number fifteen to number three on the second best team in the East, and won every match he played except one.

How was he taught to control his length? He was told to *stop* hitting right through the ball in an unrestrained manner, and to wipe off it enough to get some feel of restricting his length. Being very talented, he learned quickly, reduced his errors drastically, and suddenly became "tough"—i.e., he stopped playing giveaway. He began stroking the ball instead of hitting it. He changed in one season from a "fence buster" into a competent competitor. This is a true story, and one is led to speculate

on how many other "wild men" could conquer their frustrations if they got over this preoccupation with "hitting through the ball" with the racket as well as the weight.

CONCLUSIONS

Racket work means control. Power without control is useless. Power is comparatively easy to generate. Power comes naturally with mastery and confidence. Therefore, ninety percent of our work should be aimed at achieving control—that is, knowledgeable racket work. Every shot is based on leading off the ball with either the top or bottom edge of the racket. Doing this means to stroke, not to hit. The first thing for everyone to learn is to think in terms of stroking as contrasted with hitting, since people do as they think. A major objective of teachers should be to guide pupils' minds to a firm grasp of this basic fundamental of tennis.

QUESTIONS

1. Why does a topspin shot arc down? Explain in detail.

2. What does "hit flat" mean to you?

3. Contrast the word *stroke* with *hit*.

4. What is the function of spin in tennis?

5. What are the two racket skills, one or the other of which underlies every shot in the game?

6. Is it possible to play a topspin slice? A topspin undercut?

7. What does "hit through the ball" mean to you?

8. Do you personally think racket work is as important as the author urges? (The answer should be judged on how well the position taken is justified.)

CHAPTER 4

Footwork and Balance

HANDLING YOURSELF

Footwork and balance are the easy part of tennis technique. This does not mean that they are less important. It means that they are, as has been said, more natural and more akin to what we have already been doing for years in our daily lives: keeping our balance, running, jumping, changing direction, etc. Again the word *easy* does not mean that anyone can move exceptionally well with only a little practice. What it does mean is that anyone can realize whatever talent he has without anywhere nearly as much instruction and practice as required for similar success in handling the racket.

In spite of this "ease" there are quite a few common fallacies current about footwork, and therefore a review of the fundamentals is desirable.

SOME BASICS

Bend the Knees

Always keep the knees somewhat bent so that you feel flexible and crouchy, not stiff and straight. Almost all quick reactions are based

on having the knees bent. You start by shoving against the ground by straightening one or both legs. If the leg is not bent you must take time to bend it before you can start. This slows you down because you have to do two things instead of only one. If the knees are not bent you are not ready—for anything.

Figure 4–1. Ready position: normal. Note the crouch, the bent knees, the weight on the balls of the feet, the racket cradled in both hands.

Figure 4–2. Ready position: sophisticated. Note the off-center arrangement of the feet to favor the forehand. This is because the forehand is played from the back shoulder, the backhand from the front shoulder, so whirling for a backhand meets the ball out front and allows one to get weight into the ball, whereas the reverse is not true. Therefore, some players favor the forehand so the right shoulder, being already turned away some, can instantly come back into the ball forcefully. This permits aggressive returning off both sides and is recommended for advanced players as something to be experimented with in their return of service. The illustration is somewhat exaggerated to make the differences obvious.

Learn to Sidle

Move the right foot to the right, pull the left foot after, move the right again, etc. This allows you to move along the baseline or across the net while maintaining a neutral (face front) attitude as to which may the shot may come. By contrast, if you turn and run to the left in the usual manner (by facing left), any ball to the right catches you hopelessly "going the wrong way." This is particularly true at net, where to turn either way is pretty much of an irrevocable commitment that should be avoided until the ball has left the opponent's racket. Anyone can learn to skip in a few

moments. It is an invaluable part of footwork, even though very easy to acquire. All beginners' groups should be drilled in this a little.

Advance One Foot

Advance the left foot for forehand shots, the right for backhand shots. This is correct, but leads numerous players and some instructors into one of the great fallacies in tennis. Many people are taught and believe that they should "get the feet sideways." This is not true anywhere in the court except when stretching for a "get"—i.e., when you are *forced* to get sideways. If you stand facing the net, then advance the left foot to hit a forehand, this is quite definitely not getting the feet sideways. The left foot is pointed forward about forty-five degrees, while the right foot tends to get more completely sideways. See Figures 4–3 and 4–4. The shoulders should turn so that you are somewhat twisted, and a quick untwisting of the shoulders (or waist) is the source of much of one's power in a drive.

The object of arranging the feet in a certain manner is to facilitate moving the weight forward into the shot (any shot whatever). This is the fundamental—that each shot, as nearly as possible, should be met by your weight, thus giving the firmness and security that bring "touch." This firm security is just as important to a drop as to a drive. If you are sideways—i.e., your feet pointing at right angles to the flight of the ball—it is difficult to move the weight forward. Why? Because the knee will bend only one way—the direction the foot points. Therefore, the front foot should point at the spot where you hope to meet the ball so the knee can bend and the weight move into the shot. And you should always meet the ball in front of you diagonally to the side. Thus the rough rule "Point your front foot at a forty-five degree angle" is, while subject to variation, about right most of the time. But it is even more important for the player and the instructor to realize what one is trying to get ready to

Figure 4–3. Good forehand footwork. The left foot is pointed, aiming knee and weight forward. The right foot is braced, ready to shove. Contrast with "formy" footwork in Figure 4–4.

Figure 4–4. Poor forehand footwork. The player has "got sideways," with front foot pointed parallel to the baseline, so getting weight into the shot will be difficult. This is "formy" and purposeless. Contrast with Figure 4–3.

do. To think "get sideways" is irrelevant to the job. To think "Get ready to move into the ball, to apply the weight" is purposeful and relevant

and will lead to good useful footwork as contrasted with "formy" but ineffectual footwork.

The most common cause for poor volleying is the belief that as the ball comes the player should "get sideways." Actually there should be no turn at all at net; the player should concentrate entirely on advancing (closing in) toward the net. The worst way to volley a forehand is to put the right foot back, thereby achieving what *looks* like a correct stance: the left foot pointed forward, the right foot braced behind. See Figure 4–5. This volley will tend to be weak (since the player's weight is moving back) and ineffectual (the player has backed up and is not far enough in for a winner), and it is very frequently an error in the net (by backing up the player has in effect moved the net farther forward in front of the shot). It is quite extraordinary how many people volley in this way and wonder why "I just don't seem to be any good at net."

By contrast if you follow the principle of always advancing the left foot for a forehand volley (and the right for a backhand), thus getting as nearly on top of the net as possible, you *look* almost the same to a casual observer, but the difference is as day over night: the weight moves in, the volley is crisp, the ball is contacted much nearer the net at a point from which aces or near aces are possible and at times even easy; everything seems to go well. See Figure 4–6. Then people say "I like to get to net—I have pretty good luck, and it's fun." (This of course assumes they have good racket work.)

The fundamental is to *move forward into the ball*, not back from it, when you make a shot. Footwork should serve this purpose, and should not serve some meaningless "form" objective such as "get sideways" or "get your right foot back and your left forward," etc.

Avoid Crossing the Legs

Once the legs are crossed it is difficult to step into a shot. So you should sidle all small distances, arriving so you can advance the correct

Figure 4–5. Poor volley footwork. The player has taken the right foot back—the reverse of closing in on the net. The ball will be taken late, the shot will probably lack pace, and an effective placement will be difficult since the player is not in far enough. The form may LOOK correct, but actually this is poor volleying. Contrast with Figure 4–6.

Figure 4–6. Good volley footwork. The right foot has advanced all possible (no thought has been given to ''getting sideways''), the weight is moving into the ball, and the ball will be intercepted as near the net as possible, thus permitting a volley with good pace and good placement. Contrast with Figure 4–5.

foot as you play, thus again achieving the important objective of moving into the ball. Of course, when a long distance is to be covered you run in the normal manner, with perhaps a sidle or two as you arrive.

Take Small Steps

Any long step always results in loss of balance and poise—a feeling of being sprawled out and not under control. Small steps have the effect of keeping one altogether in one neat package, able to adjust or change direction quickly. A large number of quick neat poised steps and skips is the ideal to pursue in learning to move well.

Move Nothing but the Legs

Track men use their arms in running. Tennis players use *nothing* but the legs. From the waist up the torso, head, and arms should be carried like a passenger in a rickshaw; the legs are the coolie who carries the passenger

about. Why is this? Because the racket must be prepared and held poised for the shot, and the arms doing this cannot be diverted to help with the running by pumping.

Being unaware of this peculiar characteristic of tennis running is often the undoing of a player. He gets there—then misses the shot because the arms have been used for running and his racket is not ready to play the ball when he reaches it, and there is no time left to get it ready. Have you not heard the anguished cry, "Why do I miss it when I get there?" The answer often is that the racket was not ready to play, so getting there did no good. While of course some other reason may have caused the error, using the arms for running is frequently at the bottom of apparently stupid errors of this type.

Bend Low for Low Shots

Most players—even many good ones—miss low balls because they do not get right down there with the ball. The knee of the back leg should nearly touch the court on a low volley. You

Figure 4–7. The low volley. Note the deep crouch and the open racket face.

have to be where the ball is to handle it well. See Figure 4–7.

A Pointer for Advanced Players

Learn to run low. All the greatest exponents of the running passing shot have been masters at running—fast—while in a deep crouch. The racket is near the ground—where the ball will be when the player reaches it. Being right down there with the ball means that even though they barely reach it on first bounce they are able often to pull off a fine shot, to the surprise and dismay of a startled opponent.

THE OPEN VERSUS THE CLOSED STANCE

The closed stance means one foot is in front of the other—the left on forehand shots, the right on backhand shots. The open stance means the striker faces the net as he plays, stepping sideways with the right foot to play a forehand, the left to play a backhand. See Figures 4–8 through 4–11.

Many advanced players use the open stance. It is a compromise between the ideals of good footwork and good position. It requires extra

Figure 4–8. The open stance. Note the body will twist at the waist to get pace into the shot by turning into the ball. Note the laid-back wrist to permit the player to play either straight or crosscourt. This special racket skill is an absolute necessity if the open stance is to be used; otherwise, every shot goes crosscourt.

Figure 4–9. The closed or square stance. This is the normal correct closed stance, but many refer to it as the "square stance" to distinguish it from an excessively closed stance (Figure 4–10). Semantics can cause misunderstanding.

Figure 4–10. The completely closed stance. The left foot has been put over far beyond the right foot, which inhibits getting weight into the ball. This is not recommended. The open and square stances are to be preferred except in retrieving.

Figure 4–11. The partially closed stance. Many players use this compromise on their forehands.

racket skill. While most theorists have in the past considered the open stance incorrect and the closed stance orthodox, of late a very considerable discussion has arisen, since many fine players use the open stance—and win. This controversy is indeed a good development, since it helps slaughter the sacred cow known as "get sideways" and fosters open-minded thinking that recognizes the complexity of com-

petitive tennis. The game is not just footwork, or power, or control, or tempo, or moving, or position, or racket work: it is a combination of all these, with varying emphases, in varying circumstances, against various types of players. One cannot think of tennis as one can think of golf: that there is one "best way" to swing all the time, no exceptions permitted. In tennis it may be better to use the open stance on certain occasions and the closed stance on others. If holding position is important, the open stance is preferable. If the player is most interested in maximum power, the closed stance obviously permits more body turn and weight transfer. The one thing I would like to point out is that while the argument rages, the best players continue to use both and continue to win.

An outright attacker, whose game is based almost wholly on the thesis that the best defense is a good offense, will doubtless prefer the closed stance. His strategy is to hit the ball so well and so hard there will be no question of getting to the next ball; he intends to make his opponent do all the worrying along those lines.

A player of the type usually characterized as a "counter player" will have a wholly different attitude and will use an entirely different set of percentages. Since in considerable part he uses power generated by his opponent he is not interested in or worried about making sure he gets everything possible into the ball. His plans are concerned less with the idea of one perfect shot than with a series of shots, a war of maneuver, in which being ready for the *next* shot is of primary importance. Many such players prefer the open stance, since it facilitates recovery of position. One is not turned—a whole big step and turn are saved—and this is an enormous gain in a struggle in which a small fraction of a second often distinguishes success from failure.

Is it possible to choose critically between these two styles or between the many combinations or variations that are obviously possible? The answer generally is a flat "No" *except* each player should know his own talents and be quite decisive in choosing his own approach. The idea that one way is right and some other is wrong is wasted thought. The real question for the player is "What style will best exploit my talents?" The instructor should study each advanced player with the same attitude: do not try to adapt the player to a pet theory but adapt theory to the player. The concept that players are clay and can be molded into champions by a great coach is not only a lot of sheer rot but also repugnant if one thinks it over. Do you, if a player, wish to be considered as a lump of dirt, completely lacking in individuality, willing to assume any shape I (the instructor) choose? The very idea is an insult of the highest order, since it implies you, the player, are nothing, while I, that *great* teacher, am all. It is one thing for players to be modest and for instructors to be "the authority," but just how far do we carry this idea?

So here again we find there is no "right way" unless we first define the objective. Footwork can, like tactics, vary widely and yet remain completely legitimate and logically defensible. If an instructor adapts an immovable stand for one system, he thereby limits his effectiveness to one type of player. The tricky thing is that while the teacher should be open-minded and flexible and varied in his thinking, he should be limited and simple in any individual case.

You will not find any one of the best players using both the open and closed stance in the same context at different times. He will use one or the other *every time*, and he will be expert at it, and it will go with his talents, not against them. He has made his choice and has achieved an intelligent simplicity in his game. The instructor should be open-minded and tolerant of more than one approach.

TEMPO

Another aspect of this discussion, and doubtless the most important one, is the factor of tempo (we keep coming back to that). In play-

ing a hard-hit ball, or any ball that gives a player very little time, it is quite frequently *impossible* to assume a closed stance. In advanced tennis this situation occurs with great frequency. In returning a cannonball service, in volleying a hard drive, and in exchanges at net in doubles there just is not enough time to do anything except play the ball; any talk of arranging the feet in some theoretically desirable manner is totally academic, since arranging the feet takes time that is unavailable. The *only* move that is possible is the quickest and most minimal move: step out with the leg that gets the racket within reach of the ball, namely the right leg (the right leg carries the playing arm). Thus almost *all* fast exchanges with the forehand will be played with an open stance, while most backhands, slow or fast, will be played with a closed or semiclosed stance. To argue that the closed stance is more "desirable" in these circumstances is to ignore the factor of tempo. This is easy to do in a discussion but does not meet the facts on the court. The open stance is thus used by all the best players not because of theoretical preference, but because no player can disobey that most strict of all taskmasters: necessity.

QUESTIONS

1. Why should you never cross one foot over the other before your opponent plays the ball?

2. How can you move without crossing your feet?

3. Comment on the dictum, "Always get sideways."

4. Why should you crouch?

5. Why should you point one foot half forward?

6. Discuss footwork at net.

7. How does moving in tennis differ from moving in track?

8. Discuss the open and closed stances.

CHAPTER 5

The Service

A SERVICE FOR EVERYBODY

Scores of tennis books give very detailed descriptions of championship serving. This always involves bringing the wrist over with whip, bending the knees, flexing the back, and going through the ball just about dead flat. How many people can do this? How many have the wrist? The coordination? The dead-eye needed to get a flat service in the court? The time to perfect such a difficult skill even if they have the potential? A few in a hundred is probably not too far off as a guess. What follows here is a service that is within every-body's athletic potential, and also functions as a good easy starting point for those with more talent plus time and the desire to develop it. It is for everybody.

THE GRIP

For beginners the Eastern forehand grip is to be preferred at the start. See Figure 2–5. This permits the instructor to begin both shots with one grip, so players can serve and forehand a little almost at once. This encourages them, which is very necessary at the start, for they are all wondering "Is this game for me—or isn't it?" The truest description of this grip

(the "shake hands" grip) is to say that the palm of the hand is in the same plane as the face of the racket. If the racket is held diagon-ally in the hand—as contrasted with holding it at a right angle to the hand—the player will feel that the face of the racket is a natural continuation of the palm. The instructor should point out to the players that the flatness of the handle that is against the palm is in the same plane as the strings, so they should be able actually to feel how the strings are slanted without looking at them. The key characteris-tic of any good grip is that it gives this feeling of rapport between the player and his imple-ment, so he can say, "When I hold it this way I can *feel* what it is doing." And the "it" means the head of the racket—the strings.

THE STANCE

The correct position is the closed forehand stance: the left foot in front of the right foot, so for the right court a line between the toes of the two feet will be at a right angle to the baseline. The left foot should be pointed at approximately a 45-degree angle; the right should be parallel to the baseline. For the left court everything should be turned clockwise enough so that the same relationship to the proposed flight of the ball is established. A slight crouch is desirable, with the racket cradled at the throat by the left hand. Study Figure 5–1 carefully—all these little things are important. All beginners should be trained to take a little time. Place the left foot—is it pointed? Yes? O.K. Place the right foot—is it braced straight? Is it lined up with the left correctly? O.K. Grip right? O.K. Cradle it. Bend a little. Keep the racket up. All right—now, and only now, are you ready to start.

This sounds long and complicated. To some extent it is. But, as has been stressed, if it is done in series—*one* little thing at a time—it will all be mastered by most literally in a few minutes. As usual, racket work is the key element and the most difficult. Therefore, the instructor must *ceaselessly* watch the grip, only fussing a little about the feet now and then, as when they get really mixed up by putting the wrong one forward so their stance

is completely distorted. Beginners will soon learn to feel unnatural if they stand incorrectly, but are liable to hold the racket any old way. To start each group lesson with a grip review helps get a good habit started in place of the anarchy that tends to rule at first.

Surely someone will ask, "Why must we use this stance?" The right foot is braced so as to push the weight into the ball, so the shot is secure and firm. The left foot is pointed so the knee will bend toward the ball, not in some other direction (the knee will bend only one way—the way the foot points—so this little technicality is important). A slight crouch gives mobility and flexibility—needed for any shot. And the crouch helps the player to toss in front, which is desirable. In conclusion, this stance prepares the player to put weight solidly onto the ball—and, remember, it is weight that makes the ball go—and makes a good toss more natural and less of an effort.

Figure 5–1. The stance for service—forehand court. Note the little particulars: a line drawn from toe of left foot to toe of right will be perpendicular to the baseline; the racket is cocked head high and is cradled at the throat by the fingertips of the left hand. There is a crouch—slightly bent waist and knees. The Eastern grip—as shown here—is best for beginners. Note that the left foot is pointed at least 45 degrees.

THREE SERVICE ELEMENTS

There are three elements to the service: the backswing (getting the racket ready to play the ball), the toss (getting the ball ready to be played), and the service (playing the ball). The quickest way to learn to serve is to consider each of these separately.

The Backswing

Getting the racket ready is usually referred to as the "backswing." Much time is wasted, confusion is created, and many teaching opportunities are lost by the very prevalent habit of teaching beginners a full-fledged backswing coordinated with the tossing of the ball. Here is a true case of complicating what could and should be simple with all the frustration that often results for beginners. The backswing is not part of the serve. It is merely getting ready. There is no point (except later for rhythm) in merging it with anything else. Furthermore, if the instructor urges the player to use the preparatory motion as a chance to make his actual serve swing backwards, it can contribute materially to establishing the playing groove we are after. Therefore, to take the racket straight back past the player's head, keeping the face nearly flat—so it is ready to be placed squarely on the ball—is easy, simple, and allows a beginner to put his mind on the racket work (what the strings are doing) instead of having his attention diverted to considerations of fine points like rhythm, timing, etc. He should be told to take it back *slowly*, so he can *feel* that he is keeping the face properly slanted, and the only "extras" should be to tell him to bend his elbow a little (later on a lot but not now), cock his wrist some, and keep the elbow fairly high (most beginners tend to drop it way down). Ask the player, "Do you feel you are ready to put the racket face squarely on the ball? Yes? Then we can go to the toss." See Figure 5–2.

It has been stated that the backswing is not part of the serve—it merely gets the racket ready. It is important to realize this clearly and to discard all these fallacious theories about a continuous motion that gets ever faster until, at the instant of contact, the player has reached the moment of truth—or super-power. The backswing is actually closely comparable to the coiling up of a spring, or a snake. The sudden straightening out of these coils constitutes the strike of the snake and the service of the tennis player. An advanced server, seeking power, bends the arm as much as possible at both elbow and wrist, bends the back, bends the knees—and all of these straighten out when he hits. The important point is the absence of ever-accelerating motion; there is a coiling up to the point where no more coiling is possible, a very slight pause at the point of full compression, then a sudden release like an explosion. There is no reason to demand an instant release of the coiled-up striking mechanism; even a snake, when threatened, coils up and then strikes only if further provoked. He may stay coiled for quite a while, without striking, without undue discomfort beyond some tension. This is what a beginner should do: he should cock the arm and wrist ready to serve, then just hold them there while he applies his mind to the problems of the toss.

The Toss

The toss, like the backswing, is not part of the serve; it merely gets the ball ready to be

Figure 5–2. The beginner backswing or preparation of the racket. Note it reproduces—backwards—the forward motion that will occur in the actual serve. This is a considerable aid in developing a "groove." Note the racket is slanted just a little so a slight slice will occur; the right edge will lead. Note the crouch.

served. Here again there is no hurry, no point in getting excited, no point in being energetic. In fact, it is a good idea to practice the toss a good bit by itself, since it frequently is the last thing to improve. Why? Because the left or awkward hand does the tossing. It learns slowly. Moreover, the toss is as difficult a trick as racket work. It is completely new to the left arm and hand, and involves quite a bit of technique. See Figure 5–3.

A peculiarity of most good players is that when they toss, they take the left arm absolutely as high as it will go—straight up so the upper arm is almost against the cheek. Why? Because this cuts the size of the toss to the irreducible minimum. Carrying the ball up as high as possible leaves the smallest possible additional distance for the ball to go in free flight. The problem of tossing it straight is thus not solved—it is for the most part eliminated. This is the first thing to learn: take the left hand up high when you toss. It is not possible to take the arm up too high. When this is done the ball will naturally tend to go behind the player, when it should go in front. To achieve this a player must be told to lay back the wrist so as to keep the palm of the hand horizontal as he pushes the ball up ever higher. The ball will then tend to go more nearly

straight up. In addition he may want to bend the arm a little so he can push out front a bit —by straightening it—as he reaches the release point. Thus the toss comes to resemble a reverse one-arm push-up more than a normal tossing motion, which implies a free swing from the shoulder hinge. See Figure 5–4. Some instructors find it helpful to use the analogy of holding a glass of water on the palm, lifting it way up there without spilling, then giving it a little push-off straight up at the end, still without spilling.

It is usually better to leave most of this for lessons after the first one. The instructor should just suggest that players toss it slowly and in front; get them started and refine things later. The main effort at first should be to start them tossing with reasonable slowness and deliberation, carrying the ball up there thoughtfully as contrasted with the jittery fling or flip many beginners tend to offer at first in their nervous uncertainty.

The ideal point of contact is in front of the right shoulder, a foot to a foot and a half diagonally in front of the left foot. If the ball is lifted straight up from a point perpendicularly below the proposed contact spot, the ball will go up through the contact spot and come back down through it too; it will tend to *linger*

Figure 5–3. The toss. Lift straight up from below the proposed point of contact. Keep palm level. Take arm high. Note the bent elbow in the second photograph.

around the optimum area for playing it. Tossing from either side will not produce this very desirable lingering effect; the ball will perhaps go through the spot but then is gone; it won't come back. Therefore, lifting the ball straight up is important. It allows the player to take his time. If the ball goes just a bit too high—so that its lingering is almost all right where the player wants it—this is ideal. The ball seems to sit there, and it is easy to play it well.

A good toss makes good timing easy. The cocked racket waits until the ball sits at the right spot, then plays it. It is important to realize that a ball, when tossed, does three things (not two). It goes up, stops, and comes down. If the player can make it stop where he wishes to play it, then his task is easy; the timing is obvious, and if the racket is ready as it should be, he will soon learn to hesitate until that ideal instant occurs. And this *choosing* of the optimum instant—this is timing. With beginners much stress must be put on this idea of waiting; they want to swing right away, as soon as they toss. The instructor should always teach them, "Racket ready, *wait* (while the ball goes up and sits), play."

A good many people use a very high toss. There is no question that this is possible, because there are people who do it all the time, successfully. However, there is also no question that this is far more difficult than a just-high-enough toss. Hitting a stationary object is always less difficult than hitting a moving object; the timing is much more of a problem since the ball is moving down rapidly when hit if the toss was high. And controlling a big high toss is equally obviously harder to learn. Therefore, even if you see people serving this way, sometimes well, stay away from it in teaching or learning. Also a high-toss service is always a curse in a wind; by the time the ball comes down it is no longer where the player threw it, even if he aimed it perfectly. Another caution: any technique that is more than ordinarily difficult—and a high-toss service qualifies—will also be far more difficult to keep in order; it will tend to "go off" much more easily and frequently than a simple technique.

In concluding this discussion of the toss a last word of caution is in order. A poor toss is one of the major causes of poor serving. Most poor tosses can be attributed to a player's faulty thinking. His thought is to fling it with a free arm swing, or his thought is to flip it with his wrist, or he really believes he should toss it over his head or very high. The good players, as we have attempted to describe, *hang* the ball

Figure 5–4. The toss again. Note how it resembles a reverse push-up, with bent elbow and horizontal palm on the way up.

Figure 5–5. The beginner service from the side. Note the racket presses out as far as possible before pulling down into the follow-through. Note the bowing from the waist and the careful follow-through—very good for purposes of learning, and to show the striking face of the racket does not roll over. Note the feet. They stay put. Moving the right leg forward comes later.

Figure 5–6. Press out over the net. This draws weight into the shot, and keeps the strings on the ball longer—essential for good aim.

Figure 5–7. Service from in front. Note how everything stays in line. Observe the follow-through closely: the face has not rolled over. Notice the bent waist—to bring in weight and stay on the ball.

in the air, almost dead still, right where their rackets want it, with a shoving or push-up motion more than a free swinging motion. This entire concept or mental picture is brand new to most players, and it will help them im-

mensely if they get this idea early in the game. The caution is: don't be skimpy or careless in teaching (or learning) a good toss, or the lack of it will mean continuous trouble over the years. Last, this idea of suspending the ball in the air is not "natural," nor is the technique natural. It needs thought and careful practice to get it started and to get the mind and muscles acclimated to it.

The Service

To play the ball—the third element previously mentioned—is really the service: this propels the ball. The backswing only gets the arm and racket ready. The toss gets the ball ready. Only now do we actually serve. The first principle to stress is not to hit it. The player should put the racket on the ball and press the ball out in the desired direction horizontally toward a hole in the air three feet above the net in front of the service court to be hit. When the arm has gone forward as far as it will go, he should pull down toward the left side, so the ball runs up the strings—or the strings down the back of the ball—a little. These two motions—press out and pull down—have the effect of pulling the player's weight into the shot and, more important, keeping the racket on the ball for a long time. This is what gives the feel of guiding the ball—that is, of *aiming*, as contrasted with merely swatting it out in the general direction of the court. See Figures 5–5, 5–6, and 5–7.

A common fallacy is for the player to think, "If I swing the way the instructor said, the ball should go in." Not so, except perhaps by accident at rare intervals. The player must feel he pressed the ball out over the net and pulled it down into the court. For it is perfectly possible to swing exactly this way and pull it down too soon and too much—into the net. Or press out too much—and out you go. A feeling of pressing out just the right amount so the ball is pushed to the space above the net and exactly then begins to fall marks the beginning of a feeling of length. The pulling down is the beginning of the slice or drag that will arc the ball into the court later, with more speed.

VISUALIZING AN ARC

The concept of arcing the ball is of supreme importance in thinking correctly about service. To understand its full significance the reader is asked to do exactly as will now be directed. Stand at the baseline, ready to serve. Look at the service court at which you propose to aim. You will be looking *through* the middle of the net. If you aim directly—in a straight line—at the court, you will hit the net. If you aim above the net, you are not aiming at the court but far beyond it. *Only* if you think in terms of a curve can you picture in your mind's eye a ball that both misses the net by a good safe margin (two to three feet) and lands in the court by a good safe margin (four to six feet). These allowances are by no means too large for beginners or for intermediates. Only advanced players who have mastered the arcing service should move on to the hard flat first service, which, while it arcs a little, has more nearly a straight-line flight and a very narrow margin of error both at the net and at the service line. Work this out for yourself on the court if you doubt it. In fact, it is really advisable to do it anyway—even if you believe the written word—because it is very valuable concrete experience.

An extraordinarily large proportion of all tennis players serve so badly it has to be seen to be believed. They whale the first one in a beeline with lots of moxie—and about nineteen out of twenty go into the net or out. Then, unnerved at the horrible thought of serving doubles, they "poop" a fluttery cripple on the second ball. Many intermediate-to-advanced players do this—people with comparatively serviceable strokes and passable all-round games. They are by no means intrinsically this hopeless; their thinking is faulty. They have never thought of the arc concept—and therefore have made no effort to perfect it—so after

years of serving they still serve just like beginners.

The ball must clear the net safely—not by an inch or two—if the player is to achieve any consistency. This is the "push out" part of the service. It must then drop down into the square we call the court. This is the "pull down" or "drag" part of the service. Everybody can learn to drag the ball in by pulling down as they leave the ball. Those with weak wrists will not get any wrist or snap into it, and their ball will not go so fast. Nevertheless, they will get the feel of pressing the ball out past the net and drawing it into the court: they can serve. Those with strong wrists will naturally use their strength and will tend to get more snap into the shot as they progress. They should actually be discouraged from using this kick until they learn control—to arc the ball. Then they can concentrate on arcing it faster and faster. The point is, their strength is completely useless if it is employed merely to hit the ball rather than to stroke it and "work on it" so as consciously to make the ball "break" down as it crosses the net.

Beginners should serve so gently that the ball falls into the court for lack of enough force to go any farther. Thus they at once learn restraint in their length and get the two concepts "over the net" and "into the court"—the beginning of the arc idea. Only after they can plunk the ball in fairly consistently should they be allowed to speed up a bit. Even then this speeding up should be completely confined to the follow-through: they should still put the racket *carefully* onto the ball and press, not hit.

As will soon be stressed, the follow-through is very important, but for beginners the discipline should be confined to emphasizing that one must follow through to the left side. However inadequate this vague instruction may seem, the first thing to do is get them *pressing,* not hitting. They also have a lot of worries about backswing and toss, so the instructor should not overload them. If he can get them gripping correctly, cocking correctly, tossing correctly, and pressing the ball fairly straight, this is an impressive achievement for the first few days. The instructor should let players digest that much for a while; let it sink in before moving on. (The instructor might remind himself how long it took *him* to learn this trick.)

INTERMEDIATE SERVING

The player who says "I can push my serve in all right, but I never serve a really decent one" has reached the end of the beginner stage and is ready to move ahead. If he is to speed up the ball he must also increase the amount of "stuff" he puts on it to make it arc into the court. He must advance the right-hand edge a bit so it will lead. See Figure 5–8.

The Slice Grip

An intermediate server should not keep the Eastern grip and turn the wrist unnaturally. Rather, the player should leave the hand and wrist exactly as they are and turn the racket —i.e., change the grip. While there are always extremists who advise changing way over past the backhand, it is a fair statement that the accepted "serve grip" is roughly halfway from an Eastern forehand to an Eastern backhand. This will give some cut but not too much. In general it is wise to change the grip only a very little at a time, for, as experimentation will show the reader at once, this is like hot English mustard—a little makes a huge difference, and a lot is completely unpalatable.

Refining the Swing

At any time now the full swing may be added. From the stance position the racket is dropped straight down and kept swinging, like a pendulum, so it goes back and up behind the player until it is just about straight up. See Figure 5–9. In making this simple motion, many peo-

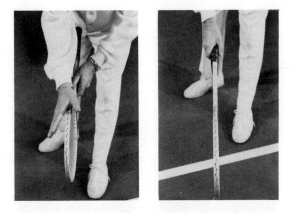

Figure 5–8. The advanced service grip. Note the thumb is more nearly straight, since the hand has moved from the forehand toward the backhand grip. With this grip the racket "wants" to cut the ball.

ple fall into one trap that can cause a lot of trouble: they turn the striking face of the racket in (toward them) as they drop the racket, instead of opening it out. Experimentation will show that turning it in gets the player all twisted up the wrong way and makes it necessary to untwist as part of cocking the racket (the next motion). This results in a lot of funny-looking twirling of the racket (first in, then out) that usually destroys the smoothness and the consistency of the serve. As with the high toss, it is *possible* to serve this way, but it is again much more difficult to learn and to keep in trim later. All players are urged to turn the face out as the racket is dropped, so that the cocking of the racket is the simplest possible motion. See Figure 5–10.

In cocking the racket, the player should cock the wrist, the forearm, and the upper arm, so good compression is obtained. The upper arm should be kept high.

There is one trick in cocking and striking that is difficult but if mastered improves the action to a marked degree. This is to partially let go of the butt of the handle with the fifth, fourth, and third fingers so the head can drop even farther down in the cocking process. Then, in striking, the racket is pushed out toward the ball and the fingers are clenched

Figure 5–9. A more advanced service. Note the increased coordination of left and right arms, the back and knee flex, the walking through with the right leg, which facilitates any advance the player wishes to make behind the shot.

Figure 5–10. Correct and incorrect backswing. Opening out the racket as in the first picture is correct. Closing it as in the second necessitates a complicated cocking motion that is very hard to make work. These little things—this and the control of the follow-through—are keys to smooth ease in serving.

tightly again as part of the wrist action that brings the head onto the ball. Obviously this is not for beginners, and it is not for others either unless they have some ability. But for those with good wrists it adds a feeling of freedom and facility and snap that is highly desirable. The important thing in learning it is to keep the fingers on the handle at all times: the player relaxes the fingers and *lets* the butt push the fingers up. At no time does the player actually take the fingers off the racket; after all, he would then lose the grip entirely. The objective is flexibility, not loss of control.

To practice this, the player holds the racket over his shoulder (cocked) and without moving his wrist lets the head drop by loosening the fingers. See Figure 5–11. Then, again with no wrist motion, he clenches so the racket head comes up again. The player should do

Figure 5-11. Finger action. Note that the action is obtained exclusively with the fingers. Many people do not appreciate the role the fingers can play in helping the wrist to give a feeling of skillful facility.

this repeatedly until he feels he is getting quite a bit of action by using the fingers alone. Then he should try coordinating it with his whole swing. The hand, wrist, and finger action should now feel more facile, less stiff, more zippy and clever. A marked increase in spin, arc, and eventual "hop" should occur. The degree of success will be great only with those who have the wrist strength and sense of timing to achieve real snap.

In learning this down-back-up-and-cock backswing it is well to practice it alone some. Then the player should practice the backswing, hesitate, *strike*—leaving out the toss. In this way he perfects the skills of the right arm and can concentrate on other skills like turning out, good cocking, making the strike go straight out off the shoulder, and above all the follow-through.

The Follow-Through

Very few players and not enough instructors have any conception of the great degree to which the control of the ball depends on the follow-through. The fundamental they miss is that whatever happens during the follow-through *begins* while the racket is on the ball.

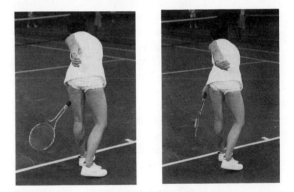

Figure 5-12. Correct and incorrect follow-through. Controlling the destination of the racket head controls the route it travels. If the right edge leads through, the ball will be sliced. The first picture is correct, while many otherwise correct serves lack "touch" (equals control) because the follow-through rolls over (second picture).

It is of *extreme* importance—please note the word "extreme"—that the right-hand edge should lead through, so that the follow-through does not roll over after the manner of some topspin forehand drives. Any reader not sure of what this means should study Figure 5-12 carefully. The player who masters this wrist motion will not have much trouble learning to control a service, for this causes what we call "slice" to be imparted to the ball.

An easy way to educate the wrist quickly is to hold the racket down by the left leg in a partially followed-through position. From here the player flips the racket through with the wrist, making sure it stays in its scooping attitude (right edge leading a little) and does not roll. See Figure 5–13. This will soon accustom the hand and wrist to the new trick, particularly if repeated ten or fifteen times without moving the arm. Next, after each flip the player takes the arm back a trifle farther up toward the hit point—farther and farther each time until a complete swing is achieved, backwards and forwards, from cocked position to the end of the follow-through, but now the follow-through is correct. In this practicing the greatest benefit is derived if the wrist is bent completely through as far as it will go. This type of cut or slice is a compound of forward and side spin, and has the effect of an out drop pitch in baseball—i.e., the ball curves to the left and down. It is the "down" that interests us most, and if the left-hand edge of the racket leads off the ball, no "down" results.

One effective method of teaching this trick is to call it "scooping." If the player follows through as though he were shovelling something up backwards off the ground alongside the left leg, to roll the racket (left edge first) will spill everything out of the shovel, while

to follow through correctly keeps the shovel going as it should. This analogy often does not read too well, but with players on the court relating a technical concept to something more familiar to them often speeds up the learning process.

Surely there will be those who will suggest this is all words, that yes we should slice, but all this stuff about edges and follow-through and scooping is unnecessary. These objectors are ignoring the fact that what happens during the follow-through begins while the ball is on the racket. Anyone who does not realize this and give it its due as an important truth would do well to reconsider. There are thousands of players who want to control the ball but say "I can't seem to do it." Many of these players try to come *to* the ball correctly but pay little attention to how they *leave* the ball—the follow-through. Its importance can scarcely be exaggerated.

Difficulties in Slicing

There are various disconcerting pitfalls that await players who first try to learn a slice service. When the grip is changed—even a little—the ball at once tends to go to the left, often quite drastically. The answer is to toss

Figure 5–13. Correct follow-through expanded. Players should practice this, emphasizing the wrist action to train the hand. This seems pretty fussy perhaps, but it controls how you leave the ball; and leaving the ball—not coming to it—gives spin. Thus a correct follow-through is essential for control through spin.

the ball a trifle to the right, aim to the right, press out a little to the right of the target. In other words, it is quite logical that a somewhat slanted racket will cause the ball to go in the direction of the slant, so one must compensate for it. Another common trouble stems from the misconception that to slice means to curl way around the ball, or even to swing in a horizontally circular manner. This of course results in a weak swish plus something approaching a forty-five-degree error in direction (to the left). The answer is to toss a bit to the right, to swing straight ahead somewhat (one service court's worth) to the right of the target, playing as flat as possible with a *slightly canted racket*. This keeps the spin, allows for it (direction), and restores the solid contact. However, with some the idea of slanting the racket keeps stubbornly producing a series of ill-guided swishes. This is again because the player has a misconception: he thinks he must turn the racket around the right side of the ball *before* he meets the ball. This idea of cutting the ball, as it were, ahead of time—which results usually in an almost complete miss or whiff (since no racket face is put on the ball)—can be quickly cured by telling the player "Put the face on the ball flat, *and then* go around it just a little as you press it out and pull down." This restores the firm contact that was lost in attempting to learn to cut. To say it again: don't slice until after you are on the ball.

Carving the Service

The idea of pressing the ball out and at the same time going around and down it is best expressed by the word *carve*. Even as we should think of the flight of the ball as an arc, so we should think of the swing of the face of the racket as a carve—i.e., the racket curls slowly and continuously around and down the ball, starting at the upper right corner of the back of the ball. This thought of carving is just one particular application of the fundamental we keep stressing: stroke the ball, don't hit it— this is the key to racket work, which is the key

to tennis. In this case the curling or carving effect turns the racket at least forty-five degrees from start to finish, and often far more with accomplished players.

To help a player get this mental picture, the instructor should have him hold his racket up at the point of contact in a nearly flat position, then have him press out and pull down slowly, curling a little as he goes. He will discover that he will follow through exactly as has been urged and not any other way. Likewise, if he contacts the ball nearly flat and then thinks *only* of following through correctly, he will *necessarily* curl and carve. Thus, far from being semantics or an unnecessary complication, stressing the correct follow-through *forces* upon the player the very skill that is often so hard to acquire. If a player puts his racket on the ball correctly and follows through correctly, it is difficult for him to play the ball badly because the start and finish pretty much control everything in between. Therefore, emphasis on the follow-through is a key teaching shortcut that is neglected or rather unappreciated by many instructors.

Coordinating the Service Elements

Thus we have the full swing preparation: the cocking of the racket, the placing of the face onto the ball, and the carving or stroking of the actual shot. With these we must coordinate the toss, and this is almost entirely a matter of timing. If a player will practice his right-hand skills alone he will get a one-hesitate-*two* effect—the emphasis of course being all on the "two" since that is the actual shot. The hesitate is usually in reality a completing of the coiling up and arranging of the racket preparatory to playing the ball; it is not mere idleness. This is also the ideal moment for the toss. So, as the racket starts dropping from the height of the backswing toward the cocked position, the left arm starts up and reaches its greatest height as the right arm reaches its lowest or fully cocked position. Just as the right arm is ready to go—there is the ball, sitting there, just asking for it.

Thus the service becomes a one, toss-cock, *play*—or a one-uh-*two* if some prefer. The one-two count describes what the right arm does but does not allow for that little hesitation between the two moves, which is vastly important because it is then that we *aim*. The one-two-three description is more complete and all-inclusive. However, here we are indeed getting into semantics. People who teach a one-two service usually advocate tossing the ball simultaneously with the backswing; this is not quite the same. I advocate tossing it simultaneously with the *end* of the backswing, but let's not quibble. The chances are that there will be few essential differences between two players taught the two different ways—the one-two player will start his toss a bit sooner, that's all. To say that either method is far superior is merely to take the narrow-minded view.

The only point deserving stress is that the teaching process will get results much faster if it uses the one-thing-at-a-time approach with beginners, no matter what the final objective may be. It is important to practice the back-swing, the cocking, the toss, the curl to the scoopy follow-through, the putting of the racket flat on the ball—each one separately. And it is important after that to go through it *slowly*, so each skill can be critically judged by the instructor and felt by the player. No matter about final objectives—teaching slowly and in series is the quickest way to accomplish the most. And racket work is the area where all players need the most guidance and drill.

As soon as an intermediate has mastered the spin of the ball he will hit the net a lot: his ball is arcing down, and he is not allowing for it. Since the player must not only get the ball over but also put it into the back part of the service court, he must now be taught to aim higher and higher over the net—for depth. "See how high you can aim and still bend it in" is a good challenge and starts him on a desirable habit: give a substantial margin of clearance over the net.

Another refinement is to bend low on the follow-through and to complete a full circle; the head of the racket ends up about where it started behind the back. While this concept is slightly exaggerated (it can leave one tied up for the next shot), it is a very good drill to make the racket leave the ball faster, thus making the spin and control more authoritative. The idea of "complete action" here embodied is a help in thorough teaching of the principles involved. It has an additional beneficial effect in that the bending necessary to get such a complete swing brings the weight more into play, increasing speed and power. Gradually the player feels he is putting his entire self into his service. He is now becoming advanced.

ADVANCED SERVING

Before the instructor attempts to proceed further, the player should be able to serve a reasonably decent slice service with good dependability and should have a pretty good grasp of what stroking means. Until this much skill is achieved the player or instructor should not bother with any of what follows, for experience negates the idea that it is good to aim for the top and set right out after the best from the word go; this is no good in tennis. A far more practical simile is to liken tennis to a ladder: the fastest way up is step by step, and one who tries to make it in one jump merely falls back down to where he started. So the instructor who says, "You are not ready for that yet" will often reach the goal sooner than one who tries to teach everything at once.

Power

Power comes from weight and wrist snap. To get maximum power the player must flex the entire body and legs like a bow—and add to this a snap-the-whip use of the wrist comparable to that of a baseball pitcher throwing a fast ball. Almost everybody understands the wrist snap if they have the strength and coordination, but not everyone by a long shot understands how to get full weight into a service. The principle usually missed is that the execution of the cannonball swing is almost entirely vertical. Most players try to move forward into the ball, thinking this puts the weight into it. It does, but only partially. The greatest weight jolt by far is produced by decisively emphasizing the downward follow-through, bending so the head goes low and the buttocks pop out backwards a little. The feet don't need to move. The backward movement of the buttocks accelerates the top of the torso forward and down. The downswing again accentuates this head and torso motion into the ball. In sum, when we swing this way we move weight forward into the ball faster than any other way. This surprises many people—but try it: swing the arm and racket and head *down* to your left side and observe how the shoulder goes *forward* when you do this. Push the buttocks out backwards and notice how the shoulders move *forward*. It sounds illogical—to make a predominantly vertical effort in order to produce an essentially horizontal result—but it is true. Last, watch some player who boasts a truly lethal cannonball; you will see what has been described here.

Players should not be confused by the fact that many "big servers" cross their right foot over as they finish. The right leg coming over adds little if anything to the service and isn't supposed to; it simply starts one to net.

Doubtless someone is already thinking: this may produce force, but doesn't it hit the ball into the ground? How does one get the ball over the net with such a vertical swing? The answer, as always, is racket work. The player puts the racket face flat on the back of the ball, swings down, and bends down, but lets the ball run up the racket enough to enable it to clear the net. This is achieved by lagging the wrist a trifle. The player literally *lets* the ball go over the net; it doesn't take much. It is easy enough to overdo it so the ball goes out, not merely just over the net. The player must swing down without taking the ball with him.

Many powerful players even use some slice and still achieve great speed. Of course, the slice aids their percentage considerably. The most striking thing to be noted here is that even the hardest, most solid, most "flat" services need to be stroked, not hit. The racket face must wipe down the back of the ball. This not only achieves better use of weight but also pulls the ball into the court.

Topspin

Most players like to use a full backhand grip for topspin. The racket is cocked at almost a right angle to the arm, so when it meets the ball it will be on top of it, with the right-hand edge decisively ahead of the left to get heavy spin. The main trick here is to move the toss back to a point just barely in front of the head so that when the racket plays the ball it will be moving *up* and over the ball, not just over it. Getting this "up" effect—so the ball would hit the fence if hit flat, followed by a big high arcing flight and a mean forward hop—these are the characteristics of the topspin service when well executed. The racket confines itself to imparting spin. The body and legs flex and rock to give weight and pace. This service is a favorite for a second service since it offers huge margins for error because of the accentuated arc.

Twist

Twist services are topspin services to which side has been added by tossing the ball more to the left and swinging back more to the right. The true American twist is the most exaggerated form of a twist. The ball is thrown behind the left shoulder, the racket is dropped well below and to the left of the ball, and then the racket is swung entirely to the right—not forward at all. The ball is propelled forward (while the racket puts side-top on it) by a violent flexing of the body and legs. Here we have two motions almost at right angles to each other: the racket goes sharply to the right and finishes on the right (ordinarily the "wrong" side), and the weight moves forward in the direction of the target. This is an extremely difficult service to learn because of these unnatural aspects, and it has caused many players to use a board instead of a bed for sleeping. If a player is naturally flexible to the point of being double jointed, so that the necessary bending and heaving are not an intolerable strain, then perhaps the American twist is a suitable service. It should be added that such players are one in a hundred or a thousand. Instructors seldom teach this service because it is physiologically difficult for the human body, particularly for the sacroiliac. Also, anyone capable of this service is capable of all the others too and so doesn't really need it. It is noticeable that while many fine players use twist, not as many as formerly go all the way and use the American twist. It is very effective and tricky and impressive—but it is also against nature.

Accuracy

The key to aiming successfully is to aim for an area, not for a line. Nobody can consistently hit a line—it is too small. Human fallibility, even among champions, demands more margin for error. The more advanced the player, the narrower the area can become, but it never reaches the status of a line. Obviously beginners should use the whole service court, then half a court, then one-third, until they can confine their service to the equivalent of a bowling alley. If a ball is that close to either side, it is difficult to run around it; and the major objective is to oblige the receiver to play his weaker stroke.

The bowling alley analogy is a good one. It may be pointed out to players that a bowler keeps his swing very straight so the ball will not end in the gutter on either side of the long narrow alley. If one thinks of serving as upside-down bowling, the idea is the same: to

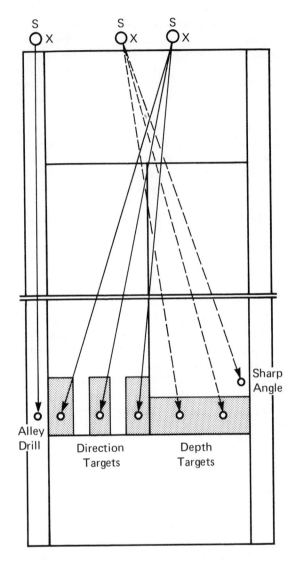

Diagram 5–1. Service accuracy. Aim for areas, not lines. This allows for human imperfection but gives effective results with some consistency. Intermediates and advanced players should master the shaded targets before attempting the very expert small target sharp angles. Those who achieve consistency in finding the targets indicated here may move on to smaller targets. Most will find these sufficiently difficult! The alley drill is very good for developing directional accuracy. Note how the service to center can be related to the center strap in aiming.

confine the swing to that small width of court that will force the opponent to play the shot he least prefers. Even in advanced serving, with lots of spin, power, etc., this concept of the long narrow area is a useful aid in acquiring accuracy. As usual, starting slowly produces quicker results: the player should try to press the ball very, very straight, and only speed it up after some success in accuracy has been attained.

Another aid to aiming is to use landmarks. For example, the center strap is a good landmark for the player to use when trying to serve to the backhand from the right court. The natural turning motion, the follow-through, and the slice all tend to take the ball to the left—to his forehand. The player should aim carefully a few inches to the *right* of the center strap. It is amazing how this trick will tend to hold a serve to the right as desired. From the left court the player should try aiming as far to the right of the center strap as possible without hitting the alley. Soon he will know just about how far over to aim without losing the percentage and will have a mental marker to go by. From the right court go to the left of the center strap for the angle out to the forehand—three feet? four feet? Experimenting will help the player determine just what *he* can do; never mind other people or theory.

Landmarks can be of great assistance to instructors and players. In teaching players to allow for the tendency of a sliced service to go left, an instructor can use everything in sight: "aim one service court's width to the right; toss the ball toward the wrong court" (when serving from the right); "toss the ball toward the netpost" (from the left); "swing straight at where the alley goes under the net"; etc. For the more advanced players more exact landmarks are needed, such as the center strap.

Missing the net is an important part of serving and accuracy. It seems obvious, yet it is necessary to point out—endlessly—that the net is something to aim *away from*, not *at*. It is a fact that most errors occur in the net. People, believing a skimming low ball is the best (though it frequently isn't), actually aim at the top of the net. It is not enough to say "Don't aim at the net." This leaves a vacuum in the player's mind. The instructor should substitute "Aim *away* from the net as far as you can and still achieve your objective." This is positive and tends to foster a good mental habit.

This apparent fussing over words is more important than most people realize. In one respect people are like moths: one's eye is attracted by whatever is the brightest object in

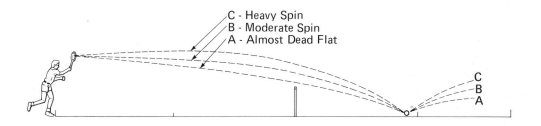

C - Heavy Spin
B - Moderate Spin
A - Almost Dead Flat

C
B
A

Diagram 5–2. Aim away from the net (advanced serving). Note the large margin of safety permitted by the spin services. Note that aiming as far as possible away from the net is MORE aggressive, since it results in better depth. Only the cannonball (A) should go close to the net. All spin serves should clear the net by from three to six feet. Note also the variety of bounces that can be achieved—from a low hard skid (A) to a high kick (C). Note that spin serves go UP from the racket, not down.

his field of vision. When you look out the window at night you will at once focus on a street light or some other comparatively brilliant object. Likewise, when the player looks from the baseline toward the other side of the net, what is the brightest object before him if it is not the white top-binding of the net? The eye is inevitably drawn to it, and *knowingly or unknowingly* the player aims either at it or in relation to it. Quite obviously it is desirable and advisable that we use this fact constructively by training players to aim—knowingly—away from the net, and to be aware of the tendency we all have actually to aim at it. In the specific case of advanced serving, the player must aim a cannonball not more than a foot above the net, while a topspin or twist should clear the barrier by from three to six feet. In any event, the player, with the instructor's help, should develop the mental habit of staying away from the net as far as possible.

Learning from Experience

Once the player has reached the advanced skill level in serving, experience is much to be preferred to books, hence the comparatively skimpy treatment given the subject here. The player will learn much if he participates in tournaments, observes how his adversary goes about embarrassing him with his serve, how he varies it, takes him by surprise sometimes, and generally uses it as a formidable weapon. Soaking up these tricks in matches where one feels the pressure is the real way to appreciate their true significance. The player should copy any tricks that fall within the scope of his natural talents. In this way he will not restrict himself to one man's limited theory (and most books have this limitation) to the exclusion of a good many plays that might be right up his alley. It is a pretty good idea for the player to be nobody's disciple but rather to get to know himself and his potentials and limitations as well as he can. Instructors should avoid all pet theories and instead try to adapt to their players.

Racket Work and Serving

With intermediate and advanced players it is often desirable to draw attention to a simple and pure racket work drill. The player holds the racket up in front of him and serves using *only* the hand, fingers, and wrist. He follows through only with the wrist, not the arm. This is his skill, his steering wheel, the kernel of the serve. If he can slap the ball flat with a little down-wipe and make it go close to the top of the net, he has a flat serve. If he can carve the ball and arc it into the court, he has a slice serve. If he can now toss over his head and snap up and over it, so a high arc shot results, he has a topspin serve. All of these will be light and will lack pace. But if the player has the hand skills (the racket work), then rocking, bending, leaning, pressing—these are *easy* to add. If he does not have the hand skills, no amount of rocking, flexing, or heaving will produce a good serve. Racket work is the key.

What of those less gifted mortals who do not have the intrinsic athletic ability to master these obviously difficult skills? The answer is that all players should move as far up the ladder as they can. Everybody can learn to press a no-swing, smooth, well-aimed—even if admittedly weak—service across the net and into the court. The next rung of the ladder is to accentuate the bowing on the follow-through, thus getting more drag (a little slice) on the ball and more weight into it. Everybody can do this; there is still *no wrist at all* required. The next step is to learn to aim for a part of the court instead of merely the whole area. Everybody can do this; no unusual talent is demanded.

We have now reached a reasonably respectable "service for everybody." To go beyond this demands more and more talent—to coordinate the full swing, wrist action, finger action, snap, etc., not to mention different tosses for topspin, twist and trick angles, the body and leg flexing for power, the varied racket work for different serves, the tournament experience necessary to make these advanced techniques useful.

Perhaps some readers are surprised and feel a little critical because this chapter does not contain more lengthy discussions and full illustrations of twists and other advanced services. These are purposely omitted so that attention will be focused on the basic "service for everybody." Moreover, as was mentioned earlier, every issue of every tennis magazine usually contains pictures, and often articles, about advanced serving. This area is covered and re-covered with great regularity and often very painstakingly. Champion after champion is pictured at his peak. Advanced players would do well to study such illustrations; the smooth grace and coordination are well worthy of imitation. This book is much more basic and is aimed at helping players to help themselves and at helping instructors deal with less experienced or less generously talented players.

Instructors and players are referred to Chapter 11 for skill tests in serving. The tests themselves are good drills.

QUESTIONS

1. What grip do you recommend for beginner service? Why?

2. Discuss the stance for service.

3. What are the three parts of a total service?

4. Why does it help to use a "straight back" backswing with beginners?

5. Why should the arm reach high in tossing the ball?

6. What do you do with the palm of the tossing hand? The elbow?

7. Where will the ball bounce when tossed properly if allowed to fall to the ground?

8. How high should the ball be tossed?

9. How can an instructor help players get a feeling of aiming?

10. How does the concept of an "arc" relate to service?

11. Should beginners serve hard?

12. How would you describe the "advanced" service grip?

13. Describe the full backswing.

14. Why is the follow-through very important?

15. How can an instructor help players get used to slicing a service?

16. How does it help to use three counts on the serve?

17. Why do players hit the net a lot after learning to spin their service?

18. Is it important to "walk through" with the right foot when serving?

19. How can a player best get weight into a cannonball serv e?

20. How does the player hold the racket for topspin and twist services?

21. How can a player help himself develop greater accuracy?

22. How should players with weak wrists serve?

23. Can a player slice a service without using the wrist?

CHAPTER 6

Baseline Play

For all the techniques covered in this chapter readers are referred to the Skill Tests in Chapter 11. The tests are themselves very good drills.

THE OPEN RACKET

Always Play Up

Solid deep crosscourt drives are the foundation of baseline play, to which we should add the lob, passing shots, defensive slicing, and the return of service. Omitting return of service, which will be treated separately, every one of these shots must go *up* from the racket. This is by far the most basic concept concerning baseline play: play up. This does not mean to hit up some of the time or most or nearly all of the time. It means to hit up *every time* with absolutely no exceptions whatsoever. Perhaps someone is already thinking, "How about very high bounding poop shots that bounce as high or higher than your head?" The answer is uncompromising: play them *up*. They seem high, but a ball as high as a six foot player is only three feet above the lowest part of the net. If hit down at even a slight angle from roughly forty feet away it will hit the net—or more probably the ground in front of it—because it must be remembered gravity is hastening its

fall also. So it is hoped the point is made beyond further question: *hit up from the baseline.*

Technique is the servant of tactics. If we wish to hit up, then the face of the racket should be open in order to make contact below the middle of the back of the ball. See Figure 6–1. It is important to explain this to each new group of players so they understand that even when using a bangboard they should aim for the top half of it if what they practice is to be useful on the court. The open or tipped-back face produces this result almost automatically on both forehand and backhand.

DRIVES

The Nature of Topspin

While missing the net—by hitting up—is our first problem from the baseline, there is a second: we must *not* miss the court. If we take such pains to aim well away from the net, thereby getting the ball pretty high in the air, what is to prevent it hitting the fence if we give it any pace to speak of? The answer is topspin, which causes the ball to arc down and hit the court instead of sailing beyond the baseline.

It is quite astonishing how frequently people —including many who have played for years —do not understand topspin. (Just in case you

Figure 6–1. Hit up from the baseline. Note that the slightly open racket face causes this to happen automatically. Players should think of playing an exact spot on the ball (a little below the middle of the back of the ball) instead of thinking "hit the ball." Instructors should tell younger players to "hit the ball in the seat of the pants."

might be one of them, please read carefully what follows.) Topspin means that the ball is rotating forward roughly in the direction of its flight. Topspin means the top of the ball turns forward and the bottom of the ball turns backward. Topspin means the back of the ball moves up. Topspin does *not* mean you hit the top of the ball. It is quite possible to play the bottom of the ball and cause the ball to spin forward. By playing the back of the ball and moving the strings up, we again get forward spin. By playing the top of the ball and moving the strings forward, we get forward spin. The most common misconception about topspin is to think that it means to hit over the top of the ball. While coming over the top of the ball will certainly produce topspin, it will also tend to send the ball down—and this is never what we wish to do from the baseline.

The first point to understand is that we can play *any* part of the ball and get topspin. (If an instructor refers to it as forward spin, the confusion caused by the word "top" can be largely eliminated, and this is recommended.) Since from the baseline we want every ball to go up a reasonable amount, it is clear we want to put the forward spin on a spot a little below the middle of the back of the ball. See Figure 6–1. To do this we must come to the ball from behind and slightly below it with a slightly open faced racket, and we must wipe up the back of the ball as we press it forward. The top edge of the racket must lead upward off the ball. The ball must roll down, not up, the racket. The racket must finish above the flight of the ball, not below it. We must follow through rather high, since the ball is going to be played up, and the racket is going even higher. To sum up, in order to achieve the two objectives of missing the net and hitting the court, even when we use speed, we must put topspin on the lower part of the back of the ball. This gives spin plus proper elevation.

This can all be expressed very simply in another way: a topspin drive is nothing more than a low forward spin lob. Many players do not realize this; their mental picture of a drive is a horizontal beeline from their racket to the court beyond the net. This level conception ignores the inescapable truth that the ball *must* rise to miss the net and then *must* arc down if it is to strike the court. The idea of the low lob takes these factors into account. One merely thinks of lobbing three to six feet above the net instead of twenty to thirty feet above it. This likening of the drive to the lob is recommended to instructors as a tried and true method of getting players out of that most common of all faults in tennis—hitting the net. Once they start lobbing they are aiming *away* from the net—so they stop hitting it. While of course this produces somewhat "poopy" tennis at first, it also produces sound consistent stroking and aiming, and playing harder and lower is comparatively easy to acquire later on. Above all, the lob idea gets across to the player the dual nature of a drive —that it must go up *and* down—not just one or the other; and it gets out of the player's head that a drive does just one thing—that is, go straight ahead, roughly horizontally, like a bullet from a gun.

Preparation

Nine out of ten (or more) faulty strokes have as their basic cause the improper preparation of the *face* of the racket. For example, if the face is turned over (closed) during the backswing, then the player *must* either (please note he has no choice) pull up violently to clear the net—a poor swing—or he must curl under the ball to lift it as he hits it—a poor stroke that will go out if hit hard because of the backspin. The person who prepares the face incorrectly *must* hit incorrectly. Another way of saying this is to state that the preparation of the face of the racket determines what a player is going to do, so that if he prepares badly it can be predicted almost infallibly that he will play badly. That is why someone with a "bad stroke" keeps hitting it badly—again, again, and again. The chances are all against him; the endlessly repeated poor shot is the *only* thing open to him once he has prepared his racket incorrectly. Until he improves his preparation, any significant improvement in his stroke production is impossible.

Therefore, the beginner should think *only* of how he prepares the face of the racket: that is, how it is slanted as he puts it out to the side ready to play. A great deal has been written about the backswing, circles, ellipses, continu-

ous motion, acceleration, etc. For a beginner, all of this should be thrown out; the crucial importance of the racket work demands that his mind focus exclusively on that aspect of the stroke until some proficiency has been developed. Only then should the instructor allow or direct the player to consider other matters. At the start it is a full assignment to control the slant of the racket face and to keep it slanted that way as it is put on the ball and pressed through and up (for topspin). Once the player has reasonably mastered preparing, coming to the ball, pressing through, and leaving the ball, there will be time enough for additional improvements. The rigidly limited program offered here is the irreducible minimum: what is essential to getting the ball over the net and into the court. See Figures 6–2 and 6–3.

There are important additional advantages to this minimum preparation. For many beginners just meeting the ball is a formidable problem. They whiff. They hit the wood. They play too soon or too late, and the shot goes radically left or right. Holding the racket out to the side, taking care *not* to take it back more than a tiny bit, enables one to line up the head of the racket with the ball so the ball is caught by the racket as a baseball is caught in a glove. Just as the ball is received it can be given a little toss back the other way (the faint beginnings of a drive!). In this way comparatively awkward pupils can learn *quickly* how to effect a contact between ball and racket.

Timing

The problem of timing—another very difficult affair for the poor athlete—is also amenable to a reasonably quick solution *provided* the preparation is minimal. When the racket is brought to the ball from a full backswing—that is, from fairly far back—the question of when to start this swing is indeed a tough one for the beginner. However, if he starts by putting his racket very close to the proposed contact spot he can *see* when the time has come to play

Figure 6–2. Minimum racket preparation—forehand. The one thing that MUST get ready is the racket face. Note that this minimum preparation can help line up ball and racket, both horizontally and vertically. More swing can come later.

Figure 6–3. Minimum racket preparation—backhand. Players will learn faster this way; they are relieved of worrying about footwork, ellipses, etc. They get the "core" going first: the racket on the ball with the racket face properly slanted. A player's attention should not be diverted with ANYTHING ELSE at first.

the ball. Of course, as soon as he is successfully meeting the ball, the instructor should then start expanding it, suggesting that he take it a little farther back this time—not much, just a little more, etc.

Backswing

This is a good point at which to discuss the old questions about backswing. Do you believe in a backswing? How much? Straight or circular (i.e., elliptical)? First, let it be said that no last word is possible on this subject, since the right answer varies with different styles of play. A hitter like Vines used a full backswing because he was just about always attempting an all-out shot. His forehand in particular was usually a complete sweep—180 degrees or more. In sharp contrast was the forehand style of Fred Perry, who relied on his incredible speed of foot to enable him to play a war of maneuver. He would often hit the ball with a sharp wrist slap—with almost no arm swing at all—as he dashed to the net. There was no backswing—and no follow-through either—just a slap. Is one of these "right" and the

other "wrong"? To exclude either style is narrow minded: no one could swing like Vines and simultaneously move like Fred Perry. To achieve Vines's devastating execution one had to get set. To take the ball on the rise and on the run—thereby getting instantly on top of the ball, the net, and the opponent to rush him off the court—required that Perry use an absolute minimum of swing and stroke. Each of these men beat everybody in his day, and the game of each was considered truly great at its peak.

Others have done well with little or no backswing, but not in Perry's manner. Instead of taking the ball as soon as possible, one style is to hesitate until the last second—possible only with a minimum swing—so that an opponent can never seem to get a good start, so cleverly is the planned shot concealed. It is a pleasure to watch such players keep first-class opponents continually a trifle off balance throughout a hard match. Here is another style of play that, when carried to near perfection, can result in greatness on the court.

Both Perry and other short swingers had strong wrists. Without much approach to the ball they could still make it go very sharply to any part of the court. Many people, including talented people, are not gifted with such steely strength. Therefore these styles are not for them. And can anyone play like Vines? Nobody ever has yet! He came closer than anybody in the history of the game to aiming every shot for an ace or a near ace. He could hit so hard that he could make (and at times did make) more bad errors than any champion before or since—and still win because he made so many winners. Any ordinary player not having Vines's amazing hitting ability would reap the harvest of errors but not the aces, and would merely be another "big misser," if he tried that style. As an aside it may be mentioned that when Vines was champion, there were more wild sluggers than ever before or since—because the youngsters always imitate the champ. How were they to know Vines's style was almost inimitable? Likewise, a lot of people tried to use Perry's extreme Continental forehand grip with inferior results because they didn't have the other ingredients: the mercurial mobility and the gifted and educated wrist.

Having established what we cannot say, then what can we lay down as limits, rules, or high probabilities? First, there must be enough swing so the racket is in motion when it meets the ball and the player doesn't feel that he can't make it go. A little experimentation will quickly establish this limit for each player. Second, no backswing may ever go back around farther than the line between the shoulders. It is quite extraordinary how the moment one goes even a trifle past this point, extreme awkwardness and lack of poise set in. So we have two limits, a minimum and a maximum, and no one should crowd either of them when learning. If you turn out to be a Vines or a Perry later on, you won't need a book to justify the direction your style has taken.

Something more can be said about backswing: namely, that a full backswing is about half as much "swing" as most people think. If you watch a good player you will often see his racket pointed straight forward as he cradles it and waits for the ball to be played to him. Then it will go back until it points at the backstop: a 180-degree change. Yet he has actually moved the racket only ninety degrees—i.e., until it points at the sidestop or along the baseline. The other ninety degrees are caused entirely by turning the shoulders and advancing one foot in front of the other. Thus, those who think of swinging their racket all the way back often get so much backswing (three right angles, not two!) that one can see the racket around behind them well over onto their backhand side when they are preparing to play a forehand. This, of course, is a real

Figure 6–4. Maximum backswing. Good poise is maintained.

Figure 6–5. Excessive backswing. Poise and balance are impaired.

haymaker that is uncontrollable, not to mention that it destroys poise. (This fault is scarcely possible on the backhand side, since the player's body stops the backswing, while on the forehand nothing prevents the preparation from being excessive. Of course, the same result can be obtained—and often is—by getting the feet too far around, but this is not a matter of backswing.)

The conclusion is that a reasonably complete and full backswing is obtained by pointing the racket along the baseline to the side on which the ball will be played. Then when the feet are arranged the rest of the backswing will occur automatically. This goes right along with the limited swing advocated for beginners, facilitates lining up the ball with the skipping already advocated (see Chapter 4) and can be easily worked into either a closed or open stance technique. If the player flicks the racket out to that side with wrist and arm, striving simultaneously to get it slanted just right, he will build a habit that is very simple and very quick, facilitates the execution of the other crucial tasks (lining up the ball and timing it), and last but not least can easily be expanded into as full and sweeping a stroke as may be desired.

One more important advantage of this very simple lay-it-out-to-the-side preparation should be brought out. A stroke, even though we aim the ball up and spin it, has as its basis a horizontal motion. More than anything else the player is coming from behind and moving the ball forward—a horizontal job. Now circular or elliptical backswings have advantages, which will be brought out in the next paragraph, but they involve introducing verticals into the swing—up and down effects that are extremely confusing to a beginner or even a lower intermediate. Here again the series approach—one thing at a time—is advocated and has been justified by experience. The instructor should not give himself or a player more than can be swallowed at one time. An exclusively horizontal approach should be used for a while.

Once a player has reasonably mastered the simplest fundamentals and can stroke the ball

with some consistency, then indeed it is time to introduce rhythm, lightness, and flow into his game. Here is where the ellipse is really good: the slight upward motion involved in going back a little high tends to take the weight off the feet, making him feel light and on his toes just at the very instant he most wishes to feel that way—as he reacts to the opponent's shot. Then as he arrives and settles down to the spot where his stroke production will actually occur, his racket and arm drop to the level of play as the knees bend and then move forward to make the shot. The swing should be taught as a quick up! that occurs *instantly* after the ball leaves the opponent's racket and stays up there until it is time to play. The arm should be crooked for relaxation. Teaching the player to dance a bit (perhaps at first purposelessly and unnecessarily) while the ball is coming helps him develop this lightness, which is so desirable in the interests of mobility, and the rhythm of really getting into the ball with the stroke he has at first laboriously and stiffly developed.

It is quite clear that until a player has mastered the basics, the preceding paragraph is to be shunned as a lot of frills that interfere with concentration on the true essentials. Many players never get to that paragraph. But have you not seen players who have lovely circular swings and a lot of jazzy footwork—and can't control the ball at all to speak of? Haven't you heard it said, "He's nowhere nearly as good as he looks"? This is merely saying that he has a lot of form but lacks the truly indispensable form: the knowledge of how to get the ball over the net and into the court. A player should learn first to be tough. Smoothness and "class" are easy to get later on.

MORE FUNDAMENTALS

Aiming

We now have a simple preparation whereby the player puts the racket to the side and lines it up with the ball by moving the feet. The next job is the actual shot itself. Anyone can whack the ball—no lessons are necessary for this. The test of the shot is how well the player can control it. A discussion of the ingredients of control is in order.

Control implies guidance. Guidance implies time duration as contrasted with a quick, almost instantaneous contact. If the player is to guide the ball, he must stay on it for an appreciable length of time, not just for an instant. If he is to stay on it, he must *come to the ball slowly.* This is fundamental number one in the art of control. This does not mean the player cannot hit hard; it is quite possible to accelerate a ball *after* the racket is on it— and this is actually the secret of controlled speed. Most players proceed on the assumption that to get any pace it is necessary to work up terrific speed before the racket meets the ball. While it is true that this method will make the ball go fast, it is also true that it is nearly impossible to control a ball played in this manner. More important, no one who

has not yet mastered control has any *right* even to attempt a fast shot; he isn't ready for it yet. So the first rule is to forget speed and come to the ball slowly.

Second, it is important to press through smoothly and with some acceleration, so that as the ball tends to leave the racket, the racket tends to keep up with the ball, relinquishing its guiding touch reluctantly and after a long time. So fundamental number two is to stay on the ball as long as possible. Obviously, if the player does this, his ability to guide the flight of the ball is at a maximum. The thought of pressing as contrasted with hitting is a very good way to persuade players to learn this feeling of keeping the racket on the ball for quite a time, thereby gaining the means to guide it truly along the path they wish it to take.

Third, the player should always meet the ball somewhat in front of him so that his weight can turn in behind the shot, and if the legs are bent at the knees he can again increase

Figure 6–6. The forehand baseline stroke. Note how the swing lifts (lobs) the ball away from the net. The high follow-through means the racket wiped (stroked) up the back of the ball for topspin.

the time on the ball by straightening them, thus pushing forward and keeping the racket longer on the ball as it goes away from him. This feeling of getting behind the ball and shoving with the legs is the real basis for feeling secure on any shot. Note in the illustrations of the drives how the weight is moving in behind, thus reinforcing and sustaining the work done by the arm, hand, and racket.

Fourth, the player should aim three ways: (1) the ball must go straight—neither to the left nor right; (2) the ball must go the right height—neither too high nor too low; and (3) the ball must go the right distance—neither too short into the net nor too long over the baseline.

Fifth, the player should spin the ball. This happens at the end of the stroke, after he has

Figure 6–7. The backhand baseline stroke. Note that the racket does just what it does for the forehand stroke. The main difference is that the ball is contacted about the width of the shoulders more in front than for the forehand, because the playing arm is the "front arm" rather than the "back arm" on a backhand. But the action of the racket face on the ball is identical.

guided the ball along the path of righteousness and is ready to let it go off on its own. If the player lifts off the ball with the top edge leading as he finishes carrying the ball along its flight, it will roll down the racket and spin forward, and this is the desired effect: it will make the ball arc and will thus enable the player to develop a sense of length—an important part of aiming. See Figures 6–6 and 6–7.

Timing

Here again is a problem that often baffles beginners: when should one swing? Good players do this so automatically they forget it is an acquired skill and is not by any means an instinct. Of all things advanced players do by habit, timing a shot is perhaps the most important yet the most unconscious. Quite often they cannot tell another player just how they achieve their obvious success in meeting the ball well again and again.

Watch a good player. What does he do? Does he prepare and then swing? Not quite. He prepares and then *waits* before he swings. Timing—choosing the best instant to play the ball—is an act of selection involving judgment. How does he judge and select? The beginner has neither knowledge nor experience on which to base a judgment. So he swings any old time—usually at a poor time—and whiffs and half misses a lot. It is necessary to point out to him how a ball behaves.

When a ball bounces it jumps off the ground going at its maximum speed right at the start. It is very difficult to judge this speed and time one's swing correctly to meet the ball when it is thus rising rapidly. In fact, if the court surface is a bit scuffy and therefore unpredictable, it is not merely difficult; it is impossible to take the ball definitely on the rise with any certainty that a wood shot won't be the result. As the ball fights gravity it loses energy and finally floats dead in the air for a brief interval: it is through rising and has not yet begun to fall at any appreciable speed. At this point there is no question of judging it badly: there it is, sitting there. This is the easiest time (therefore the best time) to play the ball. Every beginner should have the nature of the bounce explained to him and should be taught to prepare his racket, toss the ball, *wait* for it to sit still, then play. Very quickly he learns how to select this one and only time (at or soon after the top of the bounce) when it is easy to play the ball, and to plan his play accordingly. His whiffs and half misses are quickly reduced to those times when he just plain takes his eye off the ball, which makes anyone miss. Incidentally, if a player is taught to watch and wait for this optimum instant he also learns to watch the ball more constantly, and more intelligently, then he might otherwise do.

It should perhaps be added that this explanation of the nature of a bounce is quite a revelation to a lot of people, including adults. It at once distinguishes clearly between good and bad timing and places in sharp outline a subject that tends to be extremely foggy with most players. This approach is recommended as a solidly established teaching trick. It works.

Teaching in Steps

This is really too much, isn't it? How can the hapless beginner hope to carry all this rigamarole in his mind while doing something as quick as a shot in tennis must be? The answer is, as always, to use the series method and go slowly. The beginner should merely press the ball softly up to a hole in the air four to six feet over the net. It will flop into the court from sheer lack of sufficient guts to go any farther. But never mind, he is learning to prepare, to open the face, to line up the ball, to time it to meet it and to guide it a little, not to mention some footwork: skipping, advancing the left foot for forehand, right for backhand. After he has a reasonable grasp of these basics (and this may take months) the instructor should suggest that the player accelerate his follow-through a bit, leaving the ball faster, spinning it sharply, aiming a little lower as the pace is increased.

The Racket Work Method

Every shot involves three steps: preparing the racket, lining up the ball, and playing. This can be summarized, in terms of the racket, as "Ready, wait, play." Every player should be taught to play every shot this way, even when playing a ball out of the hand: the racket is laid out correctly first; then the racket waits while the ball is tossed and bounces up and hangs; then the racket plays the ball. The "wait" refers only to the racket; the player may be running across the court to get to a ball, but the racket is ready and waiting to play when the player gets there. With beginners a lot of repeated urging is needed: "Get your racket ready *first*." This is true on every shot—including the service. And this is only the most ordinary common sense: how can you play a ball when it arrives if the racket is not already prepared? After all, it won't sit there like a golf ball, awaiting your pleasure.

The point being made here is that the plan and the sequence should be related to the racket more than to anything else. The player should think of preparing the racket—and never mind preparing himself. He should think of lining the racket up with the ball—and never mind himself. And he should think of putting the racket correctly onto and through the ball. *After* these ideas are somewhat digested, he can start adding good handling of himself in order to execute the racket work even better: pressing more, staying on the ball more, accelerating more, aiming more truly, etc., by using the legs, by crouching. But notice that all these are done in order to achieve the original objective—racket work. The footwork, body turn, bent knees, etc. should not be objectives in themselves; they must be subservient to and contribute to the *prime* objective—good racket work. The function of the instructor is to focus the player's mind on this core problem of the game.

Sometimes a person of reputation will say something like "This game is all footwork" or "This game is primarily a matter of concentration." Such statements are quite common.

They seem to deny and contradict the central theme of this book—that racket work is the key—but they do not. These statements are made by advanced players speaking to other advanced players. They have good strokes, good timing, good control, good tactics—in sum, they have a good game—so the only remaining questions are: are they there in time and properly set to make the strokes they know so well (footwork) and do they play their best without letup (concentration)? So what they say is true and is good advice—for one-half of one percent of those who play tennis. This book applies to the other ninety-nine and one-half percent; the great majority of players must give heed to their racket work!

Smoothness

When the hand, forearm, and upper arm go through smoothly together a nice swing results. Unfortunately, beginners seldom cooperate: they flop the wrist or the elbow so that one or two sections of this three-part mechanism go snapping through but the others scarcely move. A floppy, uncontrolled stroke results. In addition to mentioning that we wish to swing from the shoulder more than from the wrist or elbow, there are a couple of teaching tricks that often speed the smoothing process. If the player is told to push the butt of the racket through instead of snapping the head around, wrist action is sharply reduced. On the forehand, if the player is told to take the elbow far through, it takes both upper and lower arm with it, curing the half-arm swing often seen. On the backhand, the entire arm should go back until the elbow is against the stomach; this is important to prevent poking —i.e., drawing back only the front half of the arm, leaving the elbow and upper arm sticking out forward even at the end of the preparation. This chicken wing backhand is very common among children learning the game.

Frequent mention of the joints—wrist and elbow—is recommended, since each joint controls both what is behind it and in front of it. If

the elbow goes through, both upper and lower arms must accompany it—it is physically unavoidable. If the wrist is pushed through (not snapped around), both the hand and forearm must go too. A good educational exercise is to line up a group, have them stick their forehands right out at the instructor horizontally, then have them swing (1) from the wrist, (2) from the elbow, (3) from the ball and socket joint at the shoulder, (4) with body only (from the waist). Of course, the instructor demonstrates and explains also, and the players soon understand the problems they are attempting to solve. Without this comprehension much frustration can (and does) occur with people who use the wrong muscles in attempting to swing effectively.

The Wrist

The wrist is used in tennis far more than most theorists like to admit. Its use in the service is so obvious as to need no discussion. The same applies to the overhead. We are here discussing drives. The prejudice against the wrist arises from the fact that if the wrist is used as the racket approaches the ball on a drive, a flappy rather uncontrollable stroke results. In their desire to avoid this, many instructors leap to the extreme and declare that any wrist action at all is "incorrect." This is going too far. On any topspin drive the spin is increased and made more decisive by using the wrist to make the top edge of the racket lead off the ball. The important distinction to make is that wrist is bad when approaching the ball but is good (in moderation) when leaving the ball. To teach an absolutely stiff stroke (in terms of the wrist) has been aptly characterized as "straitjacket teaching" and often inhibits the use of natural abilities.

Keeping Form in Perspective

Another important aspect of this wrist business relates to the nature of the game. We keep coming back to the fact that the game is competitive, that tempo limits what a player can do, that an opponent constantly seeks to get the player into trouble and often succeeds. The wrist is what gets the player out of all kinds of pickles, or at least it is the last resort when in trouble. The tendency when writing an article or a book is to assume that one has plenty of time and the ball is easily within reach: what then is the ideal way to play it? But in fact in a game we are often hurried, pressed, the ball gets partly by us, etc. What now, please? What good is the lovely exposition of the ideal stroke? The answer is that we should teach good form but add that while to play the ball this way is desirable, no one should think it is "wrong" to make a more wristy or snatchy shot when in trouble. In fact, an "educated" wrist is a characteristic of any good player, and this should be pointed out to players as an asset, not a liability. They should be encouraged on the bangboard to play anything and everything that comes at them, convenient or inconvenient, so they acquire not only good form but also that instant adaptability that real competition demands.

No doubt this approach can be exaggerated, but it is so commonplace to encounter instructors who assert, "You should never use your wrist stroking a tennis ball" that this is admittedly an attempt to bend the stick a bit the other way, to reopen and re-examine the question. To sum it all up in another way, is it not at least in part true to say that the wrist is the player's steering wheel, the core of his ability to control the flight of the ball, the greatest source of dexterity with the racket, his last hope when in difficulty? Granted we should keep it within bounds, but should we eliminate it and teach that it is wholly bad? This just does not square with what occurs on the court.

THE LOB

Carry It—Don't Hit It

This shot seems very simple, but many otherwise competent players will come to a pro and

Figure 6–8. The lob. Note how the wrist is kept firm and the ball is lifted smoothly and carefully by straightening the legs and lifting the arm. Of course, when in deep trouble one must often snap a lob up and pray it won't be too poor, but a player should never snap if there is time to play it smoothly.

say "I can't lob." There are certain fundamentals that if practiced a bit will give the feeling of how to execute and aim an effective lob. A lob should not be hit at all. The ball should be allowed to land on the racket almost as if one were catching it in a basket. Since the objective is to send the ball almost straight up into the air, the racket face should be wide open and below the point of contact. As the ball is caught it should be lifted with a smooth heaving motion that is the complete antithesis of a snap or a crack. See Figure 6–8. This heaving idea is the secret of control, for the player can feel how high he is lifting the ball. This allows him to aim accurately for whatever spot in the air he has selected. So much for the execution.

The trick of aiming a lob is based on the flight of the ball. This is a parabola, and a parabola of the type that is a curve with two equal sides. If the player makes one side by lifting the ball to a spot in the air, Newton's laws will make the other half. See Diagram 6–1. Usually the player is at or near the baseline when he lobs, so if he lifts the ball to a spot high above the net, it will come down pretty near the other baseline. If he lifts it well past the net, it will go out. If he lifts it not quite to the net, it will tend to drop short and be a setup. A little experimentation will show anybody that he actually *can* learn to lob well if he executes in such a manner that control is possible (i.e., if he has good racket work) and if he learns that it is possible to have a specific and definite target in making this shot, which apparently is aimed in the general direction of outer space. Aiming is vague without a target, and a vague shot is often a poor one.

The lob should be taught in two stages, each of which should be drilled: first, to learn to catch and lift the ball; second, to aim it for spots in the air to become accustomed to this type of aiming (which often seems very queer to those to whom it is an entirely new concept).

What has been described here is the standard defensive lob, which should be aimed high —thirty or more feet up—with the idea of saving the point from loss, not of winning it. There are other less basic and more tricky lobs that

can be lethal weapons in the hands of advanced players. The most spectacular is the topspin lob, which is merely a topspin drive aimed very high—high enough to be out of reach—with excessive forward spin and not much impact so it will arc into the court before it passes the baseline in spite of the great height that is given it. The trick in making this shot is to avoid putting weight into the ball. It is all whippy topspin and has scarcely any solid smack at all. The racket whips the ball very quickly, and this usually has the effect of convincing an opponent that a drive, not a lob, is what is coming, so he tends to close in on the net—to his undoing. The heavy topsin causes the ball to jump away from anyone who chases it, so it is reasonably certain to be an ace if it gets over a net player's head. This shot is a very good one and has come into its own more in the last few years than ever before. It has the added advantage of being more difficult to smash accurately because of the spin. A word of caution: this is an accurate shot or it is that worst of all shots—a poor lob. Therefore, it should not be attempted when the player is in real trouble; when on the defensive, the defensive high lob should be used. The offensive lob should be used only when the player has that little extra smidge of time to get set, aim, and put a lot of stuff on the ball.

Another tricky—but reasonably standard—

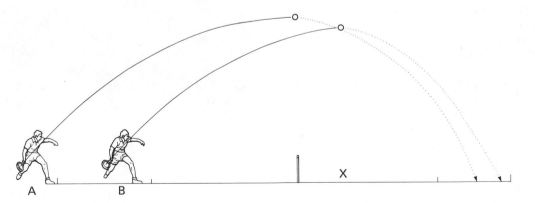

Diagram 6–1. Aiming a lob. A: From a deep position, lift the ball to a point high above the net—good depth will result (dotted line). B: From inside the baseline lift it to a point high above the opponent's head (X). Any other landmark will do, but these are always there (the net and the opposition). Of course one must allow for the wind if there is one.

lob is the quick chip return of service lob. It is made with a little poke—a very short jabby swing that pushes the lower edge of the racket beneath the ball, popping it over a net man's head in doubles. While it can be used anytime, the return of service in doubles usually presents the best chance. This lob can be very well hidden if the racket is not opened until the last second—just as the ball is met. Thus an opponent has no inkling of one's plan until it is too late to adjust to it. Here, again, clever racket work is the basis of true excellence. The secret of making this lob very deceptive—and it must be, or the net man will spot it and may smash for a winner—is to make the shot almost entirely with the body. If the player closes in on a spin service to take it on the rise, presenting the racket *exactly* as if he meant to make a chip or slice return, then the momentum of the weight will provide most of the force; the racket merely curls suddenly under the ball, popping it into the air over the net player's head.

The volley lob is a very difficult shot because it must be made quickly and is an awful cripple if executed less than perfectly. If successful it is devastating because it is nearly unforeseeable and is therefore usually a real surprise. But it requires not only great touch but also a very quick touch, so that most players—even good ones—lose out on the percentages by making too many bad ones. So the shot, while brilliant when well done, is recommended only with serious reservations as to probable percentage success. It is best tried when it is the only hope, when everything is to be gained and little can be lost that isn't already almost lost.

There is at least one time when the volley lob is legitimate and spectacular: when an opposing doubles team has a policy of moving in very close on almost every exchange it is possible to plan to lob the second shot even if it is a volley. Knowing when and over which player the lob is to go and knowing almost the whole court is open behind this player can indeed be a percentage situation and may even be the coolest and best answer to an excessively impetuous attack. And if the volley lob,

like the poke lob, is concealed by not opening the racket except by turning it under just as one plays—then again great deception is possible.

PASSING SHOTS—SUBTLE DIFFERENCES

Passing shots are not quite like ordinary baseline shots. They are usually aimed a little lower, and it is wise to give them extra topspin. Both of these changes are calculated to force a net player to volley up—that is, defensively rather than offensively. This is a sort of insurance policy: we'd like to pass him, but if we don't we still have the idea of getting him in trouble. Therefore, most passing shots should be aimed for the service line, and to this end a limited backswing and a less open face are needed to curb length. The depth that is so valuable in a baseline-to-baseline exchange is not desirable, for a deep shot presents a high

Figure 6–9. Preparation for passing shot. Note the slightly closed racket face to give more than usual topspin, the open stance to permit instant recovery of position or scrambling for the next shot, and the somewhat laid back wrist. If the wrist remains laid back, a straight shot will follow, or the racket can be brought quickly around the ball to give a crosscourt shot. Note the abbreviated backswing: the shot will be sudden, sharp, and hard for the net player to "read."

volley and allows an opponent to play very aggressively. It makes him look good.

The only exception to this is the straight hard shot down the line that is played for a clean winner. Here everything is sacrificed for speed, and no attempt is made to loop the ball heavily to make it dip; the idea exclusively is to pass the opponent so he doesn't even touch it. This shot, of course, is made like any other sound baseline drive.

Whenever possible on all passing shots a little hesitation is very desirable in order to create a little doubt and confusion in the opponent's mind. Therefore even if there is plenty of time to get to a ball it is important to try to be very quick, and be there a little ahead of time, thus making it possible to wait before playing. If to this trick a player adds another —that he *always* prepares in exactly the same manner no matter what shot he has in mind— then indeed an opponent has a hard time anticipating what is coming next.

So the technique for passing shots involves a short backswing, a less open-faced racket, the same early preparation for no matter what shot, a hesitation before the shot, a lower aim and heavy topspin, and a conscious avoidance of good depth. All this of course should be ignored until reasonable mastery has been achieved of the more ordinary baseline shots that are played mostly crosscourt for solid depth. These fine distinctions are definitely for advanced players, but it may be noted that however difficult they may seem at first reading, they are actually merely small variations of the basic strokes all beginners should learn at the baseline.

CHOPPING AND SLICING— A NECESSARY INGREDIENT

A good deal has been and will be said in favor of learning about chopping and slicing. All intermediates should be introduced to it. The necessary technique should be made clear by contrasting it with topspin technique. Every-

thing is the opposite: a topspin swing starts below the ball, chop starts above; topspin follows through higher than the flight of the ball —a high flourish—while chop and slice swings follow through lower than the flight of the ball: you hold them down by keeping the racket low at the finish. The ball rolls down the racket for topspin, up the racket for all cut shots; the top edge leads for topspin, the bottom edge leads for all chips, chops, and slices.

A great and prevalent fallacy is frequently heard: "The best players don't chop and slice." Nothing could be farther from the truth. Every good service is nothing but a gigantic big swing chop. All good exponents of the volley play the ball with backspin, which means the volley is a stiff-wristed abbreviated chop. Many—probably a majority of—good players use a slice backhand more than they use a topspin. All good players execute a dropshot with backspin, which means it is a chop. Most good players use a slice as a backhand approach shot to the net. Almost all good players block the ball back when they are forced and rushed—and they do it with a backspin shot, not a forward spin shot. While there should be no misunderstanding about the fact that topspin is advocated here for basic drives, it could be successfully argued that if one were forced to choose one spin and exclude the other, then slice would have to be preferred as the one to keep because of its versatility. Leaving that discussion aside, it is incontrovertible that the art of leading with the bottom edge of the racket is, technically speaking, at least half the game.

Now it has been said a player uses topspin to arc the ball into the court, and without it the ball tends to sail out. This is true when pace is applied. But when a player is pressed, rushed, and cannot arrange his weight properly to play a controlled forcing shot, then going down and under the ball keeps it up; instead of dropping weakly into the net, it carries back reasonably deep into the opponent's court and keeps the player in the point. (Of course, this is hopeless against a net rusher; the player must lob unless his opponent stays back.) So the very tendency to sail too far that the player avoided with his topspin shot now turns out to be his best hope.

More aggressive slices are often not what they seem. If one hits hard right through a cut shot it *will* go out because the backspin is an upshoot. Yet we hear about "vicious slices" and "hard sliced drives," etc. What is really happening here is that the bounce or kick of a good slice or chop is vicious and heavy (hard) and low. The player swings viciously, the ball spins venomously and then bounces meanly— but the actual flight of the ball through the air is *not* very fast. And knowing this opens the door to good chopping and slicing: the player should not try to make the ball *go* fast—he should make it *spin* fast *without* making it *go* very fast. How does one do this? By crossing the ball—that is, by swinging across from the

Figure 6–10. Slicing a forehand. The weight pushes forward as the racket cuts across. Note that the right leg walks through to add weight. Note the bottom edge of the racket leads decisively all the way through. Note the out-to-the-side preparation.

outside in for sliced drives and from high up, down, and in for chops. The racket crosses the ball, the lower edge cutting like a knife, but does *not* go forward through it. The arm swing is almost at a right angle to the direction of the shot and is not a from-back-forth motion but a pull in from the outside. The forward pressure or push is applied entirely by the weight, which moves in the direction of the shot. Thus the swing is a pull across (or down) that goes right off the ball in sharp contrast with the way a topspin or flat drive stays on the ball. The racket does not make the ball go—it merely spins it. The weight makes it go, and as one pushes one can feel how far he is shoving the ball. This is the feeling of length on a sliced shot—the player carefully avoids pushing it too far, no matter how much or how viciously he may spin it with the crosscutting motion of the racket. The sooner the racket is pulled off the ball, the less length will result. This can be carried to an extreme, as when a violent pull off the ball that apparently is an aggressive shot produces nothing but a fluffy floating drop shot—all spin, no pressure. The spin moreover helps make the bounce very dead.

Every player should read the preceding paragraph several times slowly, visualizing the motions described, and consulting Figures 6–10, 6–11, and 6–12 at length. Why? Because it has almost always proved to be true that no one except advanced players has any conception of what it means to slice. The idea of the racket and weight moving at right angles to each other is strange. The idea that it is desirable and indeed necessary to pull *off* the ball rather than to press through it usually contradicts what most students have already been taught. It all takes a good bit of swallowing, but it is worth the trouble. It should be added that the fact that most of this sounds strange to so many people is actually an indictment of present-day teaching. Here is an absolutely basic fundamental—how to draw down, across and under the ball, leading with the bottom edge of the racket—a fundamental that leads to excellence in over half the shots in the game, and practically nobody teaches it, and

Figure 6–11. Slicing a backhand. As with the forehand, the weight and the racket operate at right angles to each other. Note the pull-to-the-right follow-through—OFF the ball—while the weight goes straight with the shot.

many condemn it. Should such a situation be allowed to continue?

The student is cautioned again to think hard about the idea of following through off the ball rather than with it and through it. Pulling off the ball is the means of controlling or limiting length, and it should be noted that without this feel the slice will undoubtedly sail, since there will be no control. Actually a good slicer can usually outsteady a topspin player. That is why so many good players have sliced backhands. It is a very steady and dependable stroke, and since one cannot make aces from the baseline anyway, accurate dependability is the great objective.

In learning, a player should be told to prepare by putting his racket as far to the side—as contrasted with putting it back—as he can. The farther out to the side he puts it, the farther he can draw it in as he plays the ball; refer again to the illustrations, which are not exaggerated but merely correct. In playing the ball he should try to feel that he draws his racket across the ball, making eight or ten strings rake it and spin it. The ball stays on the racket for an appreciable period, and the player "works on it" with the strings and his weight. Here again the concept of stroke, drag, and draw rather than hit is of the utmost importance in getting feel.

In the case of the chop the racket is raised above the ball and carves down the back in-

Figure 6–12. Chopping a forehand. Again the racket operates at right angles to the weight, this time vertically rather than horizontally. In all these cut shots the racket "works on the ball"; it does not merely propel it.

stead of across it as for the slice. In every other way the technique is the same: the racket applies heavy backspin while the weight presses to make the ball go. On all these shots a player should feel that he grasps the ball with the strings.

There is a common misconception that causes a lot of confusion: this is the tendency to identify slice with undercut, so students will complain that every time they attempt a slice the ball pops way up in the air. To cut does not necessarily mean to cut under. Think of cutting across the back of the ball (slice) or down the back of the ball (chop), and the shot may be aimed as high or as low as you wish without altering the nature of the spin. Whether or not one wishes to go under the ball is a separate question. The fact that the lower edge of the racket leads off the ball— that is, goes through first—does not mean that it necessarily goes under the bottom of the ball. It may come from above and chop down onto the top of the back of the ball, thus hitting a shot that goes down, not up. In sum, it is possible, as with topspin, to put the spin on almost any part of the ball, thereby spinning it up, down, or level at will.

RETURN OF SERVICE

In Average Tennis

In ordinary tennis the service is not a lethal weapon, and the server is not roaring up to net behind his delivery. Usually the average player serves and awaits the return at the middle of the baseline. Under these conditions one should never hurry one's return but should take plenty of time. A good place to stand is just behind the baseline, with the toes against the line. This permits the player to step into the return so it is firm and yet avoid taking it on the rise. The ball should be taken as it comes down, after its crest, and should be played back up again for good high clearance over the net and good depth into the other court. Usually a crosscourt shot is best, but if the service is down the center one has a choice: it is just as "crosscourt" to play one way as the other. In other words, the return of

service is a standard baseline shot if the server does not come in. As a rule a solid topspin crosscourt is a good choice, or a deep sliced drive.

As the quality of play improves, and the service comes in faster and deeper, the receiver's problem becomes more difficult. He must be very quick to prepare, he must limit his backswing because of the increased tempo, and he may not be able to take the ball at exactly the height he most prefers. Still, he can use his regular baseline stroke for the most part. The game is unchanged; it is just better played by both parties.

The Block Return

Now let us assume we are up against a really good service. It has so much pace it is still rising at the baseline. There is no question of playing it "conveniently"—that is, as we'd like to play it. There is no question of making our full swing—there isn't time. There is only one thing we can do: put the racket on the ball out in front *before* it gets to us, thereby blocking it. If as we do this we move our weight forward by advancing one foot it is possible to get a firm return—a sort of bang-board effect—even when the service is a cannonball. The racket work on this shot is almost flat—we meet the ball rather than stroke it— but the bottom edge always leads a little; this shot is seldom a topspin shot but usually carries a little backspin. The greatest requirement on this shot is a firm grip to stand the shock of ball on racket. It closely resembles a volley.

The length on this shot can be varied at will by applying or withholding the weight. Thus when a server rushes the net the receiver may try for a very short return to his feet as he advances. If he does not advance, then the receiver should try to push the return deep. When a server advances, the tempo of the exchange is raised to a marked degree. A new factor has been introduced—the question of position. If the server is permitted to get far in he is in a commanding position to make a decisive shot. The receiver's job then becomes one of getting the ball back *soon* rather than getting it back excellently. He should shorten his swing until it is the merest poke, thus facilitating jabbing the ball back at the earliest possible instant, before it reaches its crest. A fair shot that catches the server half way up is more effective than a good shot when he is way in.

Here is definitely a case where the so-called best stroke is irrelevant, and a technique that might be an affront to many a dogmatic theorist turns out to be the most effective in the context in question. Once again it is pointed out that it is a mistake to think of tennis in the same terms as golf, because the factors of tempo and position-play (both missing in golf) often force a player to subordinate technical excellence to other considerations. The open stance is a case in point, the quick block return of service—often referred to as a "chip" —is another, and similar blocking and slicing are often used defensively at other times during play. It is therefore of extreme importance that all those who hope to teach tennis should avoid being too dogmatic about any one best way to play a tennis ball; the context is often a determining factor. The main point is that the higher the tempo, the less swing one may use.

The High Backhand

The high backhand return of service is another spot where the ability to slice is indispensable. The racket must be cocked straight up above and outside the ball, then must carve around the outside of the ball and down across the striker so the follow-through is low on the right side. The lower edge of the racket must lead around, down, and through. If one pivots by rotating or swivelling on the ball of the right foot as the shot is played, so the left foot steps out to the left as the shot is finished, the ball can be carved for an astonishingly effective crosscourt return. See Figure 6–13.

The high backhand is generally considered the toughest shot in the game, whether it is a volley, return of service, or merely some high bounding ball. The reason for this formidable reputation is that if it is not hit well it is usually not hit at all to speak of. The average player has quite a bit of forehand strength in his wrist (it is his natural throwing motion), so he can be off balance, on the wrong foot, take the ball late, or commit any other sin, and still be able to play the ball with a wrist snap and usually get some kind of a shot. By contrast he has comparatively little backhand strength in his wrist, so if he gets caught in any of the awkward positions just mentioned he can make no shot at all or scarcely any. If on top of this he does not know how to get his weight onto the ball, then indeed he is helpless

Figure 6–13. The high backhand. This bears a strong resemblance to the forehand chop and the service—a forehand high ball shot. Note how the butt leads and the racket drags down as the weight presses forward for firmness. Pull and push simultaneously; this is the secret. Note how the ball is kept in front of the receiver, not to the side.

when forced to play a high backhand. Just because most players have no recourse other than good execution it is important to study the shot carefully.

Good execution means to get your weight behind the racket so it presses against the ball and feels secure, not weak. To achieve this, several points must be emphasized. First, a player should never let the ball get out to his side. He should always take it diagonally out in front—and more in front than to the side. Second, he should not flap the wrist, bringing the head through ahead of the handle. This is the weakest way to play the ball. Instead, the butt of the racket should be pushed out in front toward the ball. Third, even then the player should not send the head through. The butt of the racket must be *pulled* down to the right side, while the player *pushes* right at the ball with the weight so the left foot has walked through at the finish of the shot. See Figure 6–13. Here we are at slicing again: the arm pulls, the weight pushes. To bow the head and torso as the ball is played gets even more weight into it. It is to be noted that even at the finish the wrist has not snapped through: the racket is dragged or pulled through, not sent through ahead as in a topspin shot. If one can get the ball out in front and think "Pull and push," results should come with practice. It is possible actually to combine the two words to coin a new one and tell a player to "plush" the ball (pronounced like "push").

One very frequent difficulty with the high backhand is that many players don't seem to be able to effect a firm contact between ball and racket. They get too much cut, and a swishy gutless shot results. Such players should not hesitate to change their grip a bit as they lift the racket to the ball, putting the thumb a little flatter behind the handle, thus presenting a flatter and a more solid racket face to the ball. A slight change can make all the difference between no feel and solid feel, so experimentation is very worthwhile for those who are at present stymied.

Once again the idea of stroking the ball· is emphasized. The racket is pulled down, and as

it goes down the ball rolls up it (or the racket wipes or draws down the ball; say it either way). There is a duration or time interval during which one string after another is working on the ball, and the ball does not stay in one spot but traverses a considerable part of the racket face. In this way, incidentally, like all other baseline shots the high backhand can be aimed up—by letting the ball run up the racket—even though the swing goes decisively down.

Perhaps some readers have already noticed that all this push out and pull down exhortation is pretty much duplicating the instructions given for the slice service. This is true. The ball is at about the same height, the problem is the same, and the answers are all the same. The only difference is that you are on the other side of the ball, so you do it with the other side of the racket. This is perhaps as good a spot as any to make the point that physical laws are in no way altered by the fact that a player moves from one side of the ball to the other. What the flat thing we call the racket must do to the round thing we call a ball does not change, no matter where a player may stand. This actually aids in simplifying the game: all the principles of stroking with topspin or slice are the same for both backhand and forehand. The slice service may be correctly described as a high forehand slice. The high backhand, played as suggested above, may be correctly described as a backhand slice service. There is indeed no fundamental difference except that the natural throwing motion in the forehand side gives it far more strength and kick.

High Bounding Serves

Topspin, American twist, and combination services are often directed to the backhand with the hope of getting a weak return off a high bounce. The answer is simple: don't allow them to get high. Take them on the rise before they get way up there where they make you feel weak, and also before, if angled, they carry you far out of court. To achieve success in foiling the high-bounce-to-the-backhand plot one important principle of racket work is a necessity: the face must be closed and lifted high above the ball. Because, when struck, the ball is rising, it tends to pop up; the closed face counters this. Because the service carries forward spin it tends to jump up off the racket; the downward chop swing counters this. The whole idea, in taking a service on the rise, is to hold it down, for it always tries to go high off the racket.

All such high bounders to the backhand should like other baseline shots be returned crosscourt for reasons that will be fully discussed in Part IV, "Singles." It is mentioned here because if the server moves in the receiver often thinks "I'll pass him down the line!" It is a tempting thought—but a poor one. If the service is any good a clean pass cannot be made, so all the receiver does is give the server a beautiful crosscourt opportunity for his volley. The crosscourt is the tough percentage play: make it.

Always Move into the Ball

At all levels of excellence the most basic principle to emphasize in teaching return of service is to step into the shot. The player always moves forward—never back. A great majority of tennis players fail to do this, and it is one of the most prevalent shortcomings in general play today.

Why is this so important? Because tennis is in one sense a pushing contest. The server puts his weight onto the ball and tries to press his opponent back: he gives him a shove. If the receiver gives way and moves back, he will usually make a weak return because he gets no weight into his shot. He should give as good as he gets: he should push back against the other fellow, thus hopefully creating parity in the subsequent exchange.

Why do most players fail to push back by stepping into the ball? Because they are thinking of other things, such as getting plenty of time on their shot, careful preparation, a long full swing, etc. None of these is comparable in importance to meeting the server's strength with equal strength, so that whatever shot the receiver plays will be firm and have solid weight behind it. He pushes you: push back.

All players should be taught to take a step forward with their left foot for a forehand and with the right foot for the backhand, so their weight is moving forward when they meet the ball. To make this possible against a firm service a very short backswing is usually necessary: there is no time for anything more elaborate. If the service is slower, more swing is possible, but the basic fundamental is that the swing should never be so big that one must step back in order to gain time to complete it. This is not to be confused with standing in on the service. Many players stand in courageously and then step back—to gain time— when they play the ball. They would be better advised to stand a step farther back and step in to play. Standing in is a matter of tactics, and is at times very important (see the discussion headed "Return of Service" in Chapter 13). However, we are here dealing with technique, and the point being made is that whether the player stands in or stands back, he always moves into the ball with his weight.

To get this effect several tricks must be learned. First, the player should always go after the ball at a point well in front of him. He should attack the ball and not let it attack him. Second, in order to do this, the player should develop a very quick and minimal racket preparation, avoiding big swings of all sorts, whether straight back and forth or more circular. Third, he should emphasize the follow-through, since this puts the weight through the ball. Thus instant preparation, a very short backswing, and emphasis on pressing the weight through the ball by moving forward— these are the keys to solid service returns that tend to cancel out the advantage the server has in making the first shot.

As the player becomes more advanced and frequently must contend (in both singles and doubles) with a player who advances behind his service, this technique becomes ever more crucially important in getting the ball back quickly and solidly before he has time to reach a dominant position. Thus teaching beginners and intermediates always to move forward to the ball prepares them for advanced tactics they will need later, when how *soon* you play the ball is at least as important as how well you play it.

Often students are reluctant to get too fussy about this. It is usually enough to point out one home truth: return of service is the first shot on half the points (singles) and one quarter the points (doubles) they will play for the rest of their tennis life. These points are started well or badly according to how well or badly they return service. This is all very obvious, but it is quite astonishing how many players have never thought of it that way. They understand clearly the importance of service —this is "attack" and appeals to one and all. But they usually need considerable urging to give comparable status to return of service, which starts just as many points.

QUESTIONS

1. Why should we open the face of the racket in playing from the baseline?

2. Does topspin mean "come over the ball"?

3. How does a baseline drive resemble a lob?

4. What is the most essential part of getting ready to play a ball?

5. Why do some players play the same stroke all their lives—millions of times—and still play badly?

6. What should we stress in teaching beginners to get ready to play the ball?

7. How much backswing is enough?

8. How does an elliptical backswing aid a player?

9. How do you teach a beginner to aim?

10. How do you teach timing?

11. What does a ball do when it bounces?

12. What three things must the racket do in any stroke?

13. What do the joints at the wrist, elbow, and shoulder have to do with a stroke?

14. How do you teach smoothness?

15. Comment on the dictum "Never use your wrist in tennis."

16. How do you make a lob?

17. How do you aim a lob?

18. Discuss the "offensive lob." How important is it?

19. Is the lob volley a desirable shot?

20. Is the quick chip lob a desirable shot?

21. Are passing shots different from ordinary baseline drives? If so, how and why?

22. Is slicing desirable? Why so or why not?

23. Does slice mean go under the ball?

24. How do you keep a slice from sailing out?

25. In slicing, how does the racket motion contrast with the weight motion?

26. How does the preparation for a slice differ from the preparation for a drive?

27. What are the two basic moves in slicing?

28. How does the quality of a service affect the receiver's technique?

29. Why is a high backhand so difficult?

30. What is the most important factor in getting some feeling of strength on a high backhand?

31. What is the best answer to a service that bounds high to the backhand?

32. What is the key to a solid return of service?

33. Why do so many players step back on return of service?

34. What is most important in racket technique in order to get a solid return of service?

35. Why is return of service so very important?

CHAPTER 7

Halfcourt Techniques

Drills and tests for halfcourt shots will be found in Chapter 11.

THE IMPORTANCE OF HALFCOURT SKILL

A Crucial Difference

Very few instructors—even those who are coaches at leading tennis colleges and are therefore dealing almost exclusively with advanced players—stress halfcourt technique as an important subject for study all by itself. This is an error of omission, for it is in the halfcourt that the true limits of a player's resources are most completely revealed. Any experienced tennis player knows that often two opponents will warm up and one will look just as good as the other. Then they play, and a decisive difference appears. While of course the difference may be at net or elsewhere, it is frequently a fact that one player is able to make much of his opportunities while the other cannot seem to capitalize. On any good college squad there is always a considerable group of those who have good strokes and can rally with consistency. From this group who makes the team? Those who can *hurt* you when you make a mistake—i.e., when you give them a short ball. This is always the pres-

sure one feels when up against a really fine player: the awful knowledge that if you set the ball up you are going to be beaten—just about every single time. This is why you sweat blood and make errors against the best: it is the feeling that you *must* make a good shot *every* time. The pressure is terrific, not just because he plays well but because of the potential danger that is there, just waiting for a chance to show itself. In sharp contrast is the mediocre player who rallies well from the baseline but cannot do much with your short shots. There is no pressure to speak of. Sins of all sorts may be committed, barring downright missing, and there is seldom any penalty exacted. There is no need to risk error, just get it back any old way until *he* makes a mistake. then put your own attack into action. It is easy to be steady, to wait for just the right one for your attack, because there is no pressure. The difference is primarily in the halfcourt. The good player will be able to make you suffer fully for every short ball. The mediocre player will not.

The reason for this neglect of the halfcourt skills is that few instructors or coaches appreciate that they are so different from baseline skills. All pros and coaches will drill players thoroughly on baseline forehands and backhands. Unless the instructor makes a point of providing special drills, the player gets little ractice on approach shots—i.e., attacking plays that make it difficult for the opponent to pass or lob successfully when the offensive player follows to net. In several sets of play, the ratio of such attacking, approach shots to baseline shots may be one to ten or even one to twenty. This is not enough if real skill is to be attained. And this is the crucial skill: after you fight hard and outrally your opponent and force him to give you a fat one—now, can you *do* anything with it? If you can you are good. If you can't you tend to lose when you lose the rally and also to lose when you win the rally, so how good are you? Isn't it inevitable that you will think "I guess I'm a poor competitor —I just can't seem to put it across"? Isn't such a psychologically crucial skill worth not just a little work but a lot? Though very few do it, drill on approach shots should occupy as much time as drill on baseline and net play. It is truly a basic technical aspect of the game.

APPROACH SHOTS

A Sharp Distinction

A ball that is short—so a player can move forward a step and a half or more inside the baseline—offers an opportunity to attack. The objective should not be a winner but a shot that compromises the opponent's ability to return the shot successfully. Unless played from a very low point, this approach shot should be low, sudden, deceptive, severe, and placed close to one side so as to open the other side for the volley or overhead.

Tactics dictate technique. For emphasis we repeat the description of an approach: "it should be low, sudden, deceptive, severe, and placed close to one side." Could anything be more different from a baseline shot, which should be high, long, smooth, not overhit, and aimed well inside the lines? Diagram 7–1 makes this clear and deserves a long look.

The Closed Racket

Obviously a different racket skill is involved in the halfcourt. The face should be closed— either perpendicular or slightly turned over— to keep the ball low. The backswing should be reduced; a short, sharp, jabbing attack shot is to be made, not a sweeping depth shot. See Figure 7–1. The backswing should be high, to play level or down. The ball will not travel nearly so far as when hit from the baseline area; therefore, a full swing will tend to give too much length. With a short backswing plus some hesitation, considerable deception is possible, and this is of great value in getting the opposition off balance, thus provoking that weak return we yearn for at net. The stance —i.e., the position we adopt while hesitating— should be about half open. This gets the benefit of addressing the ball properly, for by twisting at the waist the upper half of the body assumes almost a fully closed position. At the same time the feet are arranged so that a quick move forward behind the shot is possible. Study Figure 7–1.

The most important aspect of these technical points is the closed face of the racket. Most players go at a setup with the same racket

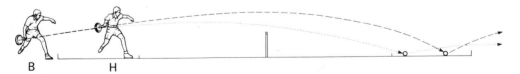

Diagram 7–1. Halfcourt and baseline shots contrasted. Note the sharp differences in the height of the flight of the ball and the depth of the shot.

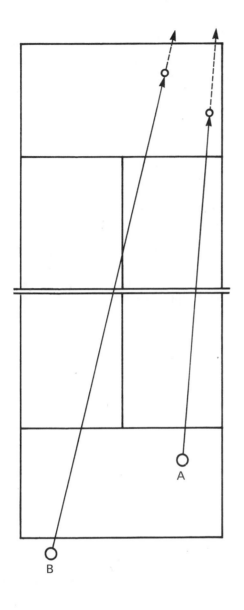

preparation they would use for any baseline shot. This will not work; the ball that goes nice and deep from the baseline goes out from the halfcourt area. The great fundamental involved here is that from the baseline we always hit up, but as we approach the net we start to hit level or even down, until finally the other extreme is reached—when on top of the

Diagram 7–2. Halfcourt and baseline shots contrasted. Note how much farther the baseline shot (B) travels. It is hit crosscourt, deep, well within lines. The approach shot is hit straight and aimed much closer to the sideline and less deep to make greater width possible and to avoid the double risk of going close to two lines. The objective of the baseline shot is depth. The objective of the approach shot is to open the court for the subsequent volley.

Figure 7–1. The approach shot. Note the high closed racket so as to cover the ball and aim low and short, the short backswing, the semi-open stance, the walking through so the player is on his way with the ball. Note how sharply this differs from a baseline drive.

net, playing a poor lob, we smash it decisively down, sometimes nearly vertically.

Decisiveness

An approach shot by definition is designed to make it possible for us to approach the net. Therefore it should get us there; by the time we finish the shot we should actually be there. This is, of course, an ideal that is seldom literally attained, but we should get as near it as possible. We should move to net as part of the follow-through so that if by chance we hit the net we are up there to pick up the ball. This concept of sweeping in *with* the ball, as contrasted with making the shot and moving in afterwards, is a very important part of half-court technique. It means we are mentally completely committed to advancing to net *before* we play the ball. Even if we play it off the wood for an absolute cripple our balance is forward so we still go in with the shot. And even if we make a great shot that doesn't come back at all we are up there ready to volley and smash in case there is a return. The key to the proper mental attitude on all halfcourt shots is to be decisive. You are or you are not going to net, and there is no messing around with maybe, perhaps, if my shot is good enough, etc. Never was it more true that he who hesitates is lost. One must either play the ball and run back to the baseline (thus frankly admitting to a supercautious—or chicken?—attitude) or play the ball and move in. One should never play the ball and then afterwards try to make a delayed decision, meanwhile remaining in a position that is unsound for either attack or defense.

Aiming Short

This brings up another characteristic of half-court technique and the approach shot in particular: do not aim very deep. This is surprising to most people. They are sure that a deep shot is the best, and so they aim deep.

The ball goes out—again and again. Why? Because, first, a lot of the court is behind the player; he has less available distance into which to hit than in an ordinary baseline exchange. Second, he is sweeping in with the shot; more body momentum tends to make the ball go a good bit farther than anticipated. Third, he is forcing—hitting hard—and this tends to give the ball added length. Fourth, he is taking a considerable calculated risk with the sideline; it is unwise also to risk the baseline. Taking two risks rather than one will quite likely cause the percentage of success to drop. So it is important to hit the approach shot severely, aim fairly close to the sideline, but aim comparatively short: about five feet behind the service line is a good rule of thumb. See Diagram 7–1. If the ball *goes* deeper—all right. If the player *aims* deeper, he will often miss one way or another. If the ball goes right where it is aimed, and it has been hit hard, the bounce will take it deep and hard so the player is all right anyway. The point is, in playing near the sideline with force, the depth doesn't matter—the shot will be effective anyway—while aiming deep presents a double risk and causes errors too frequently.

Aiming Low

Another characteristic of the approach that distinguishes it from the baseline shot is the height above the net. An attacking shot should be as low over the net as percentage play will permit—about a foot. This aim helps to control the length and keep it in the court even when hit severely, as it should be. Much has been made already of the idea of aiming away from the net, of avoiding aiming at it, and of the percentages involved—and all this is true from the baseline. But now we are no longer at the baseline, opportunity knocks, and some measure of risk is well run. From the baseline there is nothing to gain by aiming low and much to lose—namely, depth. From the halfcourt there is much to gain—a chance to force an error or make a winner on the next shot. From the baseline we hit up and play it safe. From the halfcourt we attack and take calculated risks.

SPECIFIC SITUATIONS

Method Helps

In drilling on approach shots one should start with the high forehand. Anyone who truly masters this shot has a lethal weapon ready to pounce on any flimsy shot by his opponent. First, the instructor should drill on advancing to the ball with the racket high to the side and a little in *front* and slightly closed (tipped forward), using a somewhat open stance. See Figure 7–1. Second, he should drill on aiming close to the net and somewhat short in terms of length, hitting down the line. Third, he should drill on sweeping in with it so that the player is well inside the service line before he can stop, so thoroughly does he commit himself to moving forward as he plays the ball. Fourth, the instructor should drill on refining the whole thing so the player is in to the setup so quickly that he can wait, poised, causing the opponent to wonder if *this* time it is a drop shot or a crosscourt; then a fast press with quite a bit of topspin to assure keeping it in and to give it a jump bounce, plus the follow-in that leaves the opponent parked on the player's alley (this matter of net position will be discussed in Chapter 8, "Forecourt Play"). If later he can be taught to make a drop shot from *exactly* the same preparation he is indeed well equipped; he can beat you with the drop if you lay back to handle his power, and he can overwhelm you if you hold your position. The only answer is: don't give him a setup, he'll beat you.

All this sounds rather advanced. It is. Beginners should not bother their heads with it. But in schools and colleges there are hundreds—literally thousands—of players who are reasonably steady and able to rally. They keep on practicing their baseline technique and their net play when what they really need to improve is halfcourt technique. And instructors should take this into account: every player cannot avoid getting a lot of baseline practice —he can't even warm up or receive service without using his baseline skills. But he will never stress the halfcourt unless he is specifically pushed into it; and isn't this the teacher's job—to guide? Even if his baseline play is still far from perfect he should be started on the art of handling his setups, for in the long run this is what separates the men from the boys.

Backhands: The Slice Is Preferred

Most good players with very few exceptions will slice all backhand approach shots. Why is this? There are several cogent reasons, each persuasive, but collectively making a very strong argument indeed, showing that the better players know just what they are doing. In the first place, very few people can lash a backhand—i.e., *sock* it—and at the same time control it. By contrast, many *can* hit a devastating topspin forehand off a setup and keep it in the court. But if the ball is not played with great speed, then how do we "force" an opponent? The answer is a heavy slice, which will kick and skid when it bounces, thereby making it very difficult for a defender to play an accurate passing shot. So the slice hopefully gets him in trouble. Added to this is a second powerful asset: a slice skids low, forcing a defender to play up to the attacker as much as is humanly possible. Is this really that important? Indeed it is. Stand a player at net, set a ball up for yourself so it bounces a convenient height (around the waist). Note that you can make either a straight or angled passing shot fairly easily. Now drop a ball that bounces not more than one foot off the ground. Immediately the net becomes a formidable obstacle, looming high in your path. You need more spin on your angle to make it dip (and this slows it some). You must aim quite high to clear the net on the straight shot, so again you cannot hit out with as much straight power. In other words, both shots become "tough shots" off a low bouncing ball. A third reason is more subtle but is not to be ignored: it takes several steps to get in close and steps take time. The slice, since it takes definitely longer to get there, gives you time to attain an optimum net position where only a great pass or a perfect touch lob will beat you. So all players, as they move from intermediate to advanced status, would do well to work hard on perfecting a good backhand slice approach.

The technique involves getting a heavy spin by crossing the ball: vertically on a high setup, diagonally from left to right and high to low on a medium-height shot, and straight across from left to right on a low shot.

In all cases the weight should press through the shot in the direction of its proposed flight. This pressing is needed not only to give pace to the ball but also to get the player started to the net—not a fraction of a second may be wasted. If the player hits the net he should be up there to pick up the ball, so total is the initial forward commitment. Good players seem to play the ball, and there they are—at net. To accomplish this many players prefer to walk through with the back foot as the follow-through is made, exactly as servers get a fast start to the net by bringing their right foot into the court as they follow through. Others, on the backhand slice, prefer to increase their accuracy by staying sideways (shoulders lined up with the shot) for an extra jiffy, but they shuffle-step in as they finish. In any event, the move toward the net must start as soon as is humanly possible without ruining the execution of the shot itself. Therefore, the shot should always be practiced as a "play-and-move-in" exercise, never as a "play-and-stand-there" exercise, since the latter won't do a player much good in actual play. Again, tempo and what comes next have a marked effect on technique. Playing a keep-the-ball-in-a-play slice is not the same thing at all as a slice approach. The very word "approach" defines the difference—it "approaches" us to the net; that is, getting to the net dovetails with the shot itself so that the two merge and become one operation, not two. Watch good players do it: they address the ball carefully and take aim, then seem to play it and sweep forward to good net position in one uninterrupted smooth move. It takes practice—separate special practice—but it pays off in success up front.

There is another small difference between this shot and baseline topspin drives. A slightly Continental grip gives heavier spin than an Eastern. Changing the grip an eighth of an inch toward the forehand will do this. Many fine players make these little adjustments without thought—it is automatic. Here again the concept of one grip is seriously open to question: it is difficult to adjust the shot to the grip; one must adjust the grip to the shot— that is, hold the racket in a manner best calculated to do the job. To slice, the lower edge of the racket must lead off the ball. The Continental grip lends itself to this by advancing the lower edge a trifle, even as a golfer uses differently slanted clubs to get more or less under a ball.

A very good drill is to alternate, either on a practice wall or in a rally. The player prepares to drive (Eastern), and makes a topspin shot. The player prepares to slice (Continental), and puts a heavy cut on the ball. This is equally true for forehand slices, which are discussed in the next paragraph. Some may feel all this is too complicated. It is advanced. But don't we do this with our service? We play flat serves and spin serves, and we combine following them to net with the shot itself. There really is little difference. And the "complication" is less than one might suppose: once a player masters slicing on one side, the other side comes quickly because of basic similarities. And the whole bag of tricks of a tennis player is included in the two racket skills, topspin and slice. Every shot is a variation of one or the other, and this concept is stressed repeatedly throughout this book.

The Low Setup—Slice It

Of course whenever possible a player should move in on a setup quickly so as to catch it as high as possible since this means the net is less in the way and he can hit hard with less risk.

However it frequently occurs—surprisingly frequently—that a player's shot will just happen to come over the net low, land short, and bounce low. It is impossible to take this ball high because it never is high. Furthermore, such short low shots often are made by mistake when a player means to hit deep, so they cannot be anticipated. Thus they are at times very low when the player reaches them. This poses a problem: if he hits hard and elevates the ball enough to clear the net, he'll go out. If he eases up to keep it in, the shot is not effective and he is usually passed or lobbed. There is only one good answer (assuming he wishes to go to net rather than play a drop) and that is the slice. He cannot make the shot go fast and keep it in, but he *can* make it nasty with a low side-kick bounce and keep it in. This shot is played with zero (repeat, literally zero) backswing. The racket cuts from outside in, across the lower back of the ball, and imparts heavy spin. The weight puts enough pace into it so it kicks low when it lands.

This is a difficult shot. The tendency is to hit it out continually at first until the backswing is eliminated and an out-to-the-side preparation is substituted for it. Also it goes out because the player is usually rushing in and has more momentum than he realizes plus less distance into which to play than he realizes. It is a good idea to aim only four or five feet past the service line. The idea here is twofold: the player wishes to create a bounce that is a little unpredictable and therefore hard to judge, and above all he wishes to keep the ball very low so the opponent must hit sharply upwards. Many players hit over the baseline not only for the reasons already mentioned but also because they are subconsciously trying to put the ball *through* their opponent as with a hard flat or topspin shot. They are thus attempting the impossible and fail continually. It is important that a player realize that the low point at which he takes this ball inhibits drastically what he can do (never mind what he'd *like* to do). He *cannot* make it go really fast and keep it in so he is limited to creating a low bounce that he hopes will transfer the

same inhibitions and limitations to his opponent. It is as though one said "I cannot prevent you from playing this ball, but I intend to make it as difficult and unpleasant as possible for you."

This shot should be practiced by itself as a drill by all advanced players. It is quite extraordinary how few there are—even among players of reputation—who can handle a low short ball well. It is not a matter of talent, ability, or desire: they just haven't realized that it is a problem by itself and a tough one that will not respond to less than its full due in thought, planning, and practice. In particular the techniques indicated here and in the chopping and slicing section of "Baseline Play," Chapter 6, are recommended to all those who coach at the secondary school level and on up.

A last word to the wise: a great deal is made of net play; all instructors stress volley and overhead and drill them a good bit. It is time we reminded ourselves that the quality of the approach shot determines what kind of a chance we get (if any) when we arrive at the net position. To go up behind an inadequate approach is just as foolish and unrewarding as to go up behind a poor service. All good players work hard on their services, and they should also work on their approaches, in particular on the slice since it is the only good answer to a short low ball.

THE DROP SHOT

The Key to Change of Pace

A good bit will be said about the never-ending tendency of young players to ignore or downgrade the drop shot. This is natural because most boys and girls are attracted by the philosophy that says "I don't fool around—I hit 'em!" But it is up to instructors—continually, endlessly, and with eternal patience—to point out that as the saying goes for every punch there is a counterpunch; so variety, change of pace, and mixing 'em up are not merely desirable but indispensable if we are to prevent our opposition from getting used to our style so they know just what we are going to do next and are soon standing there waiting for it—with the counterpunch all prepared of course. Now the drop shot is the shot farthest removed from the hard forcing approach; therefore, it is potentially the greatest creator of doubt and the greatest change that is possible. It should therefore be taught not so much as a shot by itself but as an adjunct to or a variation on our more usual approach shots. This brings us to the technique that will create this effect.

Identical Preparation

If the drop is to relate to the approach as just stated, then the preparation for both should be *exactly* the same. The perfect crime is the one that gives no clue. The greatest deception in tennis comes not from a lot of expert faking but from absolutely none at all. The fake is a clue, and your opponent will very probably deduce from it what you plan to do. Even if you fool him, next time he spots it at once. But if you prepare for a drop just as though you were about to hit the ball hard—get your racket, weight, feet, poise, even your facial expression, everything the same, and then merely drop the ball instead of playing it hard—how can he tell? The answer is, he cannot. He knows you *may* drop it, but you may also force hard—because he can see you are perfectly prepared to force hard—so he is in doubt until you actually play. Thus the first thing to learn about drop shot technique is that it must grow out of ordinary halfcourt technique with no variation at all.

A Vertical Shot

The second characteristic of a drop shot that surprises a lot of players is that it drops. Far from being facetious this is a sober statement of a fact all too often ignored. A drop shot is called a drop shot because it is vertical: it goes up, then it drops down. It should be *falling* when it crosses the net. Very few people realize this until it is pointed out. Study Diagram 7–3 with care if this is a new concept because it is basic to the proper execution of the shot: the ball goes *up* from the racket, floats softly until it is about to the net, then falls exhausted just on the other side. This picture of a ball that goes up and down brings up the third essential in good dropping: do not aim low. The ball should rise to about twice the height of the net. This permits it to *drop* without being at once in the bottom of the net. The idea is to aim very close to the net in terms of length but not in terms of height. Not only does the higher drop shot allow us to drop the ball closer to the net in terms of length but it also limits our risk factor to one dimension instead of two.

Backspin

The fourth ingredient in a drop shot is backspin. If it lands just over the net and has some backspin it will tend to stop dead right there. A shot that does this, after having been played with reasonable deception, is very difficult to cope with on any except the hardest courts. It is devastating on grass and wicked on slow clay or composition.

Diagram 7–3. The drop shot. Note how vertical the flight of this shot is compared with most others (except the lob). It is strictly a shot that goes up and drops down; it is not a "skimmer" as many believe.

Learning to Drop

The method of practicing or drilling a drop shot is important. The instructor must repeatedly set up the ball. The player must be required first to control his preparation so it looks the same as when he means to play a hard shot. Then he must learn to "feather" the ball. If he has already learned to do some chopping and slicing he has merely to reduce the length and increase the height. It has been said that the length of a slice is controlled by regulating how much weight we put into it. For the drop shot we put scarcely any into it: the racket puts back drag (spin) on the ball while we give it the merest whisper of a shove so it barely floats through the air and cannot be said really to have any velocity at all. This must be aimed high so it will not just fall into the net.

Usually this all seems very queer to a beginning player and often at first he cannot bring himself to do it. A very good device for instructors is to suggest that he try to push the ball up (with backspin) so it drops on top of the net. Explain that the perfect drop shot would land on top of the net and roll down the other side. This way of expressing it gives a good mental picture and a target and usually speeds the learning process. And learning the shot is mostly mental, because physically it is merely a very soft (on purpose) example of the standard slice and chop technique: pull with the racket, push with the weight.

All instructors should take care to point out that a very firm grip is essential in making a drop shot. It is a delicate shot but not a weak shot. A loose grip produces a feeble or weak and uncontrolled shot. A tight grip used with great restraint gives the proper feeling of "délicatesse." Many players tend to relax their grip as they play ever more gently and at once lose all touch and control and cannot understand why they are so poor. The distinction between delicacy and weakness is an important one to make in teaching all touch shots.

It should be mentioned that a drop shot is extremely effective against the wind—since the wind helps make it shorter and deader—and poor with the wind for the same reasons reversed. Often on a windy day when against the wind one feels he can scarcely attack at all effectively, the drop shot and other hacks and slices are about the best weapons he can find.

Many teachers look upon a drop shot as a "fine point" to be left "to the end" after other more basic skills have been acquired. This is a fallacy. Of course they never get to the end. This shot should be begun with all players who show any talent not long after they become intermediates. Why? Because perhaps the most difficult skill of all to acquire in tennis is what we call "touch." The drop shot is the touchiest shot there is. It demands that element so important in tennis and often absent in other sports: nearly total restraint. The main difference between a beginner and a good player is delicacy in control. While those with little or no ability may never reach the point where they are ready for a drop shot, all those who do have some talent should be encouraged to fool around with it as soon as they are basically grounded and able to play.

The subtle point here is that delicacy in one shot carries over into other shots, so that time put in on the extreme finesse required for a good drop shot will inculcate the neatness, exactness, and restraint needed for a good volley, an angled drive, or any other shot that involves more precision than a mere baseline exchange. Even from the baseline the extra precision is needed for passing shots; what are these if not an attempt to put the ball in a small space? So all coaches are urged to give consideration to teaching the drop for technical as well as tactical reasons.

The drop shot can be taught very effectively on the bangboard: a player can drive the ball so it rebounds conveniently, then attempt his drop shot, trying to make it touch the board *going down* just above the net line. The finesse of playing it gently enough to be going down when it reaches the board is the key to touch. Many players can be taught this shot merely by showing them on the bangboard and then saying "There, work on that for a while." This saves a lot of work setting up the ball for the player, not to mention time. It also usually intrigues them—it is a new and interesting toy to play with—and they become quite taken up with it.

ANGLES

Angle the Angle

Some forecourt shots are by no means setups. If they are well to the side they may take us right off the court into the alley as they bounce. In such a case the usual answers often will not work because of our position: we are out of court. Thus even if we have a good crack at the ball we must take into account that our position is poor. The situation is a two-edged sword: we may hurt him but we may get hurt ourselves too unless we plan against it.

The best answer is usually a very sharp crosscourt angle—so sharp it goes to the corner of the service court or better as contrasted with the deep corner. If as we advance to the ball we prepare to play down the line as usual and play crosscourt by taking the ball a little sooner and pivoting sharply just as we play—so our crosscourt intent is well disguised—we stand a good chance of getting a winner or near winner with a good angle. But the major point is that this shot carries with it a big insurance policy: even if he gets to it he cannot hit away from us. He *must* play back toward us to get the ball *anywhere* in the court because he is so far out of court on the other side himself. So here is a case where a good offense is also the best defense.

By contrast if we play straight a crosscourt will beat us; we'll never get back for it either at net or in the backcourt. If we play deeper crosscourt a straight shot will seem awfully far away; we'll never make it across to it. So really the maxim "Always angle an angle" has much in its favor and should be adopted unless clear-cut reasons are present for doing otherwise:

because of an opponent's position a straight shot looks like a clean ace, or he has a terrific weakness so play straight to press it in spite of considerations of position, or a drop looks like a winner. All these last are possibilities, but the shot to practice under these circumstances is the angle.

Technique

In good execution a fast dropping ball is produced. It is a good idea to use topspin almost to excess so the ball goes up and down a lot but does not have much length. This allows a player to clear the net well and still come down very short inside the service line. Usually to brush up the back of the ball from a bit below it after a near zero backswing, with the top edge of the racket leading decisively, gives the feeling of loop and absence of length which are desired. The feeling of the shot is that it is brushed rather than pressed solidly like a deeper drive. To call it a "tweak" is going too far but gives the idea. Some good players even pull up very sharply and finish high above their heads to get the spinning effect. The point is to get a lot of vertical motion and not much horizontal. If this shot is perfected it can be employed from either side of the court as an angled passing shot and so becomes an important part of one's defense as well as an offensive trick. See Figure 7–2.

Hiding the Angle

Study Figure 7–2 carefully. Note the player uses a closed stance, obviously threatening to play straight. This serves to conceal the planned crosscourt or at least prevent an anticipatory move by the opponent. As the shot is made the striker pivots sharply so he is actually facing crosscourt at the conclusion of the swing and his right leg has walked completely around the ball, thus turning it decisively to the left at the last minute. See Figure 7–2 again. If this turning effect is withheld as long

Figure 7–2. The topspin angle. Very much a "brush up and don't hit" shot. See text for full discussion of this valuable trick. Note preparation that threatens a straight shot (first photograph) and sharp pivot (last two photographs).

as possible it is extremely difficult for an opponent to divine one's intent, so he gets a late start on what should be a long journey.

HALFCOURT SKILLS IN THE TOTAL PICTURE

Simplification

Obviously halfcourt technique is advanced technique. It exploits the variations possible provided one has mastered the two basic skills of going across over and across under the ball, using the two edges of the racket. Only those who have reached this point in their racket work are ready for these advanced shots which demand not only tactical knowledge but the technical skill to put the ball into small spaces.

Only those who have reasonable athletic ability should be urged to develop a well-rounded technique. What about the large numbers who don't quite qualify for this rarified atmosphere?

They should be taught *one* halfcourt shot—the forehand down the line to the opponent's backhand. The instructor should encourage them to run around backhand setups so that within reason they use this one shot *all* the time in the halfcourt. It is quite surprising how well an average or slightly below average athlete can do if he limits his ambitions and puts all his eggs in one basket and works hard and purposefully to make it a good one. Surely he is caught now and again, and he'll never be a champion, but he has a game—he knows what he can and cannot do, and within these limitations he can fight with determination and get great satisfaction from his play. If he con-

fines himself to opponents who do not athletically outclass him he will be a winner far more
than half the time.

Often a player who has these limitations and
has been taught in this manner will be very
pleased for quite a while; this new shiny
weapon makes him feel he is really somebody
on the court. But there comes a time (a season
later?) when he realizes people are watching
for his one pet shot and are there ready to get
it every time. Now is the time to add a drop
shot. However, he should probably learn it with
his forehand only. One side at a time is
enough.

The message here is that an instructor, no
matter how knowledgeable, should not be anxious to pour out that knowledge to everyone
who is in a group or signs up for a lesson. The
capacity to *withhold* knowledge and feed it bit
by bit if, as, and when the pupil is ready for the
next forward step—this discretion on the part
of an instructor is one of the distinctions between top teachers and average teachers. The
point is stressed here because it is particularly
in the halfcourt that we move from comparatively crude basic knowledge to the more
refined applications of racket skills. These are
not for everybody and are not even for the
most talented except in series with time for
digestion after each bite.

While of course every instructor is entitled
to be independent in his approach, and no one
wishes to appear to insist "Do it my way,"
there are general guidelines that emerge from
a consideration of the basics of racket work.
While great variation is possible within these
divisions, it would appear to be stretching one's
right to individualism to depart from them
entirely. To play at all, to rally at all, one must
start with open-faced technique. This is fundamental number one; it is absolutely indispensable and should be taught everyone first. Let
us refer to it as the open racket. Simultaneously but with far less stress all beginners
should be initiated into the idea of the closed
racket by teaching them to volley. And those
whose performance, desire, and application
indicate a capacity for further growth—they

and they only should be introduced to the nice-
ties of halfcourt technique, in particular the
use of the closed racket on certain ground
strokes, and the slice approach.

Last But Not Least

This means halfcourt skill is the last of the
three stages to be taught, while logically one
would assume it should be second. But the
facts of life on the tennis court almost compel
a one-three-two approach. One cogent reason
is that net play represents the other extreme
from the baseline: the volley and the smash
are played decisively down, while baseline
shots are played decisively up. It is important
to introduce students to both ways of preparing
the racket (low and open and taken back contrasted with high and closed and pushed forward) at an early stage. In this connection
coaches often have difficult experiences with
players who have come to them after having
drilled for years on the proper baseline preparation but who have never tried to prepare for
the volley. They just *cannot* stop from drawing back, so strong is their habit, and of course
they volley badly because of too much swing.
Therefore just because these skills are pretty
much exact opposites they should be begun
together. While admittedly it is an exaggeration, to some extent it may be compared to the
need for learning to walk with both legs, not
just with one.

A second reason is that groups always get to
playing doubles at an early stage. There they
are, and someone is saying "You should play
net when your partner serves—or receives."
The instructor just plain *must* teach net fundamentals. A third reason, weaker but not
without psychological significance, is that net
play represents the moment of crisis and greatest excitement in an exchange. Players want
this because it is fun. They don't want to spend
a long time perfecting their baseline play before they start having this fun. So let them
have their way: make net play the closing ten
minutes of one of the earliest group lessons. It

will ensure the instructor's popularity and the popularity of the game with the pupils. At the next lesson they will ask "May we play net?" and of course you say "Oh, yes, if you work hard on your strokes and your serve." The best way to teach is also the most fun, the most laughs, the most excitement. They learn more but are less aware of it, and they look forward to their lessons with pleasure.

Thus the order of instruction more or less determines itself: the open racket because it is the only way to get going, the closed racket at net to initiate the counterbalance effect of the other extreme and to make early doubles play go more properly, and the finesse of the halfcourt skills which involve both open and closed racket work for all who exhibit sufficient native ability to encourage the faith that this will cause progress rather than hopeless confusion. While all this may sound obvious to an experienced teacher, one of the major tasks a youthful instructor faces is to build in his own mind a picture of the logical progression of tennis skills from the most basic and raw to the most refined. Such a concept enables him to get as near as possible to the teacher's ideal of taking each player up to his potential without confusing him by trying to take him beyond it. And this concept is the backbone of the idea of teaching in series; it is the master series on which all the other little series hang.

QUESTIONS

1. How does the flight of an approach shot differ from a baseline shot?

2. How does racket technique change from baseline to halfcourt?

3. How do we move in making an approach?

4. Should approaches be aimed deep? Why?

5. Should approaches have a high net clearance?

6. Is halfcourt skill worth special effort? Why?

7. What is the most commonly used backhand approach? Discuss its advantages.

8. What is the best way to handle a low ball in the halfcourt area?

9. Is it important to know how to make a drop shot?

10. How does one achieve deception in halfcourt play?

11. Describe the flight of a drop shot.

12. When should one teach the drop shot to young pupils?

13. How can you "hide" an angle shot?

14. Does the average player need a lot of halfcourt shots?

CHAPTER 8

Forecourt Play

Drills and tests on volley and overhead will be found in Chapter 11.

EMPHASIZING ACCURACY

Placement versus Power

The forecourt is the promised land—the only area from which the player can make winners. As has already been emphasized, one's attitude should be aggressive, and the plan should be not just to get the ball back but to put it away. To most inexperienced players "to be aggressive," "to put it away," and "to make a placement" imply hitting very hard. Actually there is in those three phrases in quotes above not *one word* about increased power or velocity. Only when we say "smash" or "kill" do we mean slam the ball. *All* other net shots must be played with some degree of restraint, or an error usually results. The test of any shot at net is whether it was accurate, not whether it was speedy.

The most obvious opportunity at net is a bad lob that enables one to stand fairly close to the net and slam down almost vertically. One would think this shot is all power—just hit it hard, bounce it over the fence. But many players are physically incapable of bouncing it

over the fence, so that even on this most out-and-out setup the only plan that will be successful for all players is one that stresses accuracy. On all other chances at net the area open for a winner is more restricted, and the premium on accuracy and the necessity for it are sharply increased. This point may be summed up by stating that success at net depends upon a player's ability to put the ball into a small space. This, of course, is in terms of tennis practically a definition of the word "accuracy."

THE ESSENTIALS

Self-protection

Ideally players should be taught net play when they are young, so that they feel at home in the forecourt at an early age. Unfortunately this is often not the case, and an adult, playing other adults who play with considerable speed and pace, is suddenly told to play net. It is a disconcerting experience that can be downright frightening to some. Therefore, the very first thing an instructor should tell any adult student of net play is to defend his or her person with the backhand, not the forehand. It is almost impossible to volley with the forehand a ball that is directly at one's midriff. By contrast, it is easy with the backhand to intercept any shot coming straight for you. Whenever the player does not know just what may happen at net, he should cock the racket in front of him with the backhand grip. Then he is ready to protect himself if the unexpected suddenly occurs. See Figure 8–1. Instructors should emphasize this to overcome the very natural fears of beginners.

Block and Press—Do Not Hit a Volley

At the baseline and in the halfcourt the ball has bounced, and this act of bouncing takes most of the energy out of the ball. Only extremely hard hit shots like fast serves and overhead smashes can be blocked at the baseline without having them drop hopelessly short. Most shots that have bounced must receive energy from us if they are to go anywhere. So we use swing and a lot of body pressure to give them the desired velocity, length, and pace. We produce the necessary energy and put it into the ball.

By contrast, when we are at net the ball is in the air fresh from our opponent's racket and still full of energy. Only if he lobs is the ball comparatively without force—it floats—so here again we must produce energy and impart it to the ball, and we do. The overhead and the stroked volley are the only shots at net that receive their main impetus from the striker. All others get their energy from our opponent, and we utilize this energy by blocking. This means we do not swing at all. Like a mirror reflecting light we use what comes to us and produce nothing. The best example of expert and infallible blocking is a bangboard. Does the bangboard swing? Does it produce energy? No, your own shot comes right back at you full of your own energy. A good net player uses the other fellow's shot exactly like a bangboard except that he is able to alter the position of his racket and so can change the direction of the rebound any way he likes.

Blocking and swinging are quite different.

Figure 8–1. Self-protection. Always use the backhand. The backhand, not the forehand, is your shield.

To swing, we take our racket back away from the ball. To block, we put our racket out front *to* the ball, and the ball plays our racket more than our racket plays the ball. Look at Figure 4–3 (how to prepare for a forehand drive), then look at Figure 8–2 (how to prepare for a forehand volley). Note that in addition to being out in front the racket has a closed face and is higher, ready to press down from above. But the most fundamental difference is that the racket is reaching towards the ball instead of drawing back. This concept of preparing the racket far in front is the first element to get across to all players learning to volley.

Perhaps it has occurred to the reader that the volley has been overexplained in the foregoing paragraphs. It may well read that way, but out on the court ten out of ten beginners and a large majority of those with experience will *swing* at the ball—and this is a sure way to develop a bad volley. Therefore, to spend time making crystal clear the difference between baseline and net play, and the fact that in many respects the technique of one is the opposite of the other, this is not at all to overdo it. Rather it is to get right at the heart of the problem—which is that players do not understand these distinctions. They mix their techniques and get hybrid results, and also get very frustrated. To teach by contrast and by opposites is as a rule the most successful approach.

A Tight Grip—A Rigid Wrist

A firm grip is desirable whenever the ball is met in the game of tennis, but it is an absolute necessity for a good volley. Since there is no bounce our racket receives the full impact of all the force our opponent has given the ball. A tight grip and a cocked or braced wrist are the means of meeting this shock successfully so we retain control rather than lose it. Obviously if the grip is at all loose the ball will control the

Figure 8–2. The forehand volley. Everything reaches forward—racket, arm, left leg, bent body—to catch the ball as soon as possible. Note the braced wrist for firmness.

Figure 8–3. Grit and grip when you volley. Meeting a ball that has pace requires great firmness. Note the grim expression, the tense left hand. HE will tell the ball; the ball won't tell him.

racket instead of the reverse. A good maxim in teaching the volley is to urge the player to "grip hard but don't hit hard." It is of some importance to point out at the same time that the tight gripping should occur only just before and during the actual shot, since to squeeze the racket continually soon produces extreme fatigue and an aching forearm. Relax between shots. The "bracing" effect can be seen clearly in Figure 8–2; when the wrist is cocked back as shown it cannot give way to the ball because it won't go back any farther. Thus a firm grip plus a firm wrist plus the body pushed firmly by the legs gives the ideal result: an impregnable fortress effect that cannot be shaken even by a hard drive. "He volleys like a rock" is what every player wants people to say about him.

This matter of firmness is so important it needs a lot of stress. Players should be told to grip so hard that their knuckles get white, or to grip as hard as they would if they were unscrewing a jar of peanut butter that doesn't wish to be unscrewed. Point out that the best players often make horrible faces when they volley, these facial twistings being merely what anyone does when gripping anything absolutely as hard as possible. In other words good exponents of the volley grip so hard they cannot help grimacing at the same time—which indicates that our tight grip should be *very* tight indeed, and that gritting and gripping seem to go together. Besides being good for a laugh it sometimes actually helps a player to a firm grip if he snarls a little as he volleys. See Figure 8–3.

Cut Your Volley

In preceding passages a good bit has been written about controlling the length of chops and slices by applying or withholding weight. The average volley is nothing more or less than a stiff abbreviated block chop. A low volley is an abbreviated block slice. By pulling off the ball length may be subtracted. By pressing forward length may be added. So the racket work already discussed is definitely applicable here even though everything tends to stiffen up to stand the shock of a sharp impact; and everything tends to be cut short for lack of time, which is the next subject for discussion. The point here is that the volley is a bottom-edge-first shot; it should always carry backspin, and it should be controlled with the same push and pull combination basic to all chopping and slicing.

Tempo and Simplicity

Again to deal in contrasts, compare the time a player has while the ball travels from an opponent's racket to his own racket—first at the baseline, then at net. It is quickly clear that things happen from two to four times as fast at net. This means that a player's execution—his making of the shot—must be sufficiently simple, restricted, and minimal so he can accomplish it without undue haste even in so short a time. It follows that an instructor must be rigid in insisting that absolutely every unnecessary move, swing, or mannerism of either the racket or the player should be eliminated. One good way to get this concept through is to keep saying "Do this and *nothing else!*" In this way the correct move is instilled while the tendency to do other things is curbed. And due to this factor of tempo and the need for simplicity this business of eliminating "everything else" can be half the job in teaching the volley to some players.

To achieve simplicity a player must wait in a crouch with his racket well in front of him, elbows forward. This ready position is of crucial importance since it reduces the number of moves to be made after the ball leaves the opponent's racket. If the ready position already has us in a crouch with the racket in front, then the least the racket can do is to cock itself sideways—to the forehand or backhand side. That is *all* it should do except to lift or lower as the shot may be higher or lower. If the ball is within reach the left foot steps in for a forehand, the right for a backhand. If these two things are done simultaneously a player closes in, puts his weight forward, and plays the ball securely—all with extreme simplicity.

Good players often are heard to say "Oh, there is nothing to a volley." They almost literally mean this because they have reduced their personal volley down to such a small poke-draw that there really does seem to be nothing to it. However there is a good bit of work and discipline involved in achieving this extreme simplicity. It is a paring process: put your racket out front so that it is near the ball—nearer, nearer, until there is no approach swing at all. That eliminates that. Now go diagonally down through in a stiff and abbreviated manner, shorter, shorter, until it only moves a foot or so—that eliminates all the follow-through. So there is practically no approach and practically no follow-through, just a quick little chip. There is almost nothing to it.

Closing In

We are at net to win. That's fine, but a ball cannot be taken any old time and be turned into a winner. Most players do not understand with clarity what a ball does and what this means in the matter of opportunity for a net player. Any fairly decent defensive shot (excluding lobs) will rise up enough to clear the net by a reasonable margin (a foot or more) and having cleared it will dip down so as soon to be again below the level of the net. It is only above the net for a short distance on your side and for a short interval in time. If we could run a tennis movie in slow motion and then stop it just as the ball is crossing the net: there it is, sitting above the net, just asking to be put away *provided* you can get to it and play it while it is in this vulnerable position. Now if the movie is turned on again, notice how soon the ball dives down to a level from which a winner is difficult or impossible. So one of the most important skills in the forecourt is the ability to close in fast with the realization that success at net is determined as much by *when* we play the ball as by how well we play it. Opportunity is fleeting most of the time.

Of course a beginner might suggest that we move right in on top of the net ahead of time thus making sure, but this leaves out that great spoiler shot called the lob, and the lob of course cannot be ignored. We dare not advance, before he plays, beyond a point half way from the service line to the net. The determining factor is what we do *after* he plays, after the ball leaves his racket and we see it is not a lob. If we let the ball come to us, meanwhile preparing carefully to volley it (we hope with great skill), it will cross the net, arc down, and be too low for us to handle decisively no matter how well we execute. If, on the other hand, we reach forward with our racket and spring forward with our legs, then we have a very good chance of catching the ball while it is hovering above the net, open to any sort of placement we may have in mind. The importance of closing in—that is, of going to meet the ball rather than letting it come to you—cannot be exaggerated. It is so easy to make a winner when the ball is above and near the net. It is so difficult when the ball is low and farther back.

Figure 8–4. Ready at net. The crouchy hovering attitude permits a catlike reaction to whatever an opponent offers. Note the off-center arrangement of the feet—ready for a forehand, and ready to push with the right leg to whirl for a backhand.

Some people are much better than others at this even though they are apparently about even in intrinsic talent. This is because there is a definite technique to closing in. The first and greatest essential is to be in a crouch, for if the knees are well bent a player can jump in upon the ball as soon as he sees it is a drive, not a lob. See Figure 8–4. If the knees are not bent, he must bend them in order to jump in, and this takes much too long—and the chance to win is probably lost. The second essential is for him to shove the head of the racket forward as he jumps in so that it actually helps pull him forward. Any tendency to take the racket at all back has the effect of cancelling out an equal amount of forward effort thus defeating his purpose.

The third essential is far more subtle and requires thought and practice. It is to play position in such a way as to have the most time and the fewest alternatives, thus simplifying the job and increasing the chances of getting it done well. Now, ignoring lobs for the moment, we know an opponent must play either crosscourt or straight. It would seem logical to assume a middle position, leaving equal openings on each side. But this apparently sensible plan is not the best plan, because the two shots, straight and crosscourt, are not equal. One goes directly past us via the shortest route—the straight shot—while the other lingers in front of us longer as it goes by. It is a case of the old rule about the hypotenuse being longer than the side. There is less time to move for the straight shot, and we must take this into account. A little consideration leads to the conclusion that for the straight shot we must *be there*, and leave our scrambling for the crosscourt. This also has the important virtue of eliminating one of our alternatives. Instead of worrying about moving in either to the right or to the left we now worry about moving straight in or diagonally in for the crosscourt. This permits us to use favoritism—that is, to be more ready to move to the left than to the right if we are playing to an opponent's backhand, and vice versa. This means we can move better, faster, and farther.

This sounds on first hearing as though it really couldn't quite be true, and of course it can easily be carried too far. A good rule of thumb is to approach the net so that all straight shots are within reach except one that will land within a foot or less of the line. This means the attacker is wagering his approach shot is effective enough so that the defender, if he tries a really fine shot, will miss. The attacker is backing that bet by saying "If you can put it a foot or less from the line I'll give you the point." Thus the attacker is there for all *possible* straight shots, leaving what he considers the impossible shot uncovered. Usually this position is about four feet off the center service line, and the attacker does not go to net ready to cover either side—he goes to net already covering one side and ready to break for the other side. These two mental attitudes are quite different, and the second is quite a bit more effective than the first just because it allows us to concentrate on being ready to move one way only.

There is a fourth skill to closing in on the ball: the trick of hovering as the defender plays the ball. In the preceding chapter much stress was laid on the importance of moving in *with* an approach shot rather than later on.

If the attacker does this he is "in" *before* the defender strikes the ball. The attacker can therefore stop and hesitate, deeply crouched and ready to spring, until the defender commits himself. The attacker never should be in motion when the defender plays: nine times out of ten this means he has followed a false clue and has moved ahead of time the wrong way. In other words the defender has faked him right out of his sneakers and will win with ease. By contrast, if in spite of all the defender's powers of suggestion the attacker holds his well-planned position until the defender's shot leaves his racket, then he can close straight in or in-and-crosscourt—and now the chances are that he will win, not the defender. A further refinement of this hesitating or hovering technique is to crouch, ready to spring forward, and if necessary to cover a crosscourt, ready to spring and whirl. Thus if the shot is straight one just closes in. If the shot is crosscourt one closes in but also whirls or turns quickly so that the *same* inward springing action is directed toward cutting off the crosscourt shot while it is above the net. See Figures 8–5 and 8–6.

As this method is perfected the attacker develops—with experience—the feeling that

Figure 8–5. Closing in on a forehand volley. Note every effort is made to intercept the ball as SOON as possible, not merely as well as possible. A ball cut off while it hovers above the net can be put away. If allowed to come farther back, it probably cannot be put away.

Figure 8–6. Closing in on a backhand volley. Note how everything is forward, forward, NOT sideways: the arm, racket, body. Some very athletic players actually lunge in so their feet completely leave the ground.

playing net is all quite simple. Many fine players have said "Hit your setup straight and go up the alley." This puts it in a nutshell, but it is never that simple to those who are beginning

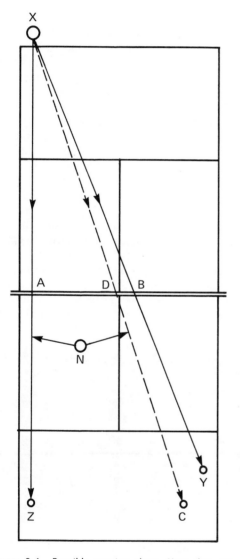

Diagram 8–1. Possible passing shots. Note that even a rather sharply angled pass (XY) crosses the net at B—not far from the center of the net—and that all easy shots (that give the striker the full length of the court) cross the net between A and D. Thus for a net player to be well to the side as at N is not overdoing it.

to develop a net game. The preceding rather elaborate treatment is an attempt to present to the student the reasons why the best players always seem to end up feeling it is quite simple, and end up covering the alley most of the time. There is one more reason that should help to reassure a player that he *really should* get over by that alley. This is the fact—completely unappreciated by most tennis players —that the ball, if placed to one side of the court by the attacker's approach shot, *must* cross that half of the net when it comes back. Even a good crosscourt passing shot is only a trifling distance the other side of the center strap *as it crosses the net.* See Diagram 8–1. Thus the attacker goes up the alley not by any means confident that he can move fast enough to get way over where that crosscourt will *land* —this is of course impossible—but hopeful that he can *intercept* the ball while it is in the air roughly over the center of the net. Here again the attacker wagers that his approach shot is sufficiently incommodious to justify confidence that a really sharp crosscourt will be missed if attempted. The point this paragraph hopes to make is that if the approach shot is any good the attacker can pursue the policy outlined in this chapter and the ball *must* come to him: the defender has no other choice except to try a shot he cannot make or to lob. This is why a good net player always seems to be there. He is indeed always there— right where the ball must come if it is to hit the court. This is why a defender will tend to make more errors against a good position player: because he does not want to hit it right to him, he aims for the very edge and risks an error.

To summarize net play: the approach should be played straight and the player should move in as part of the approach as much as possible. He should go right up the alley behind the shot. He should always hesitate or hover in a deep crouch, racket well forward, just before the defender plays; he should *never* be moving. As soon as he plays he should close in as fast as possible, reaching in with the racket, leaping in with the legs, to catch the ball before it dips low after crossing the net.

He should volley with an exceedingly small, tight, stiff, crisp diagonal chopping motion that only moves about two feet. He should play for accuracy, not speed. The player should think in terms of two shots: the approach opens the court, the volley exploits the opening.

Anticipation and Deception

Defenders have all sorts of mannerisms by which they attempt to decoy an attacker away from the shot they mean to make. They attempt to deceive in several ways: by hiding what they intend to do; by making moves strongly suggestive of a shot opposite to that which they intend; or by making it so obvious that they intend a certain shot that the attacker doesn't believe it—and is fooled. If an attacker can be persuaded to play detective it is quite possible to do a real job on him. To name a few—but by no means all—of the nefarious schemes common to all wiley defenders: (1) Line the ball up to hit it down the line, get the feet pretty well around, take the racket back a trifle extra as though to play the ball a bit later, then with a last minute move of the wrist turn the ball sharply crosscourt, leaving him in the alley. (2) Line the ball up to hit it crosscourt, use the open stance, get the racket outside the ball a bit, then by laying the wrist back at the last second let the ball slide off the racket down the alley, leaving him contemplating the center strap. (3) With a forehand, drop the racket below the ball and open it pointedly as though to say "I shall now lob"; he backs up hurriedly; you play crosscourt with a quick over-flick stroke; he is passed, having opened the court by backing up. This list could be extended to be quite a lengthy one—there are so many ways of hooking across and sliding straight, not to mention cleverly interspersed lobs.

If the defender has all these fancy resources at his disposal what chance has an attacker? Hadn't we all better stay back? Not at all. *None* of these trick plays will work unless the attacker reacts to them. He should not react.

The good net player takes up a position he knows is *right*—not too far in, not too far over—and he *holds* it. If the defender makes various suggestive blandishments, he ignores them. He reacts to one thing only: the ball. When he sees the ball start crosscourt—whether with a last minute flick of the wrist or with a more sound stroke—he lunges diagonally in to cut it off. When he sees it leave the racket going straight, he lunges straight in to volley. When he sees it rise up, he backs up to smash the lob. The entire key to a successful attack is to *watch the ball leave the racket.* If the attacker refuses to abandon his sound position until the ball has been played, then he cannot be faked out of position, and he cannot run the wrong way.

An accomplished forecourt player resembles a cat after a mouse. The cat does not wait for the mouse to run into its mouth: it waits until the mouse shows itself, then pounces. Similarly, the strong net player hovers until he sees the shot, then he pounces in for the placement or jumps back to smash. Like the cat he crouches, like the cat he concentrates and watches and waits with intensity, and like the cat he doesn't miss many chances.

This sounds easy, but it is not. Good defenders are like glib lawyers: they'll talk you out of anything and convince you every time that a fake is the real thing. They practically insert an "intuition" into your mind, so you say afterwards "I was *sure* he was playing it crosscourt." That's just what he planned—by some move of his shoulders, or racket, or one foot. And you were a sucker (that's right, a sucker) to allow yourself to be led by anything other than the ball leaving his racket. So to the rule "Watch the ball leave the racket" we must add *"and disregard everything else."* It takes will power and practice and experience, but once you get so that you follow only the ball you are on the road to being a hard man to fool on a tennis court, and only a fine shot will defeat you.

Of course there are exceptions. If a player clearly prepares some shot the same way every time, thus giving himself away, an attacker should take full advantage of such advance information. The advice given here assumes the defender knows his business and is subtle rather than obvious in his plans and moves. The reason this view is stressed is because the tendency of all inexperienced players is to react to everything conceivable *except* the ball, and the purpose here is to focus the attention where it should be—on the ball.

Position Play

In teaching a group the fundamentals of position play at net one very simple rule should be stressed: stay opposite the ball. As was already demonstrated (see Diagram 8–1) the ball must return across the half of the net in front of it, so if a player learns immediately to stay with the ball in the sense of covering that part

of the net, the pupil will find the ball coming to him most of the time. The most important thing an instructor can do is to demonstrate where the ball must cross the net by actually standing in a corner, making a shot out of his hand, and having one of the group go stand at that point where it crossed the net. Until this is done the players insist on trying to cover the entire net—and leave their alley wide open so almost any shot passes them. If one student stands where the crosscourt shot crossed the net, another where the alley shot crossed the net, then that part of the net which must be covered is clearly delineated. And since every beginner thinks of "covering the net" as meaning to cover the entire width, alley to alley, a very strong object lesson such as this is needed to make it clear that only half the net need be covered, and also to make it clear that this

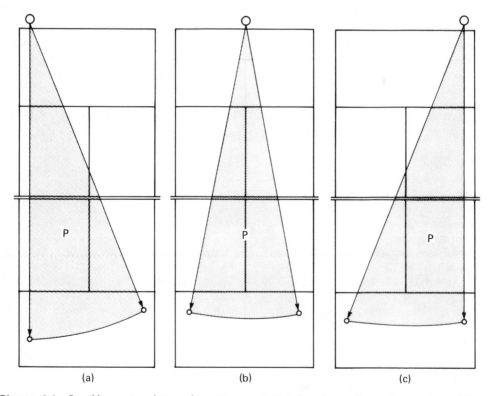

(a)   (b)   (c)

Diagram 8–2. Possible passing shots and position at net. Note how drastically good net position shifts as the source of the shot changes. Note how the easy rule clearly applies: stay opposite the ball.

half is the one most directly opposite the ball. If the object lesson is repeated from three spots—forehand corner, center, backhand corner—the lesson should be clear as to how the net to be covered moves with the ball. If the exact same thing is done with a doubles court the same result is obtained except that the net to be covered is wider because of the addition of the alleys, but of course there are now two to cover it. See Diagram 8–2.

In giving this lesson it is important to indicate that there are from any position large parts of the net over which the ball *cannot* be played and land in the court. Players are very reluctant to ignore any part of the net at first, but of course this is just what they must do if they are to cover *thoroughly* the open part of the net. So to teach by negatives contrasted with positives is effective: "Cover here, ignore there." "Cover the center, forget the alley." "When the ball is there, sit in your alley; disregard the rest of the court," etc. The instructor should stress where a player ought not to be as strongly as where he should be.

The Low Volley

The face of the racket must, of course, be opened for the low volley, but the great fundamental most often overlooked is to get down to the ball, way down, so the knee of one's back leg is not quite, but almost, on the ground. If an opponent is far back we may try for a winner by dropping the volley, but usually our main concern should be to keep the ball low so we retain the advantage by making him hit up. Of course theoretically we should not have to make low volleys very often—it means we are in trouble—so if the percentage of success is lower than ideal this must be accepted as normal.

The racket work on the low volley is the same as that on the sliced approach shot—draw across from the outside in—except it is stiffer and more of a block than a pressure by us, and as with all volleys the swing should be very small. The entire emphasis must be on

accuracy since power is out of the question from so low. See Figure 8–7.

THE OVERHEAD

Footwork

The overhead shot is closely related to serving since it is fundamentally a flattened-out sliced service. The great difference is in the toss: the other fellow tosses the ball, and he tosses it as inconveniently as he can to you. Therefore a quick reaction on your part to move your feet to get under the ball—so the toss turns out to be convenient after all—is the key to getting a good chance to kill it. It is difficult to move racket and feet simultaneously, so the quickest, most abbreviated backswing possible is desirable. The racket should be cocked back over the right shoulder, like a beginner's serve preparation, and the racket is ready to strike. This can be done so quickly that it leaves almost all the available time for footwork—and this is where it is needed. If a relatively small move is called for, the player should take the right foot back to assume the usual service stance and use the sidle step to maintain the

Figure 8–7. The low volley. Note that the right knee is almost on the ground. Few players do this well, because few players really get WAY DOWN to the ball. Note that the racket face is open and the ball is taken well in front.

proper striking position while lining up the ball. If a larger move is needed, the player should turn and run back normally but watch the ball over the left shoulder, then make final adjustments with the shuffle step. See Figure 8–8.

Figure 8–8. Lining up the overhead. Many players like to "point the ball" with the left arm to aid in setting up in proper relation to it. Note the footwork—just like service: left foot pointed, right foot braced.

Figure 8–9. Two overheads. The photograph on the left shows an advanced player taking the ball high. He will whip his wrist over and bring it down hard into the court. The photograph on the right shows a less talented player taking the ball much farther in front so it will go down without help from a talented and educated wrist. Anyone can learn to do this with practice.

Hit the Top of the Ball

In playing the ball the main emphasis should be put on hitting down. Most beginners tend to hit the part of the ball they are looking at: the back of the ball. They hit the fence. They must learn to come from above so as to strike the part of the ball they can't see—namely, the top of the ball—so as to bring it down into the court. There is one little trick that helps a lot in achieving this shift from an undesirably horizontal shot to a more vertical effect. It is to reach up with the arm and straighten up with the legs just before playing the ball. This gets the player above the ball so he can bring the racket down on it.

Another point that is of great assistance in bringing the ball down is to keep it in front; don't let it get behind you. If it is met a foot or two in front of the right shoulder, results are usually satisfactory. A little experimentation will reveal the "sweet spot" to almost any player, and henceforth the object of his footwork is to put the ball right there where his right arm wants it.

A good many books will teach that one should come over the ball with the wrist, thus bringing it sharply down. This is fine, and advisable, *if* you have the wrist. But many do not have the wiry flexible strength needed. They should be taught to start their overhead gently, to merely put the face of the racket on top of the ball and press it down (see Figure 8–9), following through as in service to the left side with the right or lower edge leading. As this technique is mastered, and only after it is going fairly well, then the pressing down can be speeded up until it becomes an effective shot.

The main thing with an overhead is, as with every shot: to try little easy ones at first. The instructor should stand inside the baseline, pop up a very short poor lob (the worst possible), and have the player press it down so it bounces over the instructor's head out of reach. He should work up from this toward a real shot off a lob that isn't such a cripple. The reason this begin-easy idea is stressed here is because almost all beginners logically connect the overhead with smashing, hitting very hard, etc., and it must be curbed, or they will tend to practice too violently—and learn next to nothing. The coming to the ball from above, the pressing decisively downward with good body bend and the carving through with the right-hand edge leading—each of these must be practiced and thought about and disciplined until the entire shot is one smooth motion down to the left side.

Talented players will naturally tend to snap their wrists and get more sparkle into the shot. Those with less ability can learn to control a stiffer, less fluid shot enough to be effective at their level of excellence. All players should carve over the upper right corner of the ball a little (not a lot, because it won't then be flat enough). As in the service, the correct grip and follow-through produces this effect, which gives a little slice, which in turn facilitates control.

Aiming an Overhead

An overhead is also called a kill or a smash. In other words it is a power shot that relies mainly on force for its effect. As has been previously stressed, it is unwise to hit hard for a small target, thus taking a double risk. The player should not try to get "cute" with the overhead; he should always take the big target. This means hitting into the widest piece of court available. If the player is on the forehand side, he should smash crosscourt at the opponent's forehand and avoid the small target to his backhand. If the ball comes to the backhand side, smash to the opponent's backhand, again taking the large width of court. While there can be exceptions to this general advice, it remains a good percentage rule and an excellent starting point for students, since it gets them making the easiest overhead every time And when exception is taken to the rule and the ball is played to the "small" side, there is another rule—and this one should not be broken even by advanced players: never angle to the small side; play the ball straight. If the

ball is on the forehand side and for some reason the player wishes to play his backhand, he should play parallel to the backhand alley. He should not try to angle, for there is not enough

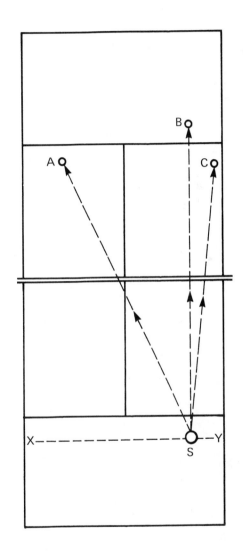

Diagram 8–3. Overhead targets. When smashing, the player should always pick a large target. Crosscourt (A) is best, straight (B) next best. Angling to the small side (C) is definitely against the percentages: it is tempting, but forget it! Note the actual differences; compare X to S distance with Y to S distance.

width across which to play. While this angle can sometimes be made, it will often be missed —too often—so it is a nonpercentage play. All instructors should stress this percentage think-

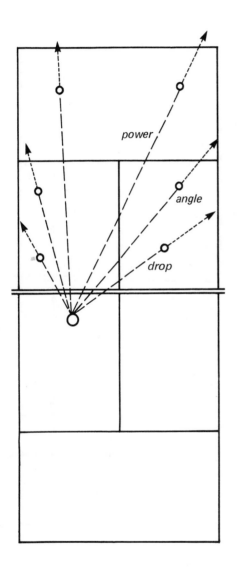

Diagram 8–4. Note the large margins of safety allowed for all volley placements. Make the angle, thus fighting your opponent; don't fight the court.

ing on the overhead, not only for the obvious reason that it is sound but because the wrong shot is a great temptation: it will win if you can pull it off. And, insidiously, if you try it you make it just often enough to encourage you to try it some more. Thus, with a team a coach has a never-ending fight on his hands to curb this continually human nature being what it is.

Talented players should practice that most difficult of overheads, the one hit going back for a tough lob. Since the entire body is moving back to get within reach of the ball, the only power sources are the wrist and a bend at the waist, this latter move throwing some of the weight forward just as he hits, even though the legs are propelling him back. This is for advanced, strong-wristed, well-coordinated players only. He who can master this jump-snap-and-bend play along with ordinary get-set-and-smash overheads has truly first-class technique.

BEING STEADY AT NET

Play for the Middle of an Area— Not the Line

Good net players do not miss many chances. This is not because they are gifted far above others but because they understand how to play for a winner *without* playing for lines. The principle is to make the angle, not the line. In fact, the object is to make the winning angle or placement or smash *as far in as possible*. See Diagram 8–4 and note how very far in most of these winning shots land. Of course, sometimes one must go somewhat closer, but the fact remains that in a game as fast as tennis even the most skillful need all the margins that are available to them.

A good teaching trick is to draw a circle about ten feet in diameter at one side of either service court and have players try to volley into it. They are soon convinced that they need to aim at the middle of an area—the larger the better—not at a line. A good maxim is "Don't play the ball over by that line: *bounce* it over to that line." We want the ball to go over there but not to land so near an error. A good bit of stress must be laid on this fundamental of aiming one's ace far inside the court, or else the beginning player usually goes through a long and painful stage of making vast numbers of errors. "I had him!" is the anguished cry. And what good is it if one misses? It is a great help to the green net player to have it pointed out to him that it is possible to be very aggressive at net yet be quite steady.

THE HALF VOLLEY

A Tough Shot

The half volley is a shot to be avoided, for the very fact that we are playing it is a confession that we are in that very poor situation—at net and obliged to play from the lowest possible position: the ground itself. However, our own ineptitude and the skill of our opponent get us into this pickle now and again, so we must be prepared to deal with it.

First and foremost a half volley is a "touch" shot that is never hit hard. The angle of eleva-

Figure 8–10. The half volley. Note there is no swing. The ball is trapped, then lifted. Note little weight is moved into the ball. The shot is all delicacy. Note the closed racket face to prevent the ball from popping up too much.

tion to clear the net is so sharp that any pace at all will carry the ball out even if we spin it. The standard play is a soft angled drop return that relies on great delicacy and accurate placement to be effective. In doubles the idea usually is to put it right back at an opponent but so low and short that he finds himself in the same difficulty in his turn. Needless to say this is much easier to write down here than to bring off on the court, and because it is so difficult a considerable percentage of failure must be taken as normal. The real answer is to avoid getting into this predicament in the first place.

Second, the ball should be played with a closed racket face the shortest possible time after it has touched the ground. See Figure 8–10. A closed face sounds illogical since the player must hit up decisively, but since the ball is bouncing up from the ground, it would go up too much if the player opened the face of the racket, thereby increasing an already sharply upward angle. So he "covers" the ball, thus tempering its inclination to pop up, and he plays it a mere instant after it leaves the ground, thus making sure the angle of the bounce cannot fool him and get off the center of the racket. Because a half volley is played in this manner it is often referred to as a "trap shot," since the ball is literally trapped by the closed faced racket held just behind where it bounces. As the ball bounces into the racket, the player lifts up with a quick vertical motion, imparting topspin and trying to carry the ball just a foot above the net and very softly short to get a drop shot effect.

QUESTIONS

1. How do you keep from being hit by the ball at net?

2. Is power very important at net?

3. Detail some differences between preparing to drive and preparing to volley.

4. Why must the grip and wrist be stiff when volleying?

5. Why is stark simplicity essential in volleying?

6. Why is "closing in" essential to effective volleying?

7. What does crouching contribute to volleying?

8. Why do some good players say "never give him the alley—give him the crosscourt"?

9. When attacking the net, what should you do just as your opponent plays the ball? Why?

10. How much of the width of the net must you cover?

11. Why should the approach shot be straight rather than crosscourt?

12. How can one avoid getting fooled by the defender?

13. How can the instructor make clear to players what part of the net must be covered?

14. What is the most important technical factor in a low volley?

15. Why is quick racket preparation needed on overheads?

16. Does the overhead resemble a service?

17. What part of the ball should be hit on an overhead?

18. What is "percentage aiming" on overheads?

19. Is it possible to be aggressive *and* steady at net? How?

20. Should a half volley be played with severity?

21. What does "trap shot" mean to you?

III

Teaching

CHAPTER 9

Successful Teaching

THE INDISPENSABLES

A Firm Grasp of the Subject

A good teacher in any subject must have a reasonably thorough grasp of the subject matter. There was a period when method was overstressed at the expense of content, but it has been increasingly recognized of late that this will not do, that the finest teacher thoroughly trained in methodology cannot get by without solid knowledge to which the methods may be applied.

Systematic Presentation

The other side of the picture is the authority whose great knowledge is unquestionable but whose ability to organize and present the material in a logical sequence has gone undeveloped. The inability to get it across is as great a shortcoming as ignorance. It is pretty hard to escape the conclusion that we must have both knowledge and communication, and both are not just desirable but indispensable. We should follow neither the fashion of the past, with its excessive emphasis on the technique of teaching, nor any rush toward the other extreme. Rather we should recognize the duality of the basic equipment required for good teaching and strive to achieve a balanced approach.

PSYCHOLOGY

Success a Must

Without making any attempt to go into an unfamiliar subject, there are a few almost childish but quite important truths about dealing with all kinds of pupils.

People like to succeed, and they abhor failure. This is obvious with children, less plain but still true with adults. People will pursue that activity which gives them a feeling of success and will turn away from that which give them little or no reward for their efforts. If we are to retain our students, hold their interest, and kindle their enthusiasm, we must make them feel successful.

So the very first (note that word "first," and that it means coming before anything else whatever) task of the tennis instructor is give every beginner a feeling that he *can* learn this game, that he is making progress. A good way to do this is to teach one or two of the easiest possible skills—such as easy little forehands against a board from fairly close or a simple "poop" serve with no backswing. Almost at once the beginner can rally a bit, can serve a little, and feels a sense of accomplishment. More, he tends to equate his teacher with this progress, and so he rates the teacher high. He goes home and tells his parents or his friends, "Tennis is fun. I like it." What he means is, "I tried it. I achieved some success. I enjoyed this. I look forward to more of the same." Such an attitude is the necessary psychological background upon which to build, and which permits the teacher to move on to more difficult skills, skills which take time to master and require that perseverance which is lacking without the enthusiasm and faith described above.

Even with adults who have played for years this is a wise approach. The instructor should look over a new player, spot his stronger side, where a little touching up will make him stroke quite well, and do that first. This makes him feel good and gives him confidence in the teacher. The instructor should then explain that his big weakness will take longer to correct, that his efforts will doubtless go unrewarded for a time. By now he is willing to go with the teacher on the more extensive repair job needed on his weakness. By contrast if one attacks the big weakness on the theory that this will take longer so let's get it started, the beginning player may well quit after a lesson or so, saying "I tried that teacher, and he couldn't seem to help me." In sum, confidence is absolutely necessary to the cooperative effort that occurs when a teacher and player work together. Without it progress is difficult, regardless of how knowledgeable a teacher may be.

Stressing Positives

The instructor's motto should be to accentuate the positive so the students as nearly as possible always feel they are moving forward and building, never moving back and tearing down. It is much more pleasant for the individual player or the group if one deals in affirmatives. The word "no" implies inferiority, failure, lack of merit. If a child swings and misses the ball, the best reaction is "That was a good swing. Now let's time it so we meet the ball."

Often adults need to be reminded that posi-

tive thinking is the only kind that gets you anywhere. "I know what I did wrong" is all well and good, but do you know what is *right*? This is the real goal.

It is not possible to do two things at once, so if a player swings correctly whatever he "did wrong" will necessarily be eliminated. This does not mean analysis is cast aside or of no use. But it does mean the player's mind must be centered on what he hopes he *is* going to do as contrasted with what he hopes he isn't going to do. Again this makes him feel he is moving ahead, not backward.

Advantages of a Light Touch

It has been pointed out that tennis is a game, and we play games for fun. Adults, too, are playing for fun and will chuck it if they do not enjoy it. So a sense of humor, a sense of fun, a relaxed atmosphere of having a good time are all desirable parts of a tennis lesson, group or individual. A disciplined and stern atmosphere with everything organized to the last detail is usually less successful than a more informal approach where everybody has a good time and the players are scarcely aware that fundamentally good muscle habits are being pounded into them. Perhaps it should be added that having fun does not mean being silly and without purpose.

With little children this attitude is of crucial importance. They are often ill at ease, scared of that big ogre called the teacher, and all tightened up. It may even be one of their first experiences in any group, so they are more or less on guard against everything and everybody. To get at them on their own level is the key to winning them over. Childish approaches are often successful—let sneer who will—with children. "We have one very strict rule in this group—everybody *has* to have a good time!" Or "This ball needs to get hit—right in the seat of the pants." (This gets them hitting that part of the ball which will give roughly the proper elevation to the shot.) Such apparently stupid gags can be invented ad infinitum and serve to break the ice with tense little beginners. Soon they are whanging away industriously with the others on the big bangboard: they are with you, relaxed, having fun, and you can easily go on from there.

Extending this principle, the use of games within games is often very effective. When they first get to net they tend to slam the ball all over with little regard for where it goes. Give them a target, such as a row of six ball cans on the service line, and offer a prize (a Coke?) to whoever can hit a can (any can) with his volley. Explain that the only hope is to cut down the swing and punch the volley with a stiff wrist. They go at this furiously, groan horribly at near misses and shriek with mad delight when a can goes down. Do they go home and say, "I had a good lesson on how to lock my wrist, keep my racket out front, put the racket head close to the ball, advance one foot, and punch the ball at a small spot"? No, they yell, *Ma! I won a Coke!*

To sum up, teachers should be unabashed and unashamed to admit that they scheme, connive, invent, experiment, and use every bit of ingenuity they possess to make it *fun.* For what good is it to state self-righteously that one gives a good conscientious, methodical group lesson, if after a while there is hardly anybody in the group? The instructor must never forget: tennis is not a compulsory subject. Wherever the game is taught one usually finds a host of competitive activities. At the seashore club there will be sailing lessons, golf lessons, summer science, theatricals, horseback riding, water skiing, deep sea fishing, and swimming. In the mountain resort there will be hiking, climbing, fishing, golf, swimming, and arts and crafts. At public parks there will be baseball, basketball, and often a pool. If the kids don't like tennis they disappear in multitudes, and they waste no time doing it. Is it very different at schools and colleges? Are not tennis and most other sports elective? Let's admit it: instructors must be salesmen first, good teachers second.

The Positive Value of Failure

Lessons are for missing. This is a basic truth in teaching, even though it doesn't sound very constructive; it is of extreme importance! The main point of taking a lesson—group or individual—is that the student is attempting something he cannot yet do. If he could do it every time without error, he'd be the teacher, not the student! Thus the instructor's attitude should be relaxed and should exhibit no irritation or disappointment when the student misses. If the student is sensitive and is obviously put out by his errors, it is important to tell him straight out "Lessons are for missing. If you could do this consistently, I'd be teaching you something else that you couldn't do—and you'd be missing again." It always helps also to point out one's own early troubles: "You should have seen me the first time I tried that shot!"

There is a follow-up to this. Having relaxed students by assuring them their mistakes are of little importance—just the normal learning process—the instructor should keep an eye out for success and jump on it. When they finally begin to play it better or hit a good one, say "Smile when you play as well as that!" Or "Aha! You told me you couldn't do it—but you just did!" This gets a little kidding into the whole thing, so it isn't all deadly serious work and no fun. It gives the beginner the feeling it is a pleasure to work with this teacher who never rams mistakes down one's throat and always believes in eventual success. The tension disappears, the player's attitude is relaxed and *positive* (because he no longer worries about his mistakes so much), and progress is usually speeded, not slowed by this absence of strictness.

With little children a lot of genial joking helps. "Isn't that awful? You *missed* it!" (with a smile). "Gee, that's funny—that's just what I did when I was first beginning." Quickly they grasp the concept that the world won't go out of orbit if they miss a few, the teacher won't jump on them, so they can keep trying, have fun, and in the end progress. The whole atmosphere of the lesson becomes friendly, because the player feels the teacher is sympathetic, not sternly disciplinarian.

This does not mean the principle of discipline is ignored. Far from it. Once the friendly rapport is established it is often effective to act horrified: "How can you play a backhand with a grip like that?! I thought you had learned how to hold a racket. You've spoiled my day." They grin, but they try to do it better, because they like you, they want to please you, and they want to improve. In other words, *friendly* discipline is what we want.

COMMUNICATION

Doors to the Mind

It has been truly said there are many doors to people's minds. But not all doors lead to all minds. The teacher's job is to find *one* door to each mind with which he is confronted. It is quite surprising how one way of saying a thing will meet a stone wall while another will bring almost instant results. An attempt was once being made to teach a player—a fairly good player—to put a little topspin on the ball. He went under it a little, and it sailed out continually. Saying "Put topspin on the ball" produced no results. "Wipe up the back of the ball." No results. "Make the top edge of your racket leave the ball first." No results. "Start below the ball, finish above it." No results. "Swing up and let the ball roll down your racket." Immediate excellent results, plus the remark, "Why didn't you tell me sooner?" The foregoing is a true—unadorned—story. Now the teacher has two choices. He may say, "I urged him to put some top on the ball, but he wouldn't do it," or he can exercise his ingenuity until he finds a way over, under, or around the pupil's obstinate muscles and mind. The high standard teacher will accept the challenge and admit failure only after a reasonably homeric struggle. A good teacher has as much fight as a good player. He wants to win, too.

Variety in communication is necessary not only because people's minds are often not open to every approach however logical but because their muscles are stubborn. At times they can understand but cannot *do* it. Great ingenuity is often—not seldom—required to achieve the result which both player and instructor perceive quite clearly to be the objective. A multitude of possible approaches, like fire power from many directions, is a desirable part of a teacher's equipment. Teachers should welcome idea exchanges, not because they cannot say what they wish to say, but because others say it differently, and this increases their flexibility and widens their adaptability and variety.

A kind of frank plagiarism is common and desirable in the field of tennis teaching. Any instructor, if he listens, will hear some other teacher express something in a superior manner. Here is a chance to improve himself, and no one should be so proud as to pass up these opportunities. The example just given is evidence that the pupil is often unable to get the message from one angle but can be successfully influenced from another. A striking case in point occurred when a ranking lady player developed forehand trouble. A few exchanges revealed she was playing the ball with her forearm only; the arm from the elbow up did not come through at all. This seemed simple: "Follow through with your whole arm, from your shoulder." No results. "Make your racket head go far out in front." No good. For one hour various approaches were stubbornly resisted. Finally a new tack was tried: "Make your elbow go through across yourself." At once, with absolutely no preliminary progress, she hit a series of first class drives and the problem was solved. She won a tournament a few days later.

Was she lacking in intelligence? Absolutely not. Her muscles were stubborn. She couldn't seem to get that upper arm through, and only when she thought of something *other* than her upper arm could she get results. But the elbow is hitched to both the upper and lower arm, and when she put it through it took everything, upper and lower, right with it. In this case a different approach was not merely desirable but a necessary prelude to success.

Actually stubborn muscles are good things to

have. If our muscles were willing to change their habits without any resistance, how would we ever establish good habits? We would learn quickly—and forget just as quickly. A person who learns only after a somewhat bitter struggle, but then *stays put*, is actually the best student, not the worst. Note that the lady referred to above is a fine player. Thus our greatest obstacle is also our greatest asset, and the difficulty we have in teaching and people have in learning is normal, not something to get upset about.

Teachers must accept this as a desirable fact of life in their work, not something to groan over, as is often the case. "I keep telling them —but they won't *do* it!" is frequently the sob story of the inexperienced teacher. A mature teacher merely says, "We must drill that," this being an unspoken admission that the player's recalcitrant muscles will only acquire the desired knowledge through hundreds of disciplined repetitions.

In the same way people's minds are stubborn—and require the same persistence, ingenuity, patience, and determination on the part of the teacher. Above all, the instructor must be flexible. Some students insist on detailed explanations of all the technicalities. Others say, "Now don't get me all mixed up!" One cannot teach them all the same way. The principle is to adapt to them; they don't have to adapt to the instructor. They merely go elsewhere if they don't like the instructor's approach. It is as easy as turning off the radio: all of a sudden the player is no longer there. If such a teacher is a professor in a college, enrollment in his courses declines. The instructor must find a way to communicate—or he will probably soon be out of business.

Generalizations about the Mind

An instructor working with a player is dealing with a mind. Are there any generalizations about the mind which will aid in the job of teaching? There are, and they are among the most fundamental concepts in this book, for they dictate everything else we do.

First, a mind can hold only one thought at a time. Haven't you said, or heard it said, "I just can't think of so many things at once"? That is a true statement, but a better and more exact way to say it would be, "I can think of only one thing at a time." How then do we do several things at once, such as make a backswing and toss simultaneously for a service? We do them by habit, not by thought. Take a beginner: he *cannot* do them both, since he has to use thought, having no habits. He must practice each separately, and only after getting them to the point where they are at least partially habitual can he put them together.

If the above is accepted, then does it not dictate that the *only* effective way to communicate is to break up complex skills, such as the service, into a series of separate single-thought skills? Thus the service should be taught: (1) backswing, (2) toss, (3) play. Many teachers present the service as a two-thought skill: (1) backswing and toss, (2) play. But people of all ages learn *much* faster if taught in three steps, thus avoiding the frustrating period involved in learning to swing and toss simultaneously. It must be emphasized that there is no desire at this point to argue the relative merits of a one-two versus a one-two-three service. The point under discussion is how best to communicate —to get the teacher's knowledge into the player's mind and muscles. The nature of the human mind urges us to adopt a series method, never a simultaneous method. Therefore, *both* the one-two and the one-two-three will be learned faster by the three-step method since it asks the mind to do what it can do, not what it cannot do.

The entire technical section of this book is based on this concept plus another: thought takes time. The phrase "quick as thought" is most misleading. It implies an instantaneous event which just does not occur. Psychological effects—emotion, fear, anger—these can be very quick, but they are feelings, not thoughts. A player can think "Backswing" very quickly. He cannot think "Drop my arm down, let it swing up high, then drop the racket into a cocked position with my hand behind the handle so I'll hit reasonably solidly" very quickly.

He must do it very slowly if his mind is to control it to any reasonable degree. Then he must concentrate on lifting the ball up in front of him, keeping the palm level, trying to toss it straight. Then he must think of putting the face of the racket on the ball and pressing the ball out over the net. All this thinking takes time. Therefore, the second generalization about dealing with people's minds is: always go slowly. The beginner needs time. If he hurries, the instructor should urge him to slow down, way down, so he can feel everything he does and thus achieve the objective: namely, to know what he is doing. Only slow practice produces this knowledge. When he puts one in slowly he will say, "I see what you mean." While the shot is nothing to brag about, the player has learned something; and isn't this the objective? Last, it is easy to speed up a correct service, but it is difficult to correct a speedy service. It is important to practice slowly to gain skill and let speed come by itself, as it will with familiarity, confidence, and the fluency that comes with mastery.

A third concept should be touched on even though it is very obvious and taken into account by all teachers: the formation of a habit (good or bad) requires many repetitions. Hence the phrase "Practice makes perfect." This point has been made many times, but there is one little twist that is often neglected. Do students—particularly young ones—understand *why* practice makes perfect, how it works, that slow practice is infinitely more productive than fast practice? They, like everyone else, must learn how to learn. Far from being a play on words, this is the sober truth. Show them how to serve, and they will almost invariably do it fast and hard since they wish eventually to serve fast and hard. They have no idea that unless they slow way down, think, control and feel what they are doing they are substantially wasting their time and will make negligible progress. So let us amend the platitude and give it new meaning by saying, "Slow thoughtful practice makes perfect." The greatest contribution the instructor can make, other than the actual technical knowledge, is to teach

the player how to practice effectively. Not only will this reach the goal of a speedy serve (or any shot) far sooner, but it will get across to the student the fundamental concept: this is the way to acquire any and all physical skills. The player's progress in every direction will tend to accelerate, even in activities other than tennis. Learning how to learn: this is job number one.

The instructor's method of communication is dictated by the mental capacity and mental characteristics of the player. While it is true that very talented people can learn more and faster than most others, and we need not be bound down rigidly by anything laid out here, nevertheless the three generalizations—one thought at a time, in slow motion, repeated again and again—are substantially true for almost everybody. He who accepts these human limitations and works patiently within them can produce astonishing results. He who impatiently tries to jump ahead of the capacity of the player to keep up merely creates a sense of frustration in both player and instructor. In his zeal to do a good job, the young teacher frequently tries to do too much at once, to move ahead too fast and to allow his students to practice too fast. Such a young person is defeated by his own idealism. All those readers headed for teaching tennis or any other skill are urged to give very serious consideration to what has just been said, for it is painful to find it all out the hard way—by experience (i.e., trial and error). It is much pleasanter (and less embarrassing) to learn from a book.

An understanding of the way the human mind works is the very core of communication, and this in turn is the heart of teaching, whether it be tennis, piano, figure skating, fly casting, or any activity whatever.

SIMPLICITY

Tempo

Nothing is more important than simplicity in teaching tennis, chiefly because of one great ever-present factor in the game: tempo. Things happen fast, not slowly, and he who has any unnecessary complications in his game often finds himself trying to make two moves in a split second that allows for only one. A long smooth backswing with an elaborate up-back-down-and-forward swing looks lovely in a movie, reads beautifully in a book, and sounds theoretically persuasive when expounded—but it is unrealistic and to be shunned. Nothing is any good unless it can be easily completed within the allotted time. Now the time is not allotted by the player, as in golf, but by the opponent's shot. The ball will not wait; it is inanimate, impersonal, and completely piti-less. This fact is inexorable and admits no argument.

Therefore, good teaching demands that a good part of the time be spent in elimination of nonessentials, instructing people not only in a correct way to do something but in the sim-plest correct way. It is quite possible to hit a ball well after a long and complicated prepara-tion provided the ball comes slowly. Instructors should employ a teaching method that will be effective against speed also. Here simplicity comes to the fore, and there is definitely no substitute for it.

Time

We have spoken in previous chapters about the limitations of the time and effort the aver-age person can and will put into tennis. This is in itself a potent argument for extreme sim-plicity in the program offered to these people. The pruning process should be severe and merciless and should leave not a motion or a flourish that is unessential. It is interesting to note that the finest players have the quietest rackets—because they make no unnecessary moves. That is why it is so frequently said, "He makes it look easy." He literally does make the game easy—by making it simple. It is not a bad simile to liken learning a stroke to ironing a sheet: wrinkle after wrinkle is eliminated until there is nothing left except a smooth

expanse, or one smooth motion in the stroke. This is the acme of simplicity and should be the ideal.

Consistency

Simplicity in stroke production is the only hope in the search for consistency. How can players hope to get something right again and again and again if it is complex and difficult? Clearly it must be as easy as walking to achieve this constant repetition without a significant percentage of failures. So the objective should not be the theoretically "perfect" stroke, em-ploying a considerable backswing, working up to great velocity, maximum power, etc.; this is good only for the fellow sitting at a desk writ-ing a book. The instructor's job is to give the player a quick simple preparation and an unadorned follow-through—something he can execute under pressure or on the run, and something so easy he can repeat it many times with few errors even after a busy week that caused him to miss his usual practice sessions. Bread and butter strokes—that is the need and the instructor's job.

Tactics

Similar simplicity is desirable in tactics. Under the stress of actual playing conditions, with sun, wind, here and there a bad bounce, plus the limitations imposed by the efforts of oppo-nents—under all this pressure can the player carry out anything complicated? The very thought is absurd. The player's best hope is to set his teeth into one or two fundamental thoughts and hang onto them throughout at least a set. If losing, he may then change to something else, but it should be equally simple. Again, only the fellow writing the book has time for complex chains or sequences of ideas. The factor of tempo is as compelling tactically as it is mechanically.

TEACHING PECULIARITIES

Watching the Racket

Perhaps no precept is so deserving of repetition as the admonition "Keep your eye on the ball." The instructor must unlearn this and substitute "Watch the player, not the ball." "Keep your eye on his racket." "Watch his feet." This is not easy. Due to playing experience, watching the ball has become so strong a habit that it has the power of an instinctive reflex. A young teacher must learn—by repeated self-discipline—*not* to watch the ball. Apprentices are asked, "Did you see what his racket did?" and the answer is almost invariably "No." They saw the ball, not the racket. Anyone learning to be a tennis teacher is urged to start at once to school himself to watch everything except the ball. Watch the racket go back, watch how it is slanted, watch the feet, note the knees, the grip, does the player prepare with two hands? etc. This may mean the teacher misses the return or plays it in a mediocre manner. Who cares? The job is to help the student, and the instructor's performance is beside the point.

Restraint

The player's objective is to win. The instructor's objective is to help someone else win. He must restrain his desire to put pace on the ball and should instead make sure the student has a good chance to play the ball. With youngsters it is necessary to use a lot of restraint, and the most effective mechanical control is to shorten the backswing. With an extremely short preparation one's stroke becomes a little tap that gives even the weakest player a good chance to do his stuff. Thus a telescopic backswing which can be opened up or closed down at will like an accordion is a good teaching trick adaptable to any and all players. It sounds very simple, but again it is relevant to point out that apprentices cannot do it at first and flounder around trying to slow down their big swings instead of making them drastically smaller.

Laziness

Once again the goal of the instructor is the opposite of the player's. The player wishes to condense all his potential effectiveness into a short time—a match—while a teacher wants to spread himself over a long period of time—six or more hours of teaching. So the instructor must learn to be incredibly lazy in the matter of footwork. Likewise he should learn to hold six balls in his left hand, enabling him to feed a succession of shots to a net player, ignoring the fact that this inhibits his own ability to manipulate his racket quickly by using two hands. So: laziness, an inadequate backswing, a full left hand, lack of pace and keeping the eye off the ball—these are all desirable attributes in a teacher. It sounds awful, doesn't it?

ORGANIZATION

Have a Plan

A plan is a necessity. One instructor's plan may not coincide with another's, and there is more than one way to skin a cat, but an instructor without a plan is pretty much out of luck. There should be a major plan that includes the whole gamut of strokes and tactics. Within this there should be lesser plans for certain areas such as baseline play and net play. Within these there should be small plans for teaching the execution of each shot needed in that area. The plans for mechanical execution should relate logically to the tactical objectives served by the various shots.

It is perhaps already obvious that an instructor needs to be somewhat of a nut on planning. Perhaps forethought can be carried too far, but if so it is a sin of which very few of us are guilty. But a well-thought-through plan adds immeasurably to the effectiveness of any teacher of any subject whatever.

From the Bottom to the Top

A good plan is one that starts with the basic concepts for beginners and builds on them, both technically and tactically, until a complete game has been expounded. It is important that the plan should start with bare essentials and move from there toward the desirable but less essential. When this view is adopted the game naturally falls into three phases or areas: baseline, halfcourt, and forecourt. These will be discussed at length in subsequent chapters. The point to be made here is that we start with the baseline (serve, return of serve, forehand, and backhand) since one cannot play at all without these. Subsequently the desirability of attacking weak shots (half-court) and following to net (forecourt) is obvious. Last come the frills: change of pace, tricky angles, etc. It is the logical sequential order that is important to the idea of planning, and makes sense out of the chaos of helpful suggestions that any good player might pass on to one of less experience.

Drills and Self-Instruction

Successful teaching is based in considerable part on self-help. If progress ceases when the lesson ends there is not much hope for the player. He should leave the teacher not only with a clear idea of what he wishes to perfect but also with a little plan of just how to go about it. For example, if strokes are taught in a three-step series—ready, time the ball, play—a very useful practice habit can be taught, too: every time the player begins a rally, he should do it in exactly that way: prepare the racket, toss the ball, let it bounce and time it, play. Thus, even when the player is merely hitting a ball out of his hand he is perfecting everything that was laid down in the lesson: the preparation of the racket, the selection of the best

instant to strike, and the execution of the stroke. This constant drilling on the series of skills that must be mastered will produce amazingly rapid progress with beginners or with anyone altering a faulty stroke because they are continually drilling it even if merely hitting for fun with a friend. The thousands of repetitions necessary in the creation of muscle knowledge are achieved painlessly in the shortest possible time.

The instructor should use his ingenuity constantly to devise such drills. Players like to go off with something specific to chew on. It is the instructor's duty to provide it, thus encouraging and guiding the student's enthusiasm to whatever extent it may be present. It may be added that a student who progresses usually gains additional enthusiasm; success engenders desire. Both instructors and players are urged to peruse Chapter 11. Many of the tests and drills lend themselves to self-drilling and therefore self-improvement. Any test is in itself a drill.

DIAGNOSIS AND CURE

The Preparation

Diagnosis is perhaps the most important aspect of an instructor's expertise, particularly with individuals—and isn't a group merely a collection of individuals? The U.S. Professional Tennis Association in its certification examinations finds many instructors comparatively weak in diagnostic skills. What is missing? A short analysis of this problem is in order.

To diagnose means to determine the cause— the first and most basic cause—of the symptoms that take the form of poor stroking. It is the word "first" that causes many to stumble. They treat the symptom, not the disease, because they have not identified the disease. This is because nine times out of ten the basic cause is not in the making of the shot but in the preparation to make the shot. Most inexperienced teachers watch the ball being played but do not see the preparation, so they cannot analyze it. Most beginning players think only of the shot and ignore the preparation—so they never improve it. Very frequently the first motion a player makes in reacting to the ball at once condemns him to a poor stroke. He prepares the face of the racket at an improper slant, or he takes the butt back before the head of the racket, or he gets it all too high or too low, or he has a faulty grip. The only way open to him is a bad way. It does no good to tell him not to pull up or not to take it so late if his preparation has made these mistakes inevitable and unavoidable. The preparation is what is behind the vast majority of mistakes, and instructors should learn to watch this more than anything else. The elimination of mistakes in preparation does not guarantee a good stroke but at least makes one possible, and it also now becomes the more natural thing to do.

Even a bad follow-through usually has its cause in poor preparation. A person who "hitches" over a forehand, turning his racket over suddenly as he plays the ball, usually does so because he prepared it too open, usually with a Continental grip. One who pulls up violently usually has too closed a racket face—he *must* pull up to clear the net. Or, he must gouge under the ball to clear the net, a second (undesirable) method of compensating for faulty preparation. These peculiar hitches and yanks often cause poor weight transfer and bad balance. It does no good to urge better use of weight; one must get at the *first* cause, or all the dominoes will again topple the wrong way. Therefore the great lesson is to become "preparation conscious."

The Cure: Exaggerate and Be Ingenious

Probably the most effective teaching method is to bend the stick the other way. If the racket is prepared too closed, the player should be urged to open it more than is desirable. His muscles will resist the new method; he'll only open it half that much, which is about what

the instructor was after. If he is learning to topspin, the instructor should urge him to spin it excessively for a bit, so that a sufficiency will be easy for him. If he volleys too "big," the instructor should insist that he place all his volleys inside the service line. A big pull-up follow-through can be helped by slicing—he *must* stay lower or the ball will go sky high. Problem after problem can be dealt with this way, by going consciously too far toward the opposite extreme. Many players fail to keep their volley low on one side or the other. They should be told to close the racket face and try for a net-cord shot throughout a volley drill. When they hit the top of the net, they should be praised. Ingenuity in devising drills that will *force* the pupil's recalcitrant muscles to make the needed correction is what all instructors need and should strive for. To say it another way: after you see where you want a player to go, can you persuade him to go there? It is often a very difficult challenge. Instructors should continually invent cures and borrow shamelessly from other teachers who have good tricks of this sort.

TEACHING AIDS

Selection

The question of teaching aids is becoming ever more complex as more mechanical gadgets are invented and advertised persuasively. Yet there are certain guidelines that can be used to establish an intelligent policy and a sense of selecting with discrimination. The primary consideration is usually money. Very few instructors have unlimited funds available. The question at once arises as to where limited funds can be put to give the greatest and most permanent return for each dollar.

Bangboards

While a practice wall is a major installation, its permanence, ease of maintenance, and general utility make it unquestionably the king of teaching aids. The best design is probably a concrete block wall with the ground surfaced for some forty-five feet out on either side so two walls are secured for the price of one. The height should be ten feet (minimum) with four to six feet of wire on top of that. The location can be anywhere that permits the recovery of wild shots. It is a good idea to have a solid line three feet six inches above the ground (the height of the net at the net post) and another dotted line six feet from the ground, this second line being where students should aim. Often a separate space is not available, in which case the wall, of wood or concrete, can be put alongside a court, replacing part of the side fencing. The two-sided concrete special area wall is merely the ideal.

The length is where the greatest unwitting parsimony often occurs. One sees many ten-foot boards, which are of course absurdly inadequate. To be truly useful in a group, a practice wall should be at least forty feet long. This is because a player rallying a ball will reach out on both sides, for forehands and backhands, and will occupy at least twelve to fifteen feet of board. A forty-foot board will just take three players nicely. To crowd them any closer, except for a service drill, is to invite disaster as someone catches a follow-through in the face. Therefore it is repeated: forty feet is a minimum dimension, and eighty to one hundred twenty feet (the length of the court) is not at all excessive wherever classes are to be held.

Bangboards seldom get out of order, are always there, are perfect for groups, even offer possibilities for games (my turn, your turn, I hit, you hit), and target practice with contests and prizes if desired. Above all, and this is seldom appreciated, bangboards are completely adaptable to players of all ages and sizes and strengths. A little girl of six can stand a few feet off and tap her ball, while a man can stand far back and boom away with his big forehand or service. This telescopic characteristic of the usefulness of a practice board is one of its chief charms.

Children love bangboards. They can practice intently, or while chattering with a friend, or in between, and the gadget doesn't care. And there is no waiting for a turn. Children *hate* to stand around. Everyone hits as often, as hard, and as continuously as he wishes. The bangboard, by its complete passivity and the fact that it does nothing but reflect what the player does, is the most tactful teaching aid one could imagine.

However, people often need to be told how to use a practice wall. Too often they whale away, miss because the ball returns too fast and get frustrated, not to mention getting tired quickly. Such players fight the bangboard, and since it never misses, they always lose. This is not so good. They must be told not to fight the wall but to *use* it. If they hit a moderate shot, the bangboard will politely return a moderate ball, thus providing a nice chance to prepare and time the next shot. By keeping this up, a player can have a quite lengthy practice and achieve considerable improvement in racket skill without getting more than pleasantly puffed.

The bangboard has one other virtue of great importance in that it makes it possible for young people to rally *at once*. Youth is impatient; it wants results now, not later. The court is huge, designed for adults, not little children, and it poses problems of judgment and timing far beyond their undeveloped and inexperienced talents. Beginners often cannot hit the ball over the net *at all*, and living intensely in the present as they do, this means failure, discouragement, and a reaction against tennis as being not for them. By contrast, the instructor should start them on the practice wall, telling them to hit little shots and assuring them that big ones will come later. They will achieve at least a partial success in a short time. Often, though they cannot play successfully over the net for several years, they love to hit on the board until they grow to the court.

Add to this the fact that children don't like to be supervised all the time. They like to be their own boss: "*Let me* do it." "Don't tell me, I can do it," they say. The bangboard permits intermittent help and guidance coupled with leaving them to go it alone a good bit. Not only do they prefer this, but the instructor can handle quite a number this way without noticeably pushing either himself or the players. A low pressure informal class like this is often more popular and more successful than a highly regimented superorganized group. And let us not forget: tennis is a game played for fun; if it isn't fun, pretty soon there are no pupils. Need one say more? Thus the bangboard helps immeasurably to get little children interested in tennis and feeling the confidence that they can do it.

For adults the board offers the opportunity to perfect what a lesson has suggested. We all know that head knowledge is easy and muscle knowledge comes only with many repetitions. The board gives the opportunity to do it again and again, alone, free to miss or err without embarrassment, under no obligation to hit to someone else or to get it in.

Mechanical Supplements

While it is clear the large practice wall should be the primary teaching aid in all programs, other gadgets can have important special uses. The ball throwers can repeat one shot indefinitely, enabling a player to practice his answer indefinitely. The ball thrower enables one to practice over the net while the practice wall does not. A stroke developer, with a ball suspended in the air, relieves the student of the problems of timing and judging, thus permitting him to concentrate exclusively on his swing. Thus the basic functions of the practice wall can be supplemented and enhanced by the more modern mechanical devices. If expense is not an obstacle, advanced players can be aided by slow motion pictures and instant video replay even as these mechanical inventions are used extensively in football. How far one carries this devotion to gadgetry is very much a personal thing though it usually is cut short by budgetary limitations.

The very great emphasis placed on practice

walls in this chapter is quite conscious. One cannot package a wall and sell it (the rebound net is scarcely the equal of a wall). No one except the local builder can profit. Therefore, while other gadgets are advertised and promoted in every possible way, the fact that a plain wall is vastly superior in utility to all other contrivances combined is seldom stressed by anyone. It is hoped this passage will draw attention to the fact—and it is a fact—that the best teaching aid available is the least often mentioned.

Today manufacturers are coming up with synthetic materials that give a totally *silent* rebound. This means that the annoying thudding from a wall may soon be eliminated, so it may be placed almost anywhere.

Group Gadgets and Tricks

A considerable number of gadgets are on the market and more are being added daily. Very small rackets, fluffy balls that won't go anywhere and can't hurt anybody, balls on elastic strings, balls held by a spring mechanism that instantly returns them to position after they are hit, finger-strengthening devices, grip springs to strengthen grip—the list goes on and on, and is ever-increasing. All of these are to some extent useful and desirable but none is *essential*. Some are quite helpful where space is very limited and crowding is unavoidable. Yet it would seem one is in danger of getting too complex, too involved, and not sufficiently direct if one uses too many of these supplements. A baby learns to walk by walking. To learn to play a ball with a racket one should play a ball with a racket, and not get mired down too much in doing something that is "preparatory," or "leads up to" or "similar." Nine children out of ten, aged eight or above, can handle a full-sized racket provided it is light. Ten out of ten adults can handle a full-sized racket. If a child is a little weak on the backhand, he can hold the racket a bit up the handle to shorten the grip and reduce the leverage of the racket head against the wrist.

If each of a group of children has a light racket, and there is a wall against which they can play, an instructor is in business.

Some instructors prefer to start with the hand, then move to a short racket, and go through tapping (up and down) and ball-bouncing routines (and others such as rolling the ball around the racket), then have tossers and players and retrievers and *finally* arrive at actually playing the ball. There is nothing wrong with such a progression; the children will learn. They will also learn (just as quickly) if they are taught, right from the start, to serve and forehand and backhand against a wall, whether it be a special practice wall, the back steps, the side of the garage, a gym wall, or whatever. The more complicated series of progressions can be very effective in crowded conditions where space is just not adequate to allow people to swing full-sized rackets because of the danger of injury (very real). The ingenious methods that have been worked out by various teachers make effective teaching possible where at first the space limitations seem insurmountable. The point being made here is that these are not necessarily *improvements* over more direct do-what-you-are-trying-to-learn teaching. Isn't it better to have *everybody* playing the ball than to have one-third of them tossing, one-third playing, and one-third retrieving? It is only when this ideal is unattainable that these clever systems of rotation, which make large groups go in a comparatively small space, are to be strongly recommended.

Therefore, each teacher must adapt to the situation in which he finds himself. If it is a practical possibility, groups should be divided into small enough numbers so that a maximum of actual playing of the ball is achieved. To whatever extent this is not possible, the rotation systems, with short rackets, soft balls, and drills such as tapping and tossing, should be used to achieve effective results in limited space.

QUESTIONS

1. What are the two most basic assets of a good teacher?

2. What motivates the average pupil?

3. Is it important to be able to say a thing in more than one way?

4. Why must complex techniques be broken down in teaching?

5. Why do good teachers always say, "Take your time"?

6. Why is simplicity essential in playing and teaching?

7. Should a teacher worry about looking good when teaching?

8. Discuss self-help as an integral part of teaching.

9. Is planning important in teaching?

10. What do you think about various teaching aids and their relative value?

11. What is most frequently the key to a good diagnosis of a faulty stroke?

12. Why is exaggeration useful in teaching?

CHAPTER 10

Teaching Beginners

The most basic function of a majority of tennis instructors is working with beginners. At this moment, when they first try the game, they form those all-important first impressions: they like the game or they don't; they like the instructor or they don't; they feel they can make progress or they feel they cannot; they decide they have a good teacher or a bad teacher. In addition they are completely helpless, without knowledge, skill, or background of any kind. They are in drastic need of assistance, more now than at any time in the future. Thus teaching beginners has an importance that can scarcely be exaggerated.

PROGRESSION IS THE SOLUTION

Limiting the Objectives

Limiting objectives is the secret of success with those who are just starting the game. They should be given one easy thing to do and should be kept at it until they achieve some slight mastery. To most of their eager questions the proper reply is (with a smile) "We'll get to that, but it comes later. Now let's do some more of those smooth easy forehands." There is little point in being secretive about it. The instructor should tell them straight out that the fastest way to learn is to drill one

thing pretty solidly, until a muscle habit is formed. He should give them the idea that they are quite smart but that muscles are sort of stupid and take a while to learn. (It is a fact that people who would resent any suggestion that they lack intelligence usually don't mind at all being told that their muscles are dumb, obstinate, recalcitrant, and worse than an Arkansas mule.) It helps, too, if the teacher creates rapport by saying "My muscles are stupid too. I remember I had a terrible time learning that shot." All this tends to create in the pupil the realization that one limited objective at a time is the proper and quickest path to progress. They acquire the very desirable habit of focusing patiently on one thing at a time. In addition they learn not to be discouraged by an initial lack of success—apparently hopeless shortcomings can be overcome by drill.

Limiting by Subdivision

Let us say we start with a forehand. Then divide it into steps: (1) prepare the racket, being careful to grip it correctly and slant the face properly, (2) toss the ball carefully so it bounces straight up, (3) wait for it to sit still at the top of the bounce, (4) put the racket on it smoothly, (5) follow through carefully, high, keeping the racket face slanted properly.

With each beginner a lot of emphasis will have to be placed on each of these five subdivisions (not to mention others such as footwork —the complete forehand is not our object here). Only when they get all of them going will they succeed in getting a shot. Really great patience is needed in instructing a student (of any age) with below-average coordination. The grip has to be corrected a dozen times running. The racket droops, must be kept up more (a dozen to twenty times). The toss is jerky, erratic, inaccurate, must be worked on separately to get it started. The timing is conspicuous by its absence. The player tosses the ball and swings at once—and whiffs of course. The instructor can hold a ball at the contact spot and have the player put his racket on it with a proper swing, then say, "You see, you have a good eye, you just aren't using it yet. Now this time, wait for the ball to sit still, then put your racket on it." After a while contact is made, but the follow-through is horrendous. And so it goes, until finally the player can hold the racket out, toss the ball, time it, and play it at least haltingly.

GIVING SERVICE TO ALL

Champions Are Few

An inexperienced instructor often thinks such a player is hopeless. In terms of ever being a champion, of course the player is indeed a lost cause. But we are talking about social tennis, tennis the lifetime sport, tennis which is fun at all levels of excellence that involve any competence at all. Actually, players who lack unusual coordination are in the majority, and a huge majority at that, in any given normal group. They are the bread and butter of a tennis teacher's existence. They are also the backbone of the sporting goods manufacturer who would soon be out of business if he depended on the few sales he makes to the gifted. It does not do to downgrade the staff of life, in this case the average aspirant.

Often they are really good students. They know they are not the best, they know they won't be world beaters, but they do so want to get that ball over and be able to play with the other kids. They will work like beavers if they get help, and particularly if that help is subdivided enough so they can handle it, bit by bit, building to a shot that is nothing wonderful in terms of true excellence but is a magnificent achievement to them. They are just as happy and as proud as the gifted player who has just won another big match. No phrase applies better to tennis than the old chestnut "Everything is relative."

Everybody Is Important

It is easy to sneer and say, "Who cares if all these mediocre athletes ever do get the ball over?" The answer is easy: they themselves care, they care very much, and in the case of children their parents care. And it has just been pointed out that they get pleasure from it, and to this we can add that this pleasure lasts all their lives in many cases. They find others of equal medium ability, have fun, close games, and a lot of healthy exercise year after year. Anyone who questions the value of work of this sort must be unwittingly judging all the labor of tennis teachers from the restricted point of view of the Davis and Wightman Cup teams.

Believing in Them

It is enormously important to believe in one's students. If they think their instructor has faith in their ability to achieve, it is quite astonishing what they will do to justify this support. And if the instructor displays real pleasure when finally the ball does go over and in—this to them is the highest praise. Particularly with children the teacher is a kind of deity, a person to whom they allot an embarrassing but wholly sincere hero worship. If the Great One approves of their efforts their day is made.

It is also easy to forget that the emotions and sensitivity of a comparative nonathlete are just as keen as those of a champion. They are human, they can be hurt, disappointed, discouraged, and cast down, or lifted way up just as easily as the top athlete. They deserve and are entitled to as much consideration as the best. Actually they need it a lot more. The born champion needs only a few hints and he starts beating his teachers. He needs guidance, yes, but not much help with his morale. There is a difference. If the general run of the crowd senses that the teacher is genuinely interested in all of them, sees good in all of them, believes all of them can achieve, then a great spirit is built up, there is a fine program, and the instructor has a host of warm friends.

One Never Knows

Now and then this policy of genuinely helping one and all will uncover a late bloomer or a slow learner who will in time astonish everybody by developing into a comparatively prominent player. This is a minor but not negligible reward that is sure to fall to the conscientious instructor, because the ingredients of talent often appear in some very deceptive mixtures. A youngster may be unusually tall for his age and go through an awkward stage during which poise and balance are very difficult. Of course, this decisively impairs performance on the court and may temporarily conceal other competitive gifts of a high order. When this person matures physically he or she may become a standout, provided encouragement and guidance have developed and maintained interest and skill. Similarly a talented person may suffer from a totally wrong sense of values on the court and play with apparently foolish wildness. As the percentage concept develops, such a player may change from one who always beats himself into a real competitor. Two assumptions are usually pretty safe: in any group there is some talent, and no teacher should feel he can make a sure judgment out of his first impressions. While the more human

reasons for helping everyone are of course the most important, this matter of hidden ability is just one more small weight in the scale.

Invisible Talent

When a teacher starts out a group who have played little or not at all, these players are unable to reveal themselves except in a physical way. Those who are glib physically will look the best at first and will out-perform the others. One tends to make unjustified long-range predictions based on these early impressions. Such tendencies should be resisted because they often lead to error. After some years when all these people have acquired a considerable technique so they can put into execution the thoughts that come to them, then and only then can an intelligent estimate be made of the total ability: physical, mental, and moral (the ability to take pressure).

One often hears of a "made player." This is usually a person endowed with unusually good mental and moral qualities but with physical shortcomings that could only be overcome with a lot of work. Other more "natural" athletes look better at first but may be surpassed by this player in the long run. The "natural" athlete has immediately visible talent. This "made" athlete has obvious shortcomings and his talents are hard to perceive. It does not always pay to leap to the conclusion that the "natural" is better.

Perhaps the greatest example of a player with concealed talent is a present champion, Stan Smith. Far from a standout as a youthful athlete, he went through a clumsy stage and was at times laughed at by his peers. This stage was a natural result of rapid growth, and no one could have foreseen that he would later be as good as anyone in the world. His outstanding *invisible* qualities could not show themselves until growth and hard work had overcome his lanky slowness in handling himself. Now that he is a champion, his inner qualities of dedication, discipline, determination, fortitude under pressure, and faith in himself are fully apparent and it is clear to all that he is both an outstanding competitor and an outstanding person.

LIMITED TECHNIQUE

Fundamentals Only

If all this faith and conscientious effort on behalf of everybody is not to founder we must stay within the limitations of the student. This must be true not only in terms of his intrinsic ability but also in terms of his stage of development. We have already seen that the majority of any group will be lacking in talent. We are also faced with the fact that they are just beginning. Therefore, the technique offered to them and the skills demanded of them must be absolutely as rudimentary as possible.

The object of this chapter is to deal in generalizations and to establish an ideal. The section on technique brings this ideal down to earth and offers specific applications of the approach delineated in this chapter. While technique is discussed in depth, nevertheless a major preoccupation of the treatment of each basic shot is the question of how best to start a beginner or a group of beginners. It is important for the reader to realize that entire sections of the book (Part II, "Technique," in particular) keep this problem constantly to the fore. How to instruct a beginner to serve is examined in depth in Chapter 5. How to make the simplest possible start on the difficulties inherent in stroking forehands and backhands is discussed in Chapter 6. Separate treatment is given to preparation, aiming, timing, grips, etc. All these often lengthy examinations of mechanics are omitted here, since they would obscure the main theme. It is hoped the reader will develop from this chapter a devotion to stark simplicity in dealing with beginners and that he will find this principle specifically applied to every basic problem in other chapters. Specific drills and tests will be found in Chapter 11.

Minimum Tactics

With little children the question of tactics does not arise since for them it all boils down to "Get the ball over the net and in the court." With an older group of beginners, such as a large physical education class whose members are thoughtful, it is important to give them a picture of what they are trying to work up to. As a rule they have all sorts of vague and erroneous impressions as to what a tennis player should attempt but have little or no concept of percentage play. It must be pointed out to them that winning is not possible until the net position is achieved, and one must work up to the net position by steady play that waits its chance. Keeping the ball in play is then seen to be objective enough for beginners (even adult beginners) and they are thus persuaded that a lot of practice on this aspect of the game is what they need. Making them see this steadiness as the foundation on which must rest all future, more ambitious plans is a significant part of teaching adult beginners, since their well-developed minds tend to run far ahead of their limited mechanical skills.

THE GROUP METHOD

Advantages

Group instruction is the cornerstone of the best programs. People of all ages like to do things together. They like to be on teams; boys and girls like to be on squads; adults like to play other groups as a team. Above all little tots love to feel they are part of a gang doing something together and will often by contrast regard a private lesson as a chore they value far less highly if at all. While the idea of the group can be carried too far, one must go a long way before this occurs.

The running, jumping, turning, and twisting involved in tennis is what draws youngsters to the game. Also tennis offers more constant activity than most games. But there is one hitch: if they feel they cannot do it they will quit and take up something that presents better hope for success. And tennis is difficult. Thus a constant program of group instruction for all the beginners (seven to eleven, roughly) is the foundation for everything else. If the beginners are well taught they take to the game—and stay with it. If not, many are soon lost, and the program enjoys limited growth.

Groups get children of the same age and sex together. They make friends or find themselves already with an established friend. This is *very* important to these children. They associate this pleasant companionship with tennis lessons, and while in the technical sense this cannot be called a gain in their tennis, it is a start at what we all get out of tennis—fun with our friends. It is of great significance that they do not get this from a private lesson. Thus if they are started with private lessons they are less likely to enjoy it thoroughly. It is this pleasure from the game that holds them more than any excellence in their early performance.

Even with adults the group concept is very popular. They can all laugh at each others' mistakes, and this tends to take away the pressure and make it all a lot of fun, even when they are working hard. The word goes around and more and more join up.

Sociological Aspects

A young beginner's attention span is often rather limited. While this varies sharply it is a reasonable generalization to say that most children from seven to eleven are not really ready for private lessons. They sense this and as a rule prefer the more informal gang lesson that gives them some instruction but not continual pressure from a teacher. The group lesson is sort of a soft sell while the private lesson tends to be more of a hard sell. If each group lesson ends with a fun game with a chance for a prize, the group lesson actually becomes something they really go for. An atmosphere is

created in which the constant stressing of the fundamentals is beautifully sugar coated with fun, laughs, games, and camaraderie. Yes indeed, it is messy—they yell, shriek, run about, and have a grand time doing it. But a good group instructor always conducts quite an orderly and purposeful group to begin with, then lets it degenerate somewhat at the end. Grind 'em at the start but send 'em home happy is a good psychological approach. It is possible to be quite frank about it; tell them right out that if they work hard at the start this or that fun game will be their reward at the end. They recognize a fair deal and try to earn it.

Perhaps the greatest benefit derived from rollicking group instruction is that it gets "the gang" coming to the tennis courts. Kids tend to congregate, and if the leaders are always at the courts the others will soon follow. Of course there are a lot of gangs—of girls, of boys, of different ages. But there should be a lot of groups, too—one for each natural cluster of tots that we call a gang. Thus the group instruction concept seeks to weld together our desire to impart technical knowledge, the social tendencies that seem to be inevitable wherever numbers of young children are involved and the fun attitude characteristic of youth. To put it in a black and white manner, the group is natural for the children, while the private lesson for the eight year old is out of character.

Planning and Organization

Both long- and short-range planning are essential to successful groups, for in spite of its intrinsic appeal a group will not sustain its momentum unless there is real content. The overall plan specifies the material to be covered and the order in which the parts will be attacked. It provides a general outline without attempting rigidly to regulate every period. The short-range planning occurs as one goes along but precedes each group. It makes decisions as to emphasis, when to move on or repeat, and when a review is in order. Certain things can be held in reserve, such as learning to score: on a very hot day the instructor might break up the lesson by getting under a shade tree and teaching how to keep score, or discussing tactics.

A typical beginners' group might be started out something like this: First two meetings: Eastern forehand grip, beginner serve, and forehand. Third meeting: backhand grip, start backhand, end with some forehand net play. Fourth meeting: practice changing the grip quickly with two hands; practice on board; forehand to backhand to forehand, etc. Fifth meeting: review, have serving contest. And so on through backhand net play, return of serve, footwork, the rudiments of tactics (play cross-court), the beginnings of doubles, keeping score, how to get along (and avoid shrill arguments), the rules, and review, review, review on the racket work. It should be noted that very early (third meeting) the class is introduced to the closed racket via the volley. Thus the two extremes of racket work are begun simultaneously: the open face and the closed face.

The basic essential is to have a theme for the day: today we are going to concentrate on preparing the face of the racket correctly, next meeting we shall concentrate on waiting for the ball to hang, etc. Some will have questionable footwork, timing, follow-through, etc.; the instructor should ignore these and stick to the theme; get them all doing one thing right. If this is done each meeting, and the groups meet twice a week or more, some gratifying results will occur after a couple of months. In a college physical education group, some should actually be playing interesting games in a halting manner, and many should be rallying with moderate success.

Group Specifics—With or Without a Wall

With large practice walls, groups are easy and literally almost run themselves. After a few sessions the students show up and start practicing without a word being said. It is significant that they also quickly learn the idea of self-practice without an instructor. The teacher's first job is to so direct the student's self-practice that a well-rounded result will be approximated in time, and to supplement the wall drills with practice over the net. Thus one very desirable arrangement is a group of about a dozen, eight of whom can be on the wall, the other four on a court trying to play across the net. Groups of four can be rotated so that everyone has equal time on both board and court. The group can be any number the facility will hold: twelve on three courts with four on a fifty-foot board; eight on a larger board with eight on two other courts.

The mechanics of the simple beginner strokes are learned on the board. Over the net stress is placed on trying to keep the ball going as contrasted with hard hitting that at once terminates the rally. Judging the ball from a longer distance, lining it up, timing the instant to play—these are all more difficult over the net than on the wall. The wall is like a first gear in a car: it is wonderful for a starter, but we do want to shift up as we improve. When to move up and how much to stress it is quite individual and the teacher must use flexible judgment. It always helps to point this out to all players of any age: "You will do much better on the wall because it is easier, and you must not be discouraged when your performance on the court is not as good as your wall play might lead you to expect." Many very young players who have not yet acquired much strength may prefer the wall to the court for several years. This should not be taken as a sign of failure. It means they are "late bloomers" who will grow to the court later. Let them go their gait. The analogy with the ungraded primary is striking and sound.

A few simple bangboard drills are:

Forehand: Arrange grip, arrange feet, racket back, toss ball, wait, play. If it returns play it again.

Backhand: Arrange feet, ball and racket, toss, draw, play.

Changing Grips: Play a forehand so it returns to the backhand and try to play it. Teach this as 'changing preparation' from one side to the other, so the pupil changes feet as well as grip.

The Rally: Ready, time it, aim. Repeat.

The Service: Arrange grip, arrange feet, racket back, toss, press it straight.

Combined practice and fun (never forget the fun idea) are obtained if the class is permitted to rally whatever comes but must begin each exchange with the shot being stressed in this particular drill. Thus the player is not rigidly constrained by the instructor, yet one thing is being pounded in again and again and more agains. The teacher purposely ignores faulty execution of shots other than the one under consideration. In this very relaxed way a bangboard can be used to grind them pretty consistently without their feeling any pressure.

Not everything can be started on the wall. Service drills can be run with four people on each side of one court (total eight per court) so they can learn to aim the service they have learned on the board. It is important not to permit rallying during this drill because someone will get hurt. One can end with a service contest and a trifling prize for the winning team. Return of serve can be combined with serve as soon as a little skill is developed. Net play must be taught on the court, not the wall. Some players should be positioned at net, some behind them (to get balls they miss), some behind the teacher (to collect balls for the teacher). The instructor should give each one five to ten chances, then rotate. If an assistant is available, he can take half the job; have six at net, he plays to three, instructor plays to three. This doubles the rotation achieved. Incidentally, any talented student can be an assistant with a bit of help. Usually such a person is honored to be permitted to help out in this way. If a target is offered with a prize for hitting it, the class will try even harder. (Here again drill and fun are combined.)

Since net play is the most exciting and the most fun, a drill of this sort at the end of the class usually brings the lesson to a very successful conclusion. They all go off thinking what a great game tennis is and what a fun teacher they have, meanwhile forgetting about the rough time they had with the backhand in the first fifteen minutes. This effect is heightened (and alertness is drilled) if toward the end the instructor looks at one but plays to another, attempting to fool them into being caught unprepared. A very little of this suffices. The instructor must not be a clown.

Wherever large practice walls do not exist, the very first job is to try to persuade administrators that practice walls (big ones) are a prime necessity. To teach groups without them means that the instructor must provide a substitute for the board at all times. The students are not skillful enough to play each other over the net with any accuracy at all. So the class must be divided into tossers, players, and ball collectors. By rotation everybody gets a chance. The tossers replace the board by returning the ball to the player nicely again and again. It will be noticed this drill keeps everybody busy, and this is essential if boredom and bad behavior are to be avoided.

"Repeat with me" drills can be invented. Students hold the racket out toward the instructor with the forehand grip and swing it back and forth, watching the instructor do it, getting rid of wrist flap, keeping the face slanted properly, leaning with it a bit, etc. The same type of exercise can be used for backhand, for beginner service, for learning to shuffle (move without crossing the feet), etc. In fact, the instructor's job is to invent a drill for each skill he wishes to inculcate. In this connection it is important to be interested in idea exchanges among teachers and pros. No matter how inventive a teacher may be, he can pick up a lot of good ideas that had not occurred to him, from others. In these professional get-togethers one will often hear "How do you teach them to change the grip for a backhand?" or some similar technical question, followed by a discussion on the best tricks to use to persuade the player to do it properly. Often there is disagreement, but there can be little question that it is stimulating to the participants if they are at all open-minded. It can almost be said that a teacher's effectiveness can be measured by his bag of tricks, and this for groups means drills of all kinds.

Thus the absence of a practice wall puts a lot more pressure on the instructor, requires more planning and makes more difficult the self-practice that is so desirable. The slow learners have a harder time and more of them tend to get discouraged, and to get the big wall idea on the budget agenda is very desirable. But many good programs are run without walls, and all teachers should take the constructive approach thinking of all they can do rather than what they can't. A theme for the day plus drilling to pound it in plus enthusiasm plus encouragement plus fun—this is a formula that always produces results.

Starting Them Young

With little children—six to nine years of age, and in particular girls who tend to be weak—enormous patience is necessary. They often just do not have enough strength to cock the racket on the backhand, so they may have no backhand at all after two whole seasons of group lessons. The court is too big for them; after all, it is designed for adults. They can play against a board and a little from the service line but that is about all. Is all this useless? Would it be better to wait until they are twelve and begin to get enough strength to do what has to be done? It is not useless, and it is a fallacy to wait. If they wait, others will not wait and at twelve will have considerable proficiency. The twelve-year-old beginner is then very reluctant to go out there and look foolish alongside her more experienced friends; she won't take up the game, claiming she doesn't like it. Again, the one who puts off tennis will not remain idle: she must do something. By the time she is twelve she has acquired other interests and just cannot be bothered with tennis. Thus, it is important to get them out there when they are young so they become

accustomed to going out on a tennis court without any false shyness and will say without hesitation, "Yes, I play tennis." In sum, as was said in Chapter 9, "Successful Teaching," if they are not with the instructor, he cannot teach them, so the first job is to sell them the game—make it a part of their lives, make it fun, make them like it and like their instructor.

How can an instructor make them like it when they can't do it? They are too small, they can't serve over the net. All right, if they stand at the service line—then they can. They can't play over the net, the ball comes from too far, they always miss it. All right, they can play against a practice board, now and then trying it over the net. If the instructor plays a ball to them so it bounces once on his side of the net before it goes over to them, it will be so soft and slow by the time it reaches them—at the service line—that they will be able to hit it. The instructor should explain that the court is built for big grown-ups, and that if they can get even one out of ten back on that *great big court* then they are *very good* for their age.

What does all this mean? It means the wise instructor uses his head, is ingenious, gives the game that enthusiasm the kids need, has serving contests, forehand contests, backhand contests, team against team, with a Coke for a prize. And he is sparing with criticism and lavish in praise for good work. He has an eye out for a discouraged laggard and gives that one a little separate attention. Above all, he sticks to the simple minimal essentials that they all can do with some measure of success, and emphasizes the positive. If they can serve and forehand but not backhand—he lets them serve and forehand, meanwhile slyly sneaking in some backhand work here and there—so that when strength comes to them they have some knowledge. A good group teacher is not just knowledgeable and conscientious but is also flexible, ingenious, and—yes—cagey.

The Proof of the Pudding

It is natural that people should wonder, "Does this really work?" The answer is, it does. Not long ago I had a surprising experience. A pair of twins, aged nine, had been in my groups for two seasons. They were average-to-good students, making satisfactory progress playing little drives against the practice wall. They then disappeared, and were not seen for six years. They returned, and asked, "May we borrow some balls and use the board?" They were now strong girls of fifteen or sixteen. They boomed away impressively, forehand and backhand. When asked, "Where did you get your instruction—you are really hitting the ball?" they replied they had had no lessons from anybody in the intervening six years. In other words, the little simple strokes learned at age nine had grown as they grew, and since their basic grips and swings were reasonably good, these shots had developed soundly without further guidance.

This does not mean they needed no more help. They could not spin their serves at all—this had not been covered in their beginning instruction. Thus they had the usual untutored youthful service: a big bang that never went in, followed by a poop second ball. They knew nothing of anything advanced such as approach shots, drops, overhead, etc. They could volley a little. They obviously needed a lot of help on advanced technique. But there never was a more striking example of the validity of the maxim, "Start them young and be patient."

I was once confronted (without warning) with a group of fifty-five adult beginners. After a short talk and demonstration of grip and how to toss and play the forehand, I lined them up all around the backs and sides of several courts and had them play into the wire. It worked: they learned quickly. But it wasn't anywhere near the fun that a rebound would have supplied. They had to go pick up the ball each time. Very dull. But they were all active and playing and acquiring knowledge. They could get a court and practice over the net between lessons, which were once a week. Each lesson taught one skill: forehand, then serve, then backhand. Subdivision of numbers was used to teach a little net. Most of them acquired

enough skill to have fun, and said so later, even though the average attention per person was necessarily one minute each per hourly lesson. Smaller groups are of course much to be preferred, but even under the above conditions a great deal can be taught by concentrating on one thing at a time and hammering it home to the exclusion of everything else.

Additional Group Situations

This chapter has stressed the economic and sociological soundness of groups for beginners and all others of poor to average skill, because these players are by far the most numerous and make up the daily fair of most instructors. It should not be inferred from this that groups are *only* for such players, and that all more advanced instruction should be confined to individual lessons. Far from it. Advanced players in groups can be taught good thinking, good tactics, and the techniques needed to put the concepts into practice. For example: a college team can be given a talk on effective service and return of service. Then half of them can serve, and the other half return. The coach moves around, court to court, making suggestions and corrections. Second example: the lob and the overhead. Third: crosscourt drills, forehand to forehand and backhand to backhand. Fourth: approach shots and defense. One of each pair sets the ball up, the other attacks, the first defends. The list could go on and on. The coach or professional can thus multiply his effectiveness by using the group method. He should, of course, single out consistent failures for special individual attention, thus using the group concept to determine just where individual instruction is most needed. The group work gets everyone thinking straight and reveals individual weaknesses. The individual work on technique sharpens up the mechanical execution wherever it shows up as inadequate.

Group doubles instruction is very effective. Specific moves can be tried out and polished. Two-shot plays can be perfected. Principles of tactics can be stressed and got across by saying it once to sixteen people instead of eight times to eight pairs.

Courses for tennis teachers (advanced players) are now being offered in various parts of the country. These courses train instructors in desirable progressions and methods. These courses are always conducted on a group basis. The advantages are very obvious: a large number of less experienced teachers can simultaneously get the benefit of the accumulated wisdom, methods, progressions, tricks, and general knowledge of a seasoned professional, and each time one of them asks a question he can answer it to all of them.

The Financial Benefits in
Group Teaching

Of all fallacious thinking, none is so unsound as the argument "You can make a lot more money by giving each one a private lesson than by running cheap groups." The exact reverse is true. A high-priced professional making $20.00 per hour is benefiting only the few who can afford this tariff. By contrast, a professional who gives one-hour group lessons to sixteen people for $3.00 per hour benefits a large number, gouges nobody, gets everybody playing, increases shop sales, and makes $48.00 per hour. The group concept is a bargain both ways: the professional multiplies his effectiveness, gets far more done, and makes more money. The customer gets expert guidance at a reasonable rate. A good pro *should* get a high rate because he is worth it. But he should also open tennis to all at reasonable cost, thus filling the enormous demand that is mushrooming in the game today, and consists in large part of people who definitely cannot

afford $10.00 per half-hour. The group concept is the coming thing because it is the only way to get the job done. Those who espouse it and become expert in it will be the "wave of the future" and will do well both in their work and in their personal prosperity.

Using Assistants

At a large club or park installation a professional can use assistants. If he trains them in the basics of group techniques he can delegate much of the work, reserving his greater in-depth knowledge for private lessons on the special problems of more advanced technique. He again multiplies his effectiveness, keeps the price within bounds, yet makes a greater total income both on the court and in his shop sales.

QUESTIONS

1. Should we worry more about teaching beginners than others?

2. Why must we talk a lot about "muscle knowledge"?

3. How do you deal with limited talent?

4. Is there such a thing as "concealed talent"?

5. What are the psychological advantages of groups for the young?

6. How would you plan a series of group lessons?

7. What do you do with young beginners when you do not have a practice wall?

8. Can groups be used effectively with adults and advanced players?

CHAPTER 11

Skill Tests, Rewards, and Drills

MOTIVATION

Many teachers like to motivate children by setting up skill tests and giving awards in the form of certificates of achievement. This gives the player a feeling of concrete progress. He has reached a goal and has something to prove it. On the other hand, such a system tends to make the game very competitive and can make it more work than fun, so if such a device is used it is important not to let the program become pressurized—pressure from the child, from over-eager parents, from playmates. It is also quite a lot of trouble in printing, testing, etc. Using this sort of plan is very much a personal thing with each teacher. Some find it excellent, others feel it is all unnecessary because the game itself is sufficient reward: once a child is playing the ball with some success he needs no other reward beyond praise from his instructor. And of course there is the most concrete reward of all right in the game itself: the player makes shots, gets balls back, wins points, games, sets, matches. The greatest incentive to use an award system lies in the fact that little beginners, aged seven to ten, usually cannot play on the big court designed for adults, and therefore need some substitute for achievement on the court until they progress to the point where they can play the game itself over the net.

In groups, team contests are very popular. If the young players choose up sides, with each taking four serves (from the service line if the instructor wishes), and cumulative

ADVANCED VOLLEY CHART

	Forehand		Backhand	
	Left to Right	*Right to Left*	*Left to Right*	*Right to Left*
Sally		X		X
Bill	X		X	
Joe	X	X		

Diagram 11–1. Advanced volley chart. This simple chart records both progress and areas needing work in the four volleys—see Diagram 11–4. This is, of course, an advanced test. It assumes the player can volley. It tests the player's ability to execute specific winning plays with his volley in the most common opportunity situations. The test also serves to prove conclusively that a player can or cannot handle a particular shot, thus eliminating possible differences of opinion. The test should be strict: all shots must bounce across the sideline, not across the baseline. Any lesser angle is easily reached and the net player is in trouble. It should also be noted that all volleys land well inside the lines; make the angle, not the line.

scores are kept, each child tries hard and feels very much a part of it. The same can be done with forehands, backhands, and volleys, with the ball being fed by the instructor.

instructor likes to start beginners ball-tapping, then tests on this skill should be first. If not, these tests should be omitted. The tests should duplicate the steps being offered in the lessons.

CHARTS AND CERTIFICATES

A simpler system for beginners is to create a chart with a number of squares opposite each name, each square representing some achievement in skill. If this chart is posted in a public place, it will make for considerable motivation. It also serves to keep the instructor informed of each player's needs: a lot of forehand squares filled in and no backhands at all is pretty obvious. See Diagrams 11–1 and 11–2.

The incentive plan, whether a chart or certificates or whatever, should be coordinated with the teacher's plan of instruction. If the

SELF-TESTING

Above all, the tests should provide incentive for self-instruction. If a practice wall is available, there should be a lot of tests that involve only the player, so the player can work on them alone and progress continually between group lessons. In addition, the instructor need not do all the work of continual testing. Assistants or advanced players can easily handle most of these chores, so the instructor can concentrate his efforts more on teaching technique to students. This is his expertise, for which a substitute is questionable except at the

BALL-TAPPING CHART

	Forehand				Backhand			
	Ten Down	Ten Up	Ten Down and Up	Two Players Alternate Ten Down and Ten Up	Ten Down	Ten Up	Ten Down and Ten Up	Two Players Alternate Ten Down and Ten Up
Bill	X	X	X		X	X		
Jean	X				X			
Sue	X	X			X			
Rob	X	X	X	X				
etc								

Diagram 11–2. A sample chart for beginner tapping tests. Note how the chart quickly reveals a typical "forehand only" beginner such as Rob, and hopefully provides incentive to correct the imbalance.

lower levels of skill. Even there an experienced eye is needed to oversee and guide assistants.

Subdivision can of course approach infinity both in numbers and complexity. The tests that follow are merely one example of an acceptable series that progresses from the bottom to the top and includes the basic skills needed to be a competent player. Teachers should feel free to modify, expand, contract, or otherwise alter these tests to accommodate them to local circumstances.

The charts can be called "Beginner," "Intermediate," "Advanced," or they can be given more colorful designations such as an animal series (chipmunk, squirrel, fox, wolf, tiger), or merely A, B, C. There is ample room for each instructor to express his own preferences, judgment, and imagination. The real effectiveness of any plan is in its content, not in the window dressing. Children like to be dramatic, so much ornamentation has appeal and is probably desirable.

On all tests, from beginner through advanced, the player should be given three tries per test; the instructor may increase the numbers if he wishes.

BEGINNERS

Ball-Tapping Skills

1. Forehand: Eastern grip.
   a. Tap the ball down ten times.
   b. Tap the ball up—no bounce—ten times.
   c. Tap the ball down so it bounces higher than the racket, reverse the racket face and tap it up, let it bounce, tap it down, etc.—ten times.
   d. Two players tap alternately: I tap, you tap—ten times. Players face each other: a tiny game.
2. Backhand: Eastern grip—same four tests.
   a. Tap the ball down ten times.
   b. Tap up ten times.
   c. Tap down and up ten times.
   d. Alternate ten times.

Comments: (1) It is important that the player be obliged to use an Eastern forehand for the forehand tests and an Eastern backhand for the backhand tests. Otherwise the player may acquire the bad and hard-to-cure habit of playing backhands with a forehand grip. (2) Proponents of tapping rightly assert that it is a practical way to begin developing feel for the racket (the grips) and the ball and timing—in a very limited space with considerable numbers, with little or no risk of injury, with everyone active, and no one "waiting around."

Practice Wall Skills

The player tosses the ball for himself for each shot.

1. Forehand drive—Eastern grip, left foot advanced and pointed, racket prepared *before* ball is tossed.
   a. From 15 feet: five consecutive shots into the entire stall area above net line.
   b. From 20 feet: five consecutive shots.
   c. From 25 feet: five consecutive shots.
   d. From 30 feet: five consecutive shots.
2. Backhand drive—Eastern grip, right foot advanced and pointed, racket prepared but not taken back until after toss.
   a. From 15 feet: five consecutive shots into stall above net.
   b. From 20 feet: five consecutive shots into stall above net.
   c. From 25 feet: five consecutive shots into stall above net.
   d. From 30 feet: five consecutive shots into stall above net.
   Note: For weak-wristed beginners one may start as close as 10 feet on the backhand, and omit the greater distances.
3. Service—same four tests.

Discussion: The players should be told they *must* perform test with correct grip, correct footwork, correct racket preparation *before* they toss, and by tossing the ball (palm up, not down) about head high so they must let it bounce, wait for it to set up, then play. (Dropping the ball palm down or throwing it down should be marked wrong.) Tossing it up develops skill in timing (i.e., waiting and selecting the proper time to play) and is an important part of the training: this is what you *must* do later on the court or in rallying off the wall. It is often easy for a careless but somewhat talented beginner to stand any old way, drop the ball, and with any old grip and a dangling preparation scoop it into the target—thus ostensibly passing the test. Testers should not allow such loose performance to receive credit. In the lessons it should be explained that while you can play it any old way on a little shot to the wall, a better stroke is necessary to play over the net on the big court: that is why you fuss about *how* they do it. So the test should be a method and form test as well as an accuracy test. In sum: the target is huge and easy but the test is fairly strict.

Without a Wall

The same tests as above are used. Players stand the required distance from the net. To control lateral aim, the shot must be required to cross the net between the center service line and the alley line on whichever side they play from. Serving may be diagonal or straight; it matters little. The advantage of the wall is twofold: there is a visible target, and they can practice by themselves all the skills of getting set, racket ready, toss, wait, play—and at the same time have the fun of attempting to play the rebound.

Beginner Volley Tests

1. Forehand volley—on the court.
   a. Player stands four feet from net, Eastern forehand grip. Instructor stands at service line, feeds ball right to player's racket. Player pokes it back, taking a little step in with his left foot. Five in a row passes test.
   b. Instructor stands halfway from service line to baseline, feeds right to player's racket. Five in a row passes test.

   c. Instructor stands at baseline, feeds to racket. Five in a row passes test.
2. Backhand volley—on the court. Same three tests as for forehand volley, step in with right foot.

Comment: These tests are the easiest possible. The tests should be marked a good bit on form: If players keep the racket in front of them and put it *to* the ball, so they put it on the ball out front and block, rather than draw back, swing, and hit, they will find these tests very easy.

3. Volley drill for laggards—on the court. Player stands four feet from net, advances the left foot, and pushes his racket out front *before* the ball is fed. Instructor stands only about six feet from net, actually hits the player's racket, saying, "When it hits your racket just give it a little push back." Often if the ball is fed by hand from very close, a beginning is made. As soon as the player can do this, the instructor should start backing up a little and expand it.
4. Volley drill on a wall. Players can be encouraged to practice volleying on a wall, by standing quite close and volleying nothing but forehands or backhands. Actually this is horizontal ball-tapping and it is good practice. When they get quite good at it (not all will), have them alternate: forehand to backhand to forehand. This requires fast grip-changing with two hands, plus accuracy in order to achieve the alternation. Most beginners will not be able to do it at all. It is suggested here only for those who show quick talent: why hold them back? Wall tests can easily be devised—five forehands in a row from six, eight, 10 feet out, etc., if an instructor wishes.

ADVANCED BEGINNERS

Practice Wall Skills

See Diagram 11–3 for targeted wall. The target is now the square or circle.

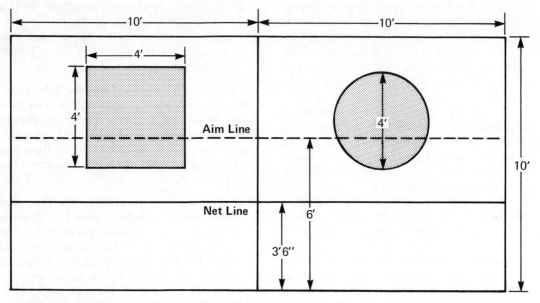

Diagram 11–3. A skill test practice wall. A practice wall marked out for skill tests. The vertical solid lines divide the board into stalls. The entire stall, above the net line, is the beginner target. The 4-foot circles (or squares) are the more advanced targets. The solid horizontal line is the net height (the netpost height is used to encourage aiming high enough). The dotted horizontal line is the height target to encourage all players to aim well above the net. The target squares are equally good for intermediates and advanced: increasing the distance serves to make the target more difficult to hit. Slightly larger stalls (12 to 15 feet) are desirable to avoid crowding if size of board permits.

1. Service (Eastern forehand grip, "scratch the back" preparation).
   a. Three out of five serves into target from 10 feet.
   b. Three out of five serves into target from 15 feet.
   c. Three out of five serves into target from 20 feet.
2. Forehand drive—player tosses the ball for himself.
   a. Three out of five into target from 10 feet.
   b. Three out of five into target from 15 feet.
   c. Three out of five into target from 20 feet.
3. Backhand drive—same three tests.

Comment: This is a tough drill, and stresses double accuracy (height and width). If the players are told to press the ball, stay on it, guide it rather than hit it, they will learn that great essential: how to aim, and how to keep the face of the racket slanted properly all the way through the stroke to guide the ball truly.

Without a Wall

The same tests as above are used. Players stand the same distance from the net, but the criteria are now that the ball must clear the net, land in the court, and be within easy reach (without moving the feet) of the instructor, who stands ready to receive them. Serves must land in the service court. Again, considerable stress should be placed on form, since what is being done is to create self-practice habits that are good, not sloppy.

Rally Tests on a Wall

1. Forehand drive—rally the ball four times in succession, the first shot being set up by hand. The ball may take more than one bounce; the target is the whole stall above the net. Again, use the gradually expanding distances.

2. Backhand drive—same as above.
3. Serve and rally: start with a service, which must be aimed to return to forehand for forehand test, to backhand for backhand test. Use varied distances.
4. Grip change test: rally forehand to backhand to forehand to backhand. Also reverse it—start with a backhand.

Comment: Item 4 is a very difficult drill for beginners, and they should be encouraged to play very gently so they have time to switch grips and aim. Many beginners, particularly weaker ones, will not be able to do this for a long time because their backhand will lag behind their forehand. However, as soon as they have strength enough to play a backhand, it is important to stress starting every rally with a backhand. This emphasis will bring the backhand along and will also force them continually to change grips, so they get past the stage of being "forehand only" players. This drill also encourages playing habitually crosscourt.

Rally Tests without a Wall

Use the same tests except that the instructor is the wall: he stands at net and volleys the ball back or feeds another quickly from his hand. In all tests the student should start the rally. The instructor should not make it too easy: he should feed one short so it takes two bounces to the player, another just right, another a little higher so the timing is slower, etc.—so the player must make varied adjustments to different types of shots coming to him. He should also feed quite quickly so the student will learn to get ready quickly for the *next* shot—the problem of tempo. This drill can be adjusted to the talent of the player: if the youngster is good, make it pretty tough. If he is less talented, make it easier, help him along. Thus the best are stimulated and the less talented encouraged.

Volley Tests

1. Beginner still stands only four feet from net, but he now stands in the proper ready position, prepared to go either way. Instructor varies feed from forehand to backhand without warning. The player is thus required to use two hands, change grips, and advance the correct foot as he plays. Again the shot should be made as easy as possible so there is no pace or pressure: the idea is to test how he does it more than to make him do it under pressure. The distances can be varied as in the beginner tests.

INTERMEDIATES

Practice Wall Skills

The square or circular targets should be used.

1. Forehand—rally the ball five times, three of which must hit target. Setting the ball up to start does not count; therefore, the ball is hit six times.
   a. From 15 feet out.
   b. From 20 feet out.
2. Backhand—same as forehand.
3. Alternating: set the ball up with a backhand, so it rebounds to forehand, then play alternate forehands and backhands.
   a. Five in a row (after setting up shot) anywhere in entire stall above net from 15 feet.
   b. Same from 20 feet.
   c. Same—two of five must hit target. Vary distances.
   d. Same—three of five must hit target; one must be a backhand. Vary distances.
4. Service—use the proper service grip (Continental).
   a. Three out of five into target—from 15 feet.
   b. Three out of five into target—from 20 feet.
   c. Three out of five into target—from 25 feet.

Comment: It will be obvious the same beginner skills, plus the service grip, are being tested more rigorously.

On the Court

1. Forehand.
   a. Player starts rally with instructor, keeps the ball going until each has played it three times. The instructor stands back (not at net), and plays softly (no pressure) to player's forehand each time.
   b. Keep it going five times.
   c. Keep it going ten times.
2. Backhand—same as forehand.
3. Alternating: instructor alternates his returns so player must alternate.
   a. Three exchanges.
   b. Five exchanges.
   c. Ten exchanges.
4. Service—using slice grip, "scratch the back" preparation.
   a. Three out of five in right court.
   b. Three out of five in left court.
   c. Seven out of ten in right court.
   d. Seven out of ten in left court.

Comment: Insist on follow-through to the left side without rolling racket over.

5. Volley—player stands eight to 10 feet from net, crouches with two hands on racket. Instructor stands at baseline, feeds ball with a little firmness but not hard. Player must put a little chip (backspin) on his volley, and must step in with the correct foot.
   a. Forehand—five in a row.
   b. Backhand—five in a row.
   c. Alternating (without much pause between) five.
   d. Random—instructor plays to either side with no advance notice.
6. Overhead—player stands four feet from net, racket cocked high, left foot ahead. Instructor stands halfway from baseline to net. Instructor makes lob just right for player (the worst possible low lob, the easiest to kill). The player must bounce this over the instructor's head by playing it straight down. (Over his head doesn't mean necessarily out of his reach: many youngsters can't bounce it that high!) Three out of five passes.

Comment: This is the most basic aspect of the overhead: getting the racket on top of the ball and pressing it down. This is the most elementary drill and the most elementary test. The follow-through *must* be to the left side.

ADVANCED INTERMEDIATES

1. The lob—instructor stands at net, player at baseline. Instructor plays ball to player, who must get it out of the instructor's reach in height and in the court behind the service line. Three out of five passes on forehand and backhand and alternating.
2. The drop shot—instructor feeds very short ball, player makes drop shot (with backspin), which must take two bounces inside the service line. Three out of five passes.
   Wall drill and test: Player stands about 20 feet out, sets up ball by playing against wall, then makes a drop shot. To be called "good" the ball must have some backspin, must be going *down* when it strikes wall, and must strike wall between the net line and the dotted "aim line." Three out of five passes.

Comment: This wall drill is *strongly* recommended for advanced intermediates. It initiates them into the concept of restraint, the meaning of "touch," and makes it possible for them to start having a change of pace when they play. This approach to the game is in general much neglected and in many cases totally ignored, although it is a fact that such "finesse" shots are the most difficult and need to be started early not only for the technique but also to develop the tactical habit of seizing opportunities to make such shots.

3. Chopping and slicing—instructor at baseline feeds a rather high bounce to player, who must chop it back. Three out of five passes. Give three tests: forehand, backhand, alternating.
   Instructor stands at service line, feeds very low bounce (by chipping). Pupil must

slice across and under and get it back over net. Three tests: forehand, backhand, and alternating—three out of five passes. If the shot pops up ridiculously high, the shot should be disallowed.

Comment: This again is a comparatively neglected area of technique, but is important to lay the groundwork for slice approaches, defensive slicing, etc. later on. Good players can play hard drives *and* can chip and slice whenever occasion demands. Practicing this also accustoms intermediates to dealing with the bounces of cut shots—a real problem.

4. Rally tests.
   a. Forehand to forehand (crosscourt). Five in a row passes. A shot down the middle is accepted.
   b. Backhand to backhand (crosscourt). Five in a row.
   c. Instructor plays straight, player crosscourt, so player alternates. Five in a row.

Comment: Note straight shot tests are omitted. A habit of playing crosscourt should first be instilled, and straight shots should be initially discouraged. This might be called "percentage instruction."

5. Overhead—player stands halfway from service line to net. Instructor stands a little inside baseline, feeds poor lobs to player's forehand side (almost right to him, requiring very little footwork). Player smashes reasonably firmly, following through to left side, aiming slightly crosscourt (almost down the middle). Four out of five passes.

Comment: This drill is calculated to teach a player how to play the ball, without putting him under the additional pressure of moving a lot or judging a higher lob. The instructor should give him an easy good chance to smash and emphasize *quick* racket preparation (scratch the back) so extra time remains for footwork even if not needed for this easy smash. The player should be told to aim inside the service line, i.e., hit *down*. The elbow should be kept pretty high, again so the play

will be decisively down. As proficiency improves, the instructor should stress the follow-through: racket not rolled over, body well bowed over to bring weight down and add pace. The instructor should advise a flat hit with some slice—not dead flat. Footwork should be confined to advancing the left foot and using the shuffle step to adjust to ball. In sum, the instructor should make it easy but make him do it correctly. It helps to say, "This is like the serve, only I toss the ball for you and you hit down more."

ADVANCED PLAYERS

There could be an endless number of these tests, because they could cover many fine points of play. What follows has been limited to the basic needs of actual reasonably competent play. Any instructor with advanced pupils should feel free to devise a drill or test for any shortcoming on the part of any pupil on any shot.

1. Crosscourt drills—forehand to forehand, backhand to backhand, with the requirement that the ball land behind the service line for depth. Five in a row. (This sounds easy. Try it!)
2. Running forehand and backhand crosscourts. Instructor places player at one side of court, hits to other side. He should not make it impossible or too tough. The idea is to teach player to prepare his racket as he starts so he can play any ball he can reach as well as any ball that comes right to him. Run him to one side, then back to other side, etc. He must learn to keep his poise, recover quickly, and still make a crosscourt each time. (When someone is running you, the crosscourt prevents him from angling away from you on the next shot; therefore, this is the shot to teach). When proficiency is developed, add the depth requirement. Five in a row passes.
3. Return of service—instructor serves firmly (but not really hard). Player must stand at

baseline, move in on the ball at least a yard, and play back crosscourt. Five forehands in a row passes, five backhands, five alternating, five random (no warning). Any ball played from behind the baseline is a miss, no matter how well it is played. Player must move into it, not back up.

4. Service drills—accuracy in direction.

   a. Each service court is divided into two halves. On a soft court this can be done merely by scratching a line with the racket handle. On a hard court white adhesive tape is easy to put down and remove. Three or four feet of tape suffices. Five serves into one half: four tests: i.e., one for each of the four halves. Four out of five passes.

   b. Service courts divided into thirds. Again require four out of five into each third: six tests.

   c. Service courts divided into quarters: Require four out of five into each of the two outside quarters in each court: four tests.

   d. A down-the-center test (right at player) if instructor wishes.

Comment: This test teaches the students to aim for areas, not lines. It also builds up competence in playing a weakness by stressing one area in a match. Instructor should stress that players should aim for the middle of the area, not at lines, so as to have a reasonable margin for error even when trying for expert accuracy.

5. Service drills—accuracy in depth. Draw a line parallel to the service line three feet nearer the net. Four out of five serves must land in this three foot area.

6. Service combined direction and depth. Combine the tests in item 4 above with item 5 above. Require three out of five: the test is difficult.

Comment: The depth tests and drills are of extreme importance: depth is the great quality —more than pinpoint accuracy—of any consistently effective service. Students should think of pressing their services a certain dis-

tance by using legs and body in a conscious effort to control how far it goes before it breaks down.

7. Service drills—spin proficiency. Instructor stretches a string or rope across the net two feet higher than the net. He requires that the student swing quite hard on his service, yet clear the rope and hit the court. The rope is raised to three feet above the net later.

Comment: This encourages aiming *away* from the net, helps get depth, and forces the concept of arc onto the player, the feeling of making the ball "break."

8. Volley tests—placement. There are four basic placements: with the forehand to the right and left, with the backhand to the right and left. The instructor stands in one corner just behind the baseline. The player stands 10 feet behind the net and three to four feet off the center service line toward the side occupied by the instructor. The instructor plays a straight shot or a crosscourt, the player closes in one good step and places the ball away from the instructor. The criterion is that the volley, after it bounces, must cross the sideline, not the baseline, of the instructor's court. See Diagram 11–4. Four tests, two from each corner, four out of five required.

Comment: Most advanced players will be able to do quite well on one or two of these tests, but will do very badly on the others. This clearly reveals their shortcomings and where work is needed. The ball should be fed with only moderate firmness and without making "line ball" straight shots or sharply angled crosscourts. The idea is to give the player plenty of time to display his technique or lack of same on each of the four most common "opportunity" situations at the net.

On crosscourt volleys stress should be laid on playing the outside of the ball (get well around it). On the others, the instructor should stress getting inside the ball by laying back the racket head with the wrist *before* playing (it

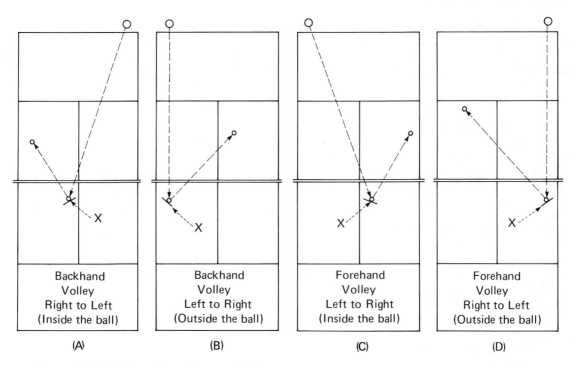

Diagram 11–4. The four volleys. These are the four most common opportunity situations at net (excluding overhead). Note the 90-degree difference in the presentation of the racket face to the ball in making the contrasting shots (A compared with B, C compared with D). Inability to quickly make these skillful racket preparations accounts for the tendency to volley back to an opponent instead of away from him. Few can do all four without special drilling. Note also that the player closes in decisively. A ball-throwing machine is ideal for drilling these skills.

must be tight and set at the impact). Sharp contrast in the racket skills is important.

Note in the diagrams that the player advances and reaches for the ball—he does not let it come to him. He wants to catch it as nearly above the net as time permits. So this is also a "close in" drill.

This is a technique test: do not inject lobs to fool the player. Give him every chance to do it well, but do not position him so close that he is woefully open to the lob. Tell him where you are going to hit it.

The second stage is to feed to either side without warning. The third stage is to combine it with overhead—inject lobs, force him to wait and watch the ball and not commit himself ahead of time. Encourage him to rush the net on all chances in play.

Various other placement tests and drills can be worked out: substitute the drop volley and require that it must cross the alley line at or inside the service line: very tough, very good to train a really advanced player to put the ball in a small space.

9. Volley tests—grip changes.
   a. Player is at net with Continental grip. Instructor stands at service line, plays high (shoulder high roughly, not a semi-lob) to his forehand. Player changes to Eastern and plays down sharply. The volley must land inside the service line. Four out of five passes.
   b. Same arrangement as above, instructor plays high to backhand. Player changes to Eastern grip, plays down.

c. Instructor moves back to baseline, plays solid but rather high drives to forehand.
d. Same to backhand: a, b, and c.
e. Alternating—no warning—low drives mixed in.

Comment: To drill on this skill the player should do one thing twenty-five or more times in a row and stay with it until the responses begin to be automatic. Two players can drill each other—one feeds twenty, the other volleys, then switch. Or set up a ball thrower to feed the desired shot. This drill is very valuable: how often (alas!) do we see players "blow" high setup volleys? Are they chicken? Do they choke? No. They just don't know how to deal with that type of ball. The instructor should teach them. The key to success is the preparation of the racket: lift it above the proposed point of contact, so as to hit down, *and* close the face with the thumb and fingers of the left hand. It is to be emphasized that these two moves are simultaneous. Anyone who tries to lift the racket and *then* close the face will definitely not have time; he would be better advised to use one grip. But if the slight turn of the racket with the left hand is mastered (the right hand contributes nothing except to be loose enough so the grip *can* change), the racket face and grip are arranged in a small fraction of a second and the racket arrives, totally prepared, at the point from which it will play down on the ball. The point is: the grip can be changed as quickly as the racket can be moved (lifted to one side in this case); therefore, the argument that "there isn't time" is totally invalid. Many players will try this once or twice and then say, "I can't do it quickly enough." Of course they can't; they are just beginning to learn. After they do it two hundred times and get the "hang of it" the process becomes almost instantaneous—and their high volley is *much* better. After a season or so they don't even know they are doing it. It just happens by itself. But now they eat up high volleys instead of blowing a good many of them. All advanced players should be given this instruction.

10. Overhead—moving. Player is positioned fairly close to the net (eight feet?). Instructor lobs a little over his head, has him move back and play it. Instructor should make it tougher as he improves. Four out of five. Stress very quick racket preparation, then concentrate on getting under the ball by moving back fast.
11. Overhead—accuracy.
    a. Lob to forehand: instructor demands a crosscourt that crosses the alley line, not the baseline. Player should lob fairly well to the side so the angle is open.
    b. Lob to backhand: instructor demands a crosscourt that crosses the other alley line. Instructor insists that he move fast enough to play it with a forehand smash, not a high backhand volley.
    c. Lob to center: student may play it either way, but it must be more than halfway to one corner from the center.
    d. Lob to forehand: instructor demands a straight overhead parallel with the alley line. Instructor should discourage player from trying to angle this one: there isn't sufficient width of court across which to angle.
    e. Lob to backhand: instructor demands a straight overhead—no angle.
    f. Lob very high: instructor demands that player bounce it, then smash. If the very high lob is deep, advise him to "second serve" it—i.e., use a lot of spin—and not try to kill it. If it is short, kill for the biggest target (crosscourt).

Comment: Instructor should not overdrill overheads in any one session—a sore arm can result. He should point out that every angle he teaches the player is across the larger width of court, never the smaller, so the target is always big. He should stress that it is nonpercentage to hit hard for small targets. A drop shot can be put in a very small space. An overhead cannot as a rule be that totally controlled.

    g. Self-practice on a wall. Ball is served into the ground in front of the wall. It will come off the wall in a high loop that can be played as an overhead. This permits self-practice at any time.

12. Approach shots.
   a. Slices—backhand: the instructor sets up the ball short on the backhand. The player slices down the line and follows to net. The objective is a low net skimmer that kicks low when it bounces.
   b. Low forehand—instructor sets it up low (by chipping), and player again cuts across it and skims it down the line, following to net.
   c. High forehand—instructor sets it up high, player hits *hard* down line and follows to net.

Comment: Players should be urged (when advanced) to put a lot of time on approaches. Playing gives insufficient practice on it, yet it is of great importance: it is the opportunity you have fought to get from your opponent. Now: can you really get him? Surprisingly few

people can. They lose at least half these points, of which theoretically they should win a huge majority. The instructor should try out his students: he should start by giving them a fat setup, then see if they can beat him. It is amazing how frequently they fail—not through the instructor's great counterplaying, but strictly because of their own inability to handle half-court chances well.

QUESTIONS

1. What are some advantages and some disadvantages of skill tests?

2. Why should we go out of our way to drill some shots more than others?

3. How does a practice wall facilitate drilling and testing?

4. Why should the instructor insist that the ball be tossed up and allowed to drop, as contrasted with throwing it down or dropping it?

IV

Singles

CHAPTER 12

Dimensions and Tactics

THE COURT

A tennis court is very long and narrow. The total length lacks three feet of being three times the width (78 feet long, 27 feet wide). It doesn't seem so when one is on the court because of perspective and the fact that most courts are marked out for doubles and look wider than they actually are for singles.

With skillful players the object is to place the ball where one's opponent cannot reach it. This is impossible from the baseline because of this narrowness. Even from part way to the net—let us say from halfway between the baseline and the service line—the task of making an unreturnable placement is too difficult; on a percentage basis it cannot be done. Only from the net position can the ball be placed decisively and quickly so far from an opponent that no return is possible. See Diagram 12–2.

Thus the dimensions of the court have determined the nature of orthodox tactics: to seek the net position at every reasonable opportunity. The present "Big Game" is merely the same tactics refined and carried to the ultimate: i.e., follow the service to net all the time; attain the dominant net position with the least possible delay the absolute maximum number of times during a match.

The current belief that this is a "modern" game, something new and different, should be shattered at once. The first national champion, Richard D. Sears (champion 1881 et seq.), sought and held the net position whenever he could. Clothier, champion in 1906, followed every service to net, both first and second, throughout the National Singles tournament—exactly as John Doeg, Jack Kramer, Stan Smith, and others have done more recently. James Dwight, the "father of American tennis," urged all his students to be net players, and he was the dominant influence in the American game for several decades. One can find books written just after the turn of the century in which the writers deplore what they consider to be an excess of net rushing and an absence of the more lengthy and interesting exchanges that "formerly" took place. Written just after 1900, these sentiments read like quotes from the sixties.

Changes there most certainly have been. The early players were often as hard hitters as any today, but the ball is now faster, so that a team of doubles champions, like the Kinsey brothers, who stressed the lob, would now quite probably find it impossible. Athletes average a good bit bigger today, there are many more of them, instruction is better, and the attitude of serious players is far more dedicated because of the economic motivation that was for the most part absent in the early days

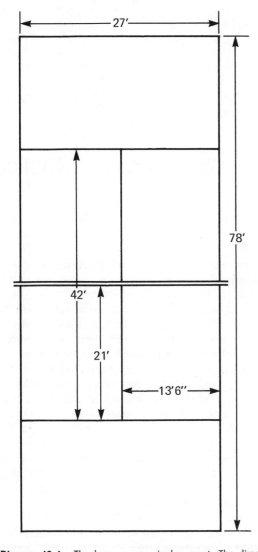

Diagram 12–1. The long narrow singles court. The dimensions of the court make it impossible to aim the ball anywhere far from one's opponent except when at net. We usually see a doubles court—alleys included—so the general mental picture of a singles court tends to be less cigarlike than the actuality. Note that it is within three feet of being three times as long as it is wide (3 × 27 = 81).

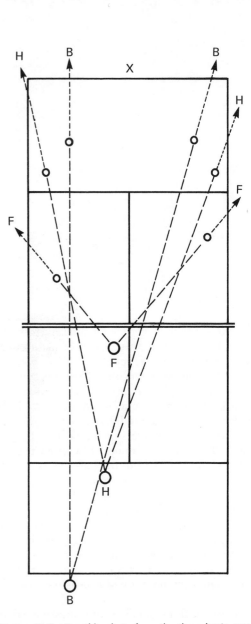

Diagram 12–2. Possible shots from the three basic areas. Note that only from F can the ball be placed decisively away from a defender. Therefore the objective of all advanced players should be to gain the net position, since only from there can one win.

when the game was regarded as a diversion rather than a profession. Yet it would seem probable that if a player like Malcolm Whit-

man—champion in 1900, a very big man with solid powerful strokes on both sides and a tactical attitude that stressed forcing to the net at all times—could be brought back, he would find today's big service superior to his but not much else. As long as the court remains unchanged the dimensions will continue to define inexorably what is possible and not possible and what is percentage and nonpercentage. Every time someone emphasizes one aspect or another, sports writers proclaim a "new" style, but it is really not so. One should not forget that even in Bill Tilden's day, when his famous and fabulous ground strokes were dominating the game for a decade, he also boasted what has always been recognized as one of the biggest services of all time and a great net game. His ability at net was amply demonstrated by the fact that he won the doubles title with an amazing variety of partners: any first-class player would do, it seemed. In singles he was so proficient off the ground that he often just didn't bother to go to net, letting cripples float back, land and set up—so he could streak another devastator into the corner. It was obviously more enjoyable this way with strokes like his. And so effective were his approach shots that he was never obliged to develop a superlative net game: he moved in merely to finish off; the winning was all done before he got there except for a comparatively easy placement.

Who was Tilden's sidekick and rival who beat him many times? Vincent Richards—whose entire game centered around the fact that he was one of the great maestros of all time with the volley. He had dead-eye accuracy plus severe backspin on his volley, so that even if an opponent reached the ball it was low and heavy and almost impossible to play effectively on a skiddy surface like grass. Even Tilden could not give Richards the net position with impunity. And who upset Tilden in the Nationals and took the U.S. title one year? John Doeg, whose thunderous lefty service, powerful overhead, and excellent volley more than made up for an incomplete stroke equipment that offered nothing more than a chopped forehand and a sliced backhand. His winning was done exclusively at the net. No matter what era one investigates, the entire

history of the game is filled with masterful exponents of net play, and only the greatest baseliners of all have been able to make headway against them. The shape of the court cannot be denied nor its consequences avoided.

The Big Game, while logical and backed by the best argument of all—it wins—is nevertheless not for most of us. We do not have the ability, technique, or stamina for it. Moreover, all the great titles are won on fast surfaces, and the pro tour is on fast surfaces, while the majority of tennis players in many sections of the country play on clay and composition surfaces, which are slow. Even the greatest players, on clay or composition, abandon their ever-rushing tactics and adopt an attitude more like Tilden's: keep the ball going until a weak shot offers an excellent opportunity, then go to net. This is made mandatory because the slower surface aids the defense by giving it time and makes a net player vulnerable unless he comes up behind a truly forcing shot. If the champions cannot always play the Big Game on clay, it would seem no further argument is needed for the rest of us. *But:* the objective is still the net—one just is obliged to be more cautious and circumspect about getting there.

The average player should on any surface play the all-round game that starts at the baseline, waits for a weak shot in the halfcourt area, forces from there and follows to net. The game divides itself naturally into these three areas: baseline, halfcourt, forecourt. In each area the objectives and therefore the techniques required are sharply different, and so it is logical to consider each separately.

SPECULATING ON DEVELOPMENTS

As this is written, serious consideration is being given to changing to slower surfaces for important tournaments. If this occurs, it will be a great improvement both for the spectators and players. The big money events are for the most part played on fast surfaces that put too great a premium on offense. No one wants tennis changed into a defensive game in which courage defeats itself. But if the balance between offense and defense were shifted a little in favor of the latter, we would at once be treated to more varied styles, more numerous rallies, fewer two-shot points, and a better chance for the receiver to break service. A greater variety of shots and a greater element of doubt about winning service would both be decided improvements in an already exciting spectator sport. Let us hope this change occurs or at least is given a try.

QUESTIONS

1. What are the length and width of a singles court?

2. How do the dimensions of the court affect tactics?

3. How does the speed of the surface of the court affect tactics?

4. Should the average player imitate the "Big Game"?

5. Why does a very fast surface tend to make the game less interesting to watch?

CHAPTER 13

Area One—The Baseline

THE BASIC RALLY

Playing Crosscourt

A player is at the greatest distance from his opponent when he is playing from the baseline, and winning shots are next to impossible. The objectives must be mostly negative: don't miss and don't set the ball up by hitting short. One is mainly concerned with waiting out the other fellow until an opportunity offers to move to the attack. Baseline shots should have two characteristics: they should all be aimed high over the net to get depth, and they should all be hit crosscourt unless a pronounced weakness in one's opponent dictates otherwise.

Why is this? Because a crosscourt shot goes over the lowest part of the net (safer), goes on the long diagonal (safer), and above all forces an opponent to hit the ball back toward the player who hit the crosscourt: the opponent can play parallel to the striker but cannot play away from him. By contrast, if the striker plays straight the opponent can run him very hard by angling crosscourt. See Diagram 13–1. Also swinging crosscourt is more natural than down the line. So a crosscourt is more natural, gives more margin for error over the net and inside the baseline, is a stronger shot defen-

sively and a stronger shot offensively. It seems to have every desirable attribute, leaving none for the straight shot. This is true, yet very few average players realize it. In fact, most of them play more straight shots in an attempt to run their opponent when he has hit crosscourt. One cannot run an opponent much this way, and the attempt merely sets up his next crosscourt. A good proof of this is to have two players take the court with these instructions: one is to hit everything crosscourt, the other everything straight. It is soon evident who is doing the running.

Someone will surely ask, "What if he too plays crosscourt?" Then fight it out. If you make it the cornerstone of your baseline game to have good crosscourts, and he chooses your game, you should be able to do well. Of course, if he outdoes you at it—always change a losing game. Even though you do not always win, this sound plan means he must defeat you at a shot to which you have devoted considerable practice, or else he must make the unsound straight shot. This is not only a good way to go at it, but it also sends you onto the court able to fight harder because you have no doubts as to what you are going to do. So if he plays crosscourt, crosscourt him back until you get a setup. Let him try the other shot—and run him if he does.

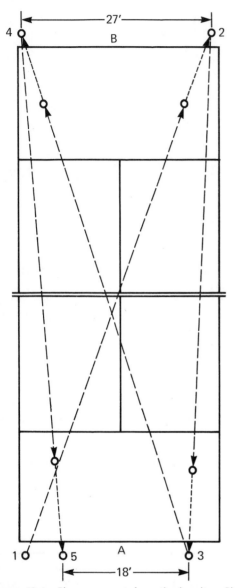

Diagram 13–1. Play crosscourt from the baseline. Player A plays crosscourt from 1. Player B plays straight from 2. Player A crosscourts from 3. Player B plays straight from 4 to 5. By scale, player A has had to move 18 feet (from 3 to 5). Player B has had to move 27 feet (2 to 4). If allowance is made for reach and the length of the racket, the percentage contrast would be even greater—say 2 to 1 instead of 3 to 2. AND, player A is in each case making an easier shot. Thus he has every advantage, and the more expert he is in angling his crosscourt, the more decisive his advantage becomes.

The Twisting Tactic

The obvious and apparently logical way to run someone is to play to one side, then the other. This is true sometimes but not all the time. If you play crosscourt and he plays straight— then, yes, crosscourt to the other side. *But:* if you play crosscourt and he plays crosscourt, your best answer is to crosscourt right back. Very often this play of putting two shots in the same place has the effect of working him much harder. After his shot to you, he must return to position. If you play straight he merely keeps going, smoothly, to the other side. By contrast, if you play another crosscourt he must stop, turn, and go the other way. He must fight his own momentum, make a U-turn, reverse the direction of his motion. In other words, he must twist. This has an isometric effect (fighting himself) that is much more fatiguing, much more disturbing, and more likely to get him off balance than merely continuing in the direction he is already moving.

If this is done subtly it can be very effective. The player should take care to prepare, quickly, and make it obvious that he *could* and *may* play straight. If, after this preparation and a slight hesitation, the player pivots the shot crosscourt, his opponent is very frequently caught "going the wrong way" and must wrench himself back to the spot he just left. So this apparently stupid play of "hitting it right back to him" can be used with extremely annoying effect, often provoking a poor return due to bad balance. *And,* it is to be noted that the whole process is the soundest procedure defensively as outlined in preceding paragraphs. Thus playing crosscourt from the baseline, if refined and used with subtlety, can be effective offensively in addition to being the sound play from the general tactical approach already described.

One of the more common opportunities to make this play is in returning a service that goes wide to your forehand in the right court. Most servers at once think, "He will hit it to my backhand" (i.e., straight). If you make it look as though he is right, by preparing quickly and lining it up for a straight shot, then swing it decisively crosscourt, it is quite astonishing how many players will be caught going the wrong way. Sometimes the crosscourt, in this context, is an outright winner, even though he served from the side to which you are playing the ball. In any event, it frequently has the twisting effect that is so disturbing and tends to make opponents lose balance and play badly. Quite often they will become disgusted and feel they are having a "bad day," instead of recognizing that you are outplaying them—i.e., *making* them have a bad day.

THE SERVICE

Depth

The service is a baseline shot. Contrary to general belief, aces are comparatively unimportant. There are seldom more than a few in an entire match. But a first-class player almost always serves well enough to retain the initiative and keep an opponent on the defensive. This means the server is calling the plays, as it were, and the receiver seldom gets a chance to make any plans of his own. The greatest attribute a service can have is to land consistently deep in the service court with reasonable weight behind it, thus holding the receiver back as far as possible. It is comparable to the way boxers often use a left jab; as long as that is in your face how can you get at him? A firm deep service can be returned, but it is very difficult to play it aggressively unless it is put right up to one's forehand.

Most tennis players have neither the skill, the wrist, nor the accuracy to use a cannonball effectively. They make one or two aces a day, and the rest are faults: a reasonably unintelligent use of large amounts of energy. But a "pressure serve"—in which body weight rather than wrist snap imparts firmness and pace to the ball—is definitely within the potential ability of almost everybody. It is covered in the

technical section of this book (Chapter 5). Suffice it to state here that respectability, not brilliance, should be the goal, and it is a fact that most players pursue the opposite tack: they whale away—and miss and miss. Even quite a few teachers and writers emphasize the hard flat service with lots of wrist action as the ideal everyone should pursue; and this is sad, since it is for the best only, and even the best should develop a reliable, respectable smooth spin service before they fool around with jazzy cannonball aces. Anyone who doubts this has only to observe the best players: what do they do when they miss the first ball? They fall back on a spin service that *always* goes in and has enough kick to inhibit a counterattack. Watch a mediocre player: he falls back on nothing—i.e., a hapless "poop shot." Such a player has no right to attempt brilliant shots since he has as yet no average shot. Don't try to run while you still should be learning to walk.

Playing a Weakness

Any respectable service can give the server one great advantage: to put the first ball to his opponent's weakness. This is again incomparably more important than achieving maximum power. Furthermore it is within anyone's talent, while the big ace is definitely beyond most players, even fairly good ones.

A tennis match is decided not by the merits of the players but by the *relative* merit of the two players. If by continually obliging an opponent to play from his weaker side you can make him play beneath his best potential, then even if you are not the greatest you may be better than he is when thus at his worst. Your service is the big chance to force him to make his poorer shot—again and again. Keep at it: you may achieve a breakthrough—i.e., he will blow up. In average tennis this sort of strategy is of extreme importance, for few average players are equally effective on both sides. When you serve remember that an ounce of intelligence is worth a pound of power.

Variety Plus Brains

If you are playing a good defensive player, he will continually be developing counterplays to your best efforts. (See the subsequent topic, "Return of Service.") If you just keep on doing the same thing, you will find yourself having more and more trouble, because he is adapting to your play. What "got him" at first doesn't get him any longer. If you just keep at it he will soon be breaking your service. Change for the sake of change is pointless, but you must vary your delivery at times to retain the initiative. How? By varying the speed, the amount of spin, the placement, and the "break" of the ball. Many players hate a service that is right at them. Others have trouble with a ball that breaks into them. An occasional "bloopy" ball —a high, slow, deep service with heavy spin— can upset the other fellow's timing just when he thinks he has accustomed himself to your serve and can handle it well. Some players are thrown off by an occasional wide breaking ball to their forehand in the right court. This also prevents them from "laying" for the serve to the backhand.

This all sounds very complicated. But once you learn how to put a *lot* of spin on your service you can use *any part* of this spin—a little, quite a bit, or a lot. This permits a variety of deliveries, which is very disconcerting to an opponent and fosters the defensive attitude you wish him to have.

Obviously this is advanced tennis. But it is within the reach of many players who now never think of it. They have a big first one and a standard second ball. Whenever they have a spell of missing the big one—and everyone does—they are in trouble, because a good defender soon accustoms himself to the set problem of the second ball. Such players would be well advised to vary their *first* service, use spin, and *get it in*, only occasionally using their much beloved bomb. Their results, on percentage, would be far higher, without any increase in their intrinsic athletic ability.

THE RETURN OF SERVICE

Limited Options

The return of service is the receiver's attempt to minimize the advantage the server has of making the first shot. There are several possibilities, and one's choice is not a free one—it depends on the server. If he follows to net, then the receiver's job is to stand in just as far as he dares with the object of getting the ball back as soon as possible. A very short or zero backswing is necessary because of tempo and the desire to land the ball short: at his feet is ideal. It is foolish to attempt a winner since the action is too fast for sharpshooting if his service is at all a forcing one. The receiver should try to avoid setting it up, try to make him volley from as far behind the net as possible, try to get him in trouble with a view to passing him on the next shot—or lobbing him if he gets way in.

If the server does not take the net, the receiver should give himself a little more time and try for a good deep return, thus achieving parity in the exchange that will follow.

Once in a while someone has a lefty twist or something else that is just too tough; the receiver is baffled, cannot seem to get a decent return. There is still one play to make: drop back and lob high. The receiver should make him earn the point instead of giving it to him. While this is of course an admission of defeat in one sense, it is right in line with the best thinking: "Try everything" is what we are told, and this is good advice.

One rule should never be broken in returning service. *Always* move forward into the ball. If the receiver moves back, the return is inevitably weak, short, and often pops up. The pressure of the body weight gliding forward as the racket plays the ball is what makes the shot firm, whether it is a topspin drive, a chip, a hard slice, or a lob. This is not always easy to remember in a long match. The player must keep reminding himself, "Move into that serve, move into that serve."

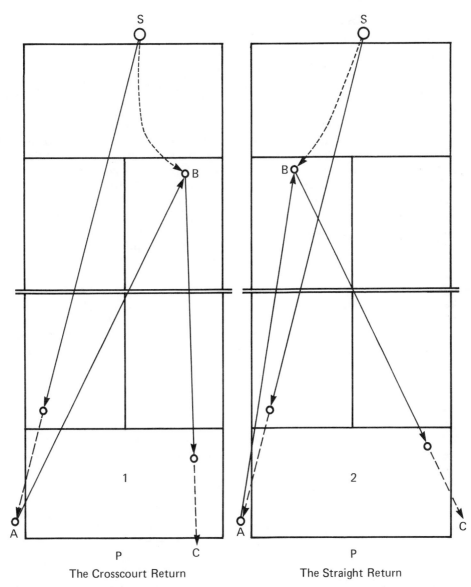

The Crosscourt Return   The Straight Return

Diagram 13–2. The crosscourt return of service is best. A wide service returned crosscourt (1) cannot be angled away from the defender as it can be if played back straight (2). Note how the defender, at C, is much closer to good position (P) in making his second shot. Note that in (2) the defender is completely off the court at C. This defensive gain is even greater if the server does not rush the net.

Pancho Gonzalez was most famed for his big service, but many observers were more impressed by the fact that Gonzalez was a great serve breaker. Anything to his forehand was whipped back hard and viciously with top-spin that made it arc decisively downward after crossing the net so it was difficult to volley for a winner and often got the attacker into trouble. His backhand return of the high bouncers they fed him was heavily sliced and taken as high as possible so he could angle it sharply crosscourt and downward. He had this slice so perfected that he could place it repeatedly as much as halfway from the service line to the net—a truly phenomenal angle. Gonzalez was completely a percentage player, keeping his return low, scrambling like a cat, very observant to find which side of an opponent's volleying was more prone to err, always making it tough, making trouble, refusing to make the error. Too much has been written about his service, reflexes, and general athletic ability. His most important characteristic was astuteness: like all great champions, he always seemed to find a way.

The return of service should always be crosscourt for the same reasons one should hit other baseline shots crosscourt. As with other drives, the straight shot should be avoided unless the player feels he has an ace coming up, or is making a strong approach off a weak service, or wishes to pull a surprise.

Breaking Service

A good player will very rarely "lose" his service. The receiver must break it. The great champions have always been amazingly aggressive, to the point of recklessness, in their returns. Why? Because against a first-class opponent they know they have everything to gain and nothing to lose; they are losing his service anyway. This attitude can be systematic—planned ahead—which markedly increases its chance of success. Perhaps the best plan is for the receiver to develop a very aggressive forehand return: attack the ball, hit it hard, even follow it to net if he has half a chance. If he can pull off even a few of these, it cannot help but affect his opponent's thinking. The server becomes wary of his forehand and this is a defensive attitude. He tends to serve always to the receiver's backhand, which means the receiver is now controlling his thinking, forcing him to play where he expects

it, and this permits the receiver to anticipate far more effectively on that side. So the whole process of winning his service becomes more difficult for the server, because his options become limited and his attitude more cautious.

Jack Kramer was a player of this type—very aggressive and dangerous with his forehand return, solid and always there for it on his backhand. A more recent and very effective exponent of this approach is Stan Smith. He keeps banging away at his opponent's service, very aggressively with his forehand, and he is bound to get lucky somewhere along the line, meanwhile supported by his own almost unanswerable delivery. It is very hard indeed to break Stan Smith more than he breaks you, even if you have the talent and the experience.

For most of us this discussion is seemingly academic, dealing as it does with all-time greats of super ability. But the lesson applies at every level of advanced play. Leaving out the money players and dropping down to ordinary "good" tennis, there are many players who have quite strong services but are not good at breaking service. The mental attitude is what is important: develop a plan for breaking service. Note the word "break": it implies a positive act, as when we smash or shatter something. It is not a defensive word. It implies aggression and attack, taking the initiative away from the opponent, making him react to you instead of you to him.

The average good player can improve his effectiveness considerably by developing a plan like those described above. Too many players of considerable ability have no plan: they just try to get the ball back and hope for a break. They are thus open to all the variety of options possible for a good server, and the pressure is all on them, little if any on the server. By contrast, the most effective defenders somehow manage to get a lot of the pressure back on the server, making him do a lot of worrying, too.

This can all be expressed in another way. It has been said that any short ball should be attacked. A short ball was described as any shot that lands near or inside the service line.

Certainly any ordinary service fits these specifications perfectly. If it lands a little short, if it lacks good pace, if it comes right to the racket without necessitating much footwork, it qualifies as an opportunity to take the net. The reason most players don't take the net when returning mediocre second services is because they tend to be defensive minded when receiving. This should not be the case. A service to a player's forehand is a short ball that bounces up fairly high to what should be his most aggressive shot. He should attack it. A second service that is a little short to his backhand is a chance to make a slice approach and move in. Any advanced player can, by practice, become very dangerous as a receiver, and can thus hope to break through opponents of equal ability more than they break through him. One doesn't have to be a Stan Smith to make the most of one's talent and technical equipment. Good thinking pays off at any level of advanced play.

Courage

There is yet another way to come at this problem of breaking service. If a player has a fine service, and is defeating you on his service with inevitable regularity, what have you to lose? If you try five different ploys and they all fail, are you any worse off than before? Therefore, you should never let fear of missing hold you back from trying anything and everything. Stand in and block and chip; stand back and whale away; stand back and lob; whack it back right at him and scramble for the volley; leave your forehand a little open and cover the backhand better; take the second service on the rise and follow to net. Try whatever is within your technique, so you either find a way or prove beyond any question that you cannot break his service; and in the process do not let fear of failure inhibit your courage, for then you will not only lose but will also have the worst feeling of all: you didn't do your best. Breaking service is in considerable part a matter of being reasonably daring in the use of your resources.

Develop a positive attitude and work on him; don't just stand there and let him work on you.

Working for Success

All the above reads inspiringly, and perhaps leads a reader to think he can now rush out and tear peoples' serves to pieces. It's not quite that easy. Learning to hit a ball hard with minimum preparation (almost no backswing) on the forehand isn't easy; it requires practice and initial failure. Taking a spinning service on the rise and chipping it to a net-rusher's feet is a tough problem in itself that comes only with much practice. Lobbing a spinning service is difficult. The spin "takes" on the racket and the ball goes askew. Just enough chip or top must be imparted to knock his spin off and substitute your own feel. It is not easy. Even more difficult is the skill involved in taking a rising ball quickly on the backhand, with a closed-face racket, and topspinning it back for a dipping return. The combined move-press-and-chip involved in turning a return of service off the backhand into a net attack is much easier to conceive than to execute.

These are the arts of "breaking" service, of achieving a counterplay that establishes parity and occasionally even wrests the offense away from the server. They should be drilled by advanced players, one at a time, repeatedly, until the defender "gets the hang of it." If one adopts a basic attitude that is constructive, aggressive, and reasonably versatile, the results can be remarkable over a period of time. By contrast, if a player is passive in his defense against service, he will win only when his opponent gets sloppy and makes bad errors. He will never "break" anyone's service—he will win only when an opponent loses his service. Thus the proper mental attitude toward defense is the first essential; if followed up with intelligent practice, it can build that indispensable skill: the ability to break even a good service from time to time. It should be added that this attitude and skill increases the fun of the game—for the defender—to a marked degree, because he now has plans, ideas, much more hope of success, and welcomes the challenge. The work required to achieve skill is amply repaid.

DEFENSE

The Lob

There is only one truly defensive shot—the lob. And the lob, 90 percent of the time, *is* a defensive shot. There is altogether too much folderol written about the "offensive lob." While this is a legitimate shot, it is a tricky addition to one's game, but the defensive lob is fundamental. One can get along very well without the offensive lob, but no one can do without a defensive lob. It is the best shot whenever one is in trouble, particularly if one's opponent is at net.

The best lob is a high lob. Most people try to sneak the ball just above an opponent's racket; he takes one step back and kills it. When a player lobs, the idea should not be to win the point but to avoid losing it. A high lob that is at all deep is extremely difficult to kill, even for those with good overheads. A player who has mastered the touch of a high lob may be down, but he is never out.

The offensive lob is an option shot. It is made with a sharp loop swing to get heavy topspin. This deceives an opponent—hopefully—into thinking the player is attempting a passing shot. He closes in only to see the ball go over his head, arc into the court, and jump toward the fence because of the spin It is impossible to catch up to it. It can be quite devastating against a player too eager to commit himself in closing in at net. It is also useful in doubles when both opponents are close in. However, it is a very difficult shot to execute and should be ignored until one's basic game is pretty well developed. The player should get a dependable high defensive lob first—and all the other basic shots too—then try the tricky ones like the offensive lob.

There is another offensive lob: the quick chip or poke on return of service in doubles. This is effective when a server's partner is playing very close to the net. The receiver moves in on the serve and pokes it quickly over the net man's head with a little chip stroke. This ball, not having any topspin, is easily retrieved —but the retriever has lost the net position. Moreover, the net man will henceforth tend to be more careful, thus giving the receiver more room for a regular crosscourt return. This shot is much easier to acquire than the topspin lob.

Passing Shots

The knack of passing an attacking net player is a real art. No one can become at all proficient at it except by experience. Above all it is a battle of wits, with each player attempting to fathom the other's intent. The defender should try his very hardest to be ready (racket out) a little bit ahead of time so he can hesitate uncommitted for a split second. This forces the net player to hesitate, too, and the hope is he gets stuck or filled with inertia, so that when the shot is suddenly unleashed he will get a bad start for it. There is nothing like a little doubt to bust up an attack.

It is as a rule unwise to try a clean pass. This is too difficult and leads to an excess of errors that more than cancel out the aces. It is better to attempt a two-shot play: the defender should make his opponent stretch and volley up on the first one, then pass him or lob him with the second. He should get the opponent in trouble and give him a chance to miss. This takes pressure off the defender and adds to the opponent's load.

An artful defender always prepares the same way whether he intends to go crosscourt or down the line or lob. If he always prepares for the straight shot, he can either play straight or take the ball a jiffy sooner and pivot to carry it crosscourt. From the same position he can lob. Thus by assuming a perfect position to hit straight, he has actually prepared three shots. The sense—or intuition—of where to hit depends on the context (What happened last time?) and on experience, observation, and a knowledge of when one's pet shot will "get him."

There are several types of passing shots. The hard flat streaker, straight down the line, is calculated to go right by him: speed counts. This shot should be made uncompromisingly or not at all. The defender must know if he is sufficiently set to pull it off; it is a try for a clean pass and should not be attempted unless things are at least a little favorable. The more usual passing shot carries a good bit of forward spin so it will dip soon after crossing the net. While a little speed is sacrificed to get this effect the advantages outweigh this loss. An opponent is often forced to volley up and so cannot be decisive, whereupon the defender gets another improved chance to pass or lob. Again as a result of the spin the ball can be made to drop shorter, and this permits a considerably sharper crosscourt angle than one would dare to attempt with a flat shot.

This matter of spin can be carried to extremes, and this produces what one might call a teaser: a ball that doesn't go fast but makes a very sharp angle. In doubles particularly this

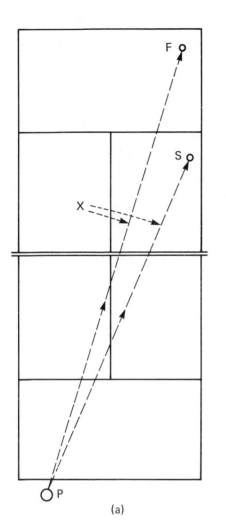

(a)

Diagram 13–3a. Topspin sharpens the angle. The defending player (P) can put the ball much farther away from his opponent (X) by using considerable topspin to make the ball dip into the court at S. By contrast, a hard flat shot needs the full depth of the court to allow it to drop, so must be aimed to F, passing much closer to X.

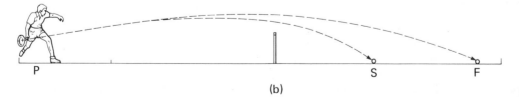

(b)

Diagram 13–3b. Flight of the ball: with spin (S), without spin (F), played from P.

permits a player to attempt a pass when any other stroke would merely play the ball stupidly to a net player. Some make their teasers with slice, particularly on the backhand, and if the direction is well disguised this shot can be effective.

Topspin verging on the excessive can also be used to advantage to get the ball to a man's feet at net, setting up the next shot for a winner. This type of passing shot is vulnerable to a player who closes very fast and catches the ball while it is hovering above the net. However, when combined judiciously with the lob —to prevent a premature advance by the net player—it can often get him into a lot of trouble.

On the forehand side many players use the open stance, which facilitates return to position and scrambling for the next volley. If one masters a "slider" (a forehand that is made with a crosscourt swing but a laid-back wrist so it goes down the line by sliding off the racket to the right) and a similar backhand trick, this defensive attitude can be very effective. It is particularly adapted to the two-shot plan previously discussed: loop to his feet, scramble for the volley, pass or lob on the second shot—the "get him in trouble first" approach.

The most important principle that needs to be learned by young players about defensive play is that the objective is to get the attacker in trouble rather than to ace him. The latter course puts too much pressure on the defender, who, if he thinks this way, often attempts the nearly impossible and of course fails too often. The cagey defender will go for an *easy* pass every time, but he tries very hard to avoid errors, meanwhile giving the attacker as many low nasty loops as he can, mixing in high lobs that are tough to kill. On any surface this attitude is the best; it makes the other fellow earn all he gets, gives him many chances to miss, and takes full advantage of any lapses— and who doesn't fall off now and then in his accuracy when rushing in? The best defense is to play tough; let the other fellow try to be brilliant. You will win more than your share.

Another aspect of passing shots should be

touched on: position play. The straight passing shot goes directly past an opponent, while a crosscourt shot tends to linger in front of him longer. The crosscourt is the hypotenuse; the straight shot is the side. Therefore, if the attacker does not cover his alley well, much capital can be made by playing hard and straight. As will appear in the section on the halfcourt (Chapter 14), the attacker supposedly covers the alley if he knows his business, but perhaps he is worrying about a crosscourt at the moment and leaves an opening. Every lapse of this sort is an open door to a keen defender, who should watch for them and seize the chances so presented. The point is that the straight shot goes past so quickly that one cannot scramble for it—one must *be there*. By the same token, if the attacker is not there he is open to being passed. Here again experience is the great teacher—to sense that now is the time to shoot one straight down the line. But this intuitive knowledge is based on a feeling for whether or not the attacker is covering his alley thoroughly.

The lob has been discussed, but no treatment of passing shots is any good without considering the essential role played by the lob. A basic concept of any good defender is that he *must* lob here and there all along, even if the opponent has a good overhead. Why? Because if he does not lob, the attacker can move in very close to the net, and it is then just about impossible to pass him. See Diagram 13–4. If he must hang back a step or two for a possible lob, a crosscourt may now make him stretch or be very low when he reaches it. If he comes in a step farther over to cover the crosscourt, he is open to the straight shot. But what makes *both* shots possible is the fear of the lob, so lob one must no matter how lethal the overhead. This, of course, is the defensive lob, high and deep.

In defending against a net rush one should never ignore the wind, and there usually is one. To pass downwind is to invite disaster. If you aim it extra far in so it won't blow out, he gets it easily. The smart play is to aim at the upwind side, play the shot pretty close to the line, and

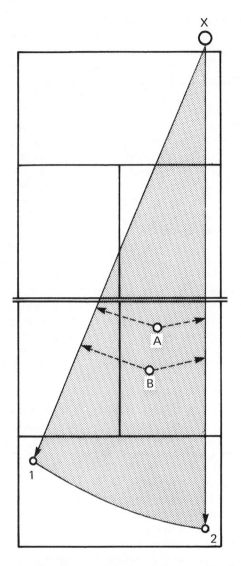

Diagram 13–4. From X a defender must play to the shaded area. Judicious lobbing forces an attacker to hover at B. Without this restraint he could close to A from where passing shots are easy to reach and easy to kill.

trust to the wind to keep it in. Thus the wind can be used and is not entirely a curse. Of course, the net player may cover the upwind shot, attempting to force a downwind error. In this case the defender should lob, or loop for his feet right at him. In any event the player

should not let the opponent get him playing against the percentages.

Often the sun is important. It is wise to lob much more when the attacker is looking into the sun and try more passing shots from the other end. This sort of astute play is by no stretch "mean"; it is good tough competitive tactics just as available to one's opponent. And a player can be fairly certain that if the opponent does not take advantage of these opportunities it is due not to a noble heart but to an empty head.

The Importance of Defense

Enough has been said to show that defensive tennis is not to be frowned on and ignored in favor of the more appealing idea of the offense. An effective campaign to stem an opponent's attack requires an excellent varied technique, imagination, ingenuity, and a lot of fight. And one great truth that is often overlooked in discussions of tennis is the fact that all the truly great champions have had *both* a good defense and a powerful offense. This book does not wish to espouse the fallacious position that tennis is not an offensive game. It is definitely an offensive game, but it is also a defensive game (50 percent of the time). Young players should be aware of this and should be persuaded to see the crucial importance of an effective defense even if it is less glamorous. Last, defensive play is a lot of fun *if* you are good at it. To work and work until an opponent's ability to hold his service is undermined, this is as important as holding your own service.

Today Chris Evert is a shining example of the importance of defense. She is still developing her net game and is recognized as being in the growth stage offensively. Yet so staunch, canny, and rocklike is her defense that she is already a top player and a threat to any other woman in the world. If she ever develops an offense comparable to that of Billie Jean King, she may well become one of the all-time greats. Return of service, deception, and accuracy in passing shots, mad scrambling, and fine touch on the lob—these are just as important, as exciting, and as rewarding as a big service, volley, and overhead.

Slicing

Most of this defensive play requires a lot of skill. A good question sure to arise would ask how a learner should get started; it all sounds pretty tough. The first answer is the lob. If a beginner learns first to keep the ball in play and to lob whenever attacked, he can proceed from there to add passing shots and all the rest if he has the time and talent to keep progressing. But there is a second answer that is important; it is used by just about all players who get any reasonable distance beyond the beginner stage but is almost never taught by teachers: this is to slice. It can be used whenever a ball comes so deep one must take it on the rise, or so fast one is hurried a little or a lot, or so high one cannot play it comfortably, or so low it is hard to dig it up. In sum, just about whenever one is pressed the answer is a slice (the word *slice* as used here includes all cut balls, chops as well as slices). A flat block is always sliced a little. All so-called chips are actually small swing slices. Digging up a very low ball often forces a player to go under it (slice) in order to lift it enough to get it over the net. And a quick chopping stroke when flattened out horizontally is what we call blocking back a very fast shot such as a hard service.

All these shots are admissions that we do not have time to execute our "ideal" stroke or that things are too inconveniently arranged (too high or low) to make our regular stroke possible. In golf this would be inexcusable, but in tennis these compromises are merely the recognition of the facts of life: an opponent is continually trying to get us in trouble, and sometimes he succeeds. A book can ignore the effects of tempo and an opponent's skillful plans, but a player cannot. A look through several tennis books will show how many advocate

practicing this sort of defensive racket work. Many books point out that it is an inferior way to hit the ball and should be avoided like the plague; meanwhile, all good players continue to do it, not by preference but because they *must*: it best does the job of keeping them in the game when in trouble.

It is of crucial importance not to try what is impossible, and it is equally important not to teach it. If an instructor tells a student, "Always play your backhand in this manner," he should be sure to add, "provided you can arrange things decently to execute it, but you must (note the 'must') also learn to chop and slice when in trouble."

Here again we come to racket work. Versatility with the racket is the key to approaching that ideal we describe as "knowing all the answers." Again it is pointed out that much more time should be put on this as contrasted with footwork or any other aspect of play.

Defensive slicing can be carried to great heights by great players. Of course, average players cannot hope to attain these heights, but they can and should appreciate the function of chops and slices and other so-called wrong ways to play the ball. And one doesn't have to be a champion to learn to block-slice and "hack" when pressed. This should be part of the instruction given intermediate players: make them slice the ball back and forth until they can both produce a slice and handle it; the kick bounce presents a real problem to those unfamiliar with it.

The ability to deal with a cut ball is another aspect of tennis technique that all too often is left out of the curriculum. Any kind of a slice or chop will completely confuse inexperienced players. If they are taught to practice cutting, then they also automatically acquire experience in dealing with it. They learn to recognize the various kicks and to anticipate enough so they are not hopelessly unprepared. Above all they learn never to take a cut ball on the rise, because the kick is to some extent unpredictable; therefore, any attempt to prejudge it is too often doomed to failure on a percentage basis. While this is less true on a hard surface, it is a real trap on a clay or composition court, where to rush a cut ball invites nearly certain disaster. Any average tennis player can learn these things and needs to learn them; some of his opponents are sure to use slice—and what then?

One note for doubters: watch Rod Laver, one of the latest great players. He slices, loops, and hits flat—all with ease and with full knowledge of when each is most effective. As in Tilden's time there are other equally fine athletes but few with comparable racket technique. Even those of us (all of us) who are not his equal still need to learn these tricks: at *any* level of athletic ability racket work will make the difference between otherwise equal contestants.

QUESTIONS

1. Why should baseline tactics be mostly negative?

2. What shot is best from the baseline? Give reasons.

3. How can a player "twist" his opponent?

4. What is the most basic attribute of a sound service?

5. Which is more important: a big first service or a reliable, respectable second service?

6. How can a player inhibit an opponent with his service?

7. How can a player keep the receiver in doubt in advanced tennis?

8. Why is adaptability indispensable in returning service?

9. How should one react to a net-rusher's service?

10. How should one react to a server who does not follow in?

11. What is one's last resort in returning service?

12. How important is the use of one's weight in service return?

13. Where should one aim a return of service as a general policy?

14. What mental attitude is desirable in trying to break service?

15. Does a conservative attitude work well in trying to break service?

16. Is it possible to have a plan for breaking service?

17. What sort of serves can be attacked?

18. Can a defender control the play to some extent when the other fellow is serving? How?

19. How can a player perfect his ability to break service?

20. Is the offensive lob an important shot?

21. What should be the objective when one lobs?

22. What are the two most important characteristics of a good defensive lob?

23. Describe two types of offensive lobs.

24. Is it wise to go for a winner on a passing shot?

25. What technical skill is necessary to the use of the open stance in defending?

26. Why is *very* quick preparation necessary for deception?

27. Is spin important in passing shots?

28. Does it do much good to lob against a good overhead?

29. Do great players lob much?

30. How much of tennis is defensive?

31. Can defense be fun and a source of pride, as in football?

32. What has slicing got to do with defensive play?

33. Is it important to know how to slice?

34. Name some uses of slicing.

CHAPTER 14

Area Two—The Halfcourt

ATTACK

The hope from the baseline is to win the rally, not the point. Winning the rally means that one's opponent makes the first poor shot—that is, one that lands short and permits the player to advance a couple of steps or more inside the baseline to play the ball. If he tries to attack and rush before he gets such an opportunity he is reckless and foolish. If he fails to attack once this chance occurs he is "chicken," as the saying goes. Many players vary between the extremes of overeagerness and excessive caution. The attempt here is to draw a line in an area that is admittedly gray, but it is a line that every player of any quality must draw for himself. The line drawn here is a good starting point and can be subject to modification per individual preference when players become advanced.

As in defensive baseline play, one who attacks from halfcourt should not try for or expect an ace. It may happen—through deception or unexpectedly good execution—that one gets a winner, but it is not percentage to try for so much success with one shot only. Again the percentage play is to get him in trouble with the first shot, finish him off with subsequent shots—at net. If the approach shot does its job, it will force a return sufficiently weak so that the attacker will be given a reasonable opportunity to make a telling volley or overhead. If the approach shot is placed to one side, the other side must be open for a placement.

The Center Theory

There is a lot of talk about the "center theory": place the approach shot directly down the middle of the court, thereby reducing the angles open to the defender. While the angles are indeed reduced, this type of attack is only for the very finest exponents of the volley, because the approach shot puts the defender into perfect position, leaving no opening for the attacker's subsequent volley. This means the attacker must plan on two volleys—one a preparatory forcing shot and a second to kill. Thus a considerable extra burden is placed on the attacker's net play, and it is obvious only a few players are sufficiently accomplished to make the system work. Likewise, not many defenders are so versatile off both wings as to inspire the caution implicit in the center theory: the attacker is admitting he is afraid to attack either side of his opponent's game. So we are left with the rare occasions when we have two players of unusual talent and skill. Another way of saying it is that the center theory is a fallacy except in the top 2 percent

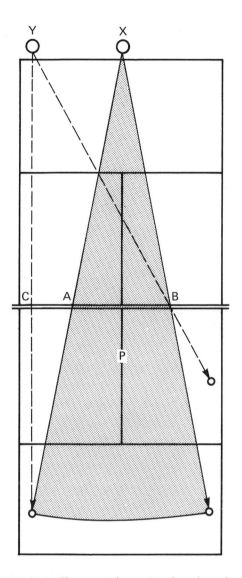

Diagram 14-1. The center theory. Attacking down the center to X gives the defender no decisive angle either way, and reduces the width of net that must be covered from the net position (P). Note how much more width of net is available from the side Y—that is, from C to B, while the center attack limits the defender to A–B. The other side of the coin is that the center attack leaves the defender in perfect position, while attacking one side opens the other side. Thus the center theory limits BOTH the attacker and the defender, and is recommended only for topnotch exponents of the volley and overhead. The diagram is slightly exaggerated to make the difference clear. The angle shot Y through B is pretty tough!

of all players. The other 98 percent will do better to open the court with their attacking shot by placing the ball to one side, with the idea of advancing to the net to exploit the opening thus created. The center theory sounds tricky and unusual and intriguing, and there is no harm in trying it if one is looking for an out, but it is a good generalization to state flatly it is not for most of us. Like the "offensive lob," it falls into the frill class as contrasted with basic skills.

Attack a Weakness

There are two standard methods of attack. The first is to avoid all theory and play a pronounced weakness at every opportunity if such a weakness is present. The second, advisable when an opponent is equipped in a reasonably balanced manner, is the theoretically correct approach: hit straight, go to net covering the alley, volley and overhead to the open side.

The first method would seem not to need any discussion, but it does. Very few players realize what "playing a weakness" means. They hit the first shot there, then when a poor return comes back they play the other side—whereupon the opponent plays his strong shot and is back in the saddle. Playing a weakness means to play *every shot with no exceptions* to the vulnerable side until an error occurs or a clean ace is possible to the strong side. The ideal objective is that the opponent shall never play his strong shot—not even once—throughout the match. If his backhand is poor, the attacker should keep the ball going to that side until a weak shot occurs, then put the approach shot to his backhand and go to net; then volley or smash to his backhand until such a weak return is presented that a sure winner can be made to the forehand side. The only exception is that one must play an occasional—but *very* occasional—shot to the strong side if an opponent shows too much of a tendency to cover up his weakness in his position play.

This unrelenting policy against a weakness requires more mental discipline than most people realize. So many other possibilities keep popping up—*all* of which must be resisted and discarded. It doesn't take much of a letup to allow an opponent to make a comeback. To be effective the plan must be applied with true thoroughness without any relaxation after a lead has been built up. This is not easy, for psychological reasons: forcing an opponent to play his worst shot repeatedly tends to create the impression that he really isn't very good after all. So carelessness follows and gives him a lot of chances to show his strength, and the whole complexion of the match changes. As the saying goes, the fish gets off the hook because you slack up on the line. So a player shouldn't say, "This fellow is easy to beat; all I have to do is play his backhand." Instead he should say, "I can win this if I concentrate on his backhand and never let up." The second way of putting it is much nearer the truth. It recognizes that although he has a weakness he is not "easy to beat," and it recognizes the concentration, determination, and mental follow-through necessary to do the job. When one plays a weakness, he must play it 100 percent all the way.

Hit Straight—Cover the Alley

The second method of attack is to play the approach shot straight down the line and follow straight in behind it. Note the repeated use of the word "straight." The emphasis is on getting well in toward the net before the ball returns. As Diagram 14–2 shows clearly, attacking crosscourt forces one to move across the court instead of forward (there is rarely time for both). This is why a crosscourt approach cannot be justified on theoretical grounds and is to be preferred only if used to maintain a sustained concentration on a recognizable weakness.

This theoretical rule—and it is a very good one—can be stated very simply: play the ap-

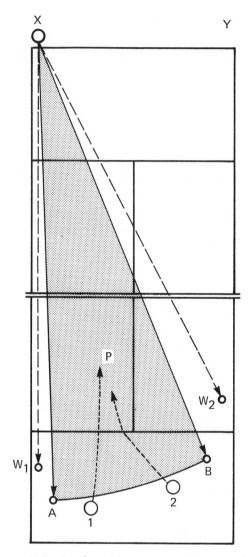

Diagram 14–2. Attack straight—get way in. A passing shot played from X must be somewhere in the shaded area between A and B. If the attacker forces to X from (1), he can go directly in behind his shot; all of his movement is forward, and he can achieve a commanding position (P). If he forces to the same place X from (2), he must move across the court to cover the straight return, and cannot get very far in. He may be in trouble. When playing from (2) he should attack the backhand side (Y). When executed properly, this tactic forces an opponent to give the attacker a chance to win, or forces him to attempt the winners W_1 and W_2, which are nonpercentage if the approach shot was at all severe. Note how decisively the attacker covers the alley in going to P.

proach down the line and go straight in behind it, guarding against the straight shot more than against the crosscourt. As has been previously pointed out, a straight shot will go right past the player—he does not have time to scramble for it—he must almost be there waiting for it. A crosscourt shot tends to linger in front of him, giving just a little more time to dig for it. Therefore a very important rule that must be learned by all net players is: cover the alley, scramble for the crosscourt, not vice versa. This further reinforces the preference for the straight approach shot: he can follow the path of the ball he has hit, and he will be just about in position. Usually a spot about four feet off the center line is not too far over. (This means one's inside foot will be about four feet off the center line.)

It is now apparent that everything done in the halfcourt is governed by the percentages of what will happen immediately thereafter. A forceful straight approach should bother a defender enough so that he cannot have the touch needed for the sharp angle. All other shots must go roughly to where the attacker has stationed himself. He has actually forced the defender to play the ball back to where he is and he hopes to put it away with his volley or overhead. The only recourse left to the defender is to hope for the error or attempt a nonpercentage shot such as the very sharp angle.

Consistent net rushers like Jack Kramer and Pancho Gonzalez in the past, and Stan Smith plus a host of others today, always keep right on coming in even when things go badly for a spell. They have confidence that the relentless march of the percentages will eventually reward the efforts of him who has them on his side. Most of the exploits of the greatest players are accomplished on fast surfaces—hard, grass, canvas, synthetics (most of which are very fast)—so they go right in behind service all or most of the time. However, when they do play on clay or any slow surface they modify their tactics and do not rush the net behind every delivery. Great as they are, their opponents are good also, and a slow surface puts

more premium on caution and patience, so they adjust to the conditions and play with less dash and more circumspection. Immediately halfcourt skills—the ability to pave the way to the net with something other than a service—assume great importance and can be crucial in deciding the winner. This latter situation is the one in which the vast majority find themselves. Unable to make the big serve-volley game go, they must work up to the net by rallying from the baseline until an opportunity occurs, then move in behind an approach. Thus for all players except the very best, halfcourt skills are an unavoidable necessity if they are to attack successfully.

There has been a great tendency for younger players to try to play on clay the way Stan Smith plays on a fast surface. This whole idea is of course unsound and it is important not only to discourage it but to make clear why it represents fallacious thinking.

HALFCOURT AND BASELINE DIFFERENCES

The techniques required to carry out halfcourt tactics present a sharp contrast with baseline techniques. At the baseline one plays high above the net, hits crosscourt, and aims deep. From the halfcourt position he must aim low, hit straight, and aim short. Why aim short? Because he is partly in to the net when he plays the ball, so it is easy to hit it out; there is less available distance between him and the other baseline. Again, the player is moving in, and this momentum tends to carry the ball out, making it advisable to aim short to counter this risk. Third, if we aim a bit short we can make a greater angle and open the court wider. Usually to aim about five feet behind the service line gives good results; a good many of the shots go somewhat deeper, but few go out, and more angle is possible. See Diagram 14–3.

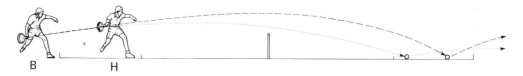

B   H

Diagram 14–3. Baseline and halfcourt shots contrasted. One is long and high, the other low and short. One goes up, the other straight to down.

DECISIVENESS AND DECEPTION

If deception can be even partially achieved it often makes that half-step difference that hurries the defender just enough to impair his touch. So a very short backswing, a closed face in preparing the racket, a little hesitation before striking, a quick sharp swing and a carry-through of everything behind the racket (for the player is rushing the net)—these are the technical characteristics of a good approach shot. When properly executed, the finish of the shot leaves the attacker at the net; he sweeps in as part of the shot rather than as an aftermath. If he hits the net he should be there to pick up the ball.

A very common fallacy with learners is to make a shot and then assess the situation: was it good enough to warrant following in? This is dead wrong, for the late start usually leaves the attacker in "no man's land"—not far enough in to be decisive offensively, not far enough back to be in a sound position to continue the rally. The decision must be made ahead of time and it must be irrevocable—a total commitment without any reservations—or it is that worst of all sins, an indecisive decision. It is better to be wrong than to be hesitant.

The whole approach shot must be planned on this basis. The decision to go in is made as soon as the short ball is seen to emerge from an opponent's racket. If the attacker is very alert and quick in preparing the racket and feet, he will have a little bit of extra time to *wait*—just before he hits. This tiny hesitation is invaluable, not only for deception but to aid in achieving an exact aim. To draw back and swing at once resembles firing from the hip with a six-shooter. While there are all kinds of legends about putting out the eye of a gopher at a hundred yards while galloping across rough terrain and firing instantaneously from the hip, the fact is nobody can ever hit anything that way except by luck or after an unbelievable amount of practice devoted to this one skill. In spite of the westerns this is true: to hit a target consistently one must take aim. To take aim requires time—time which is used to line up the racket, ball and target area, so the ball can be pressed truly to an exact spot. While this principle of aiming is true for any shot any time, it is far more emphatically necessary in the halfcourt from where a player tends to sharpshoot—i.e., pick a smaller target as his objective, striving for a truly excellent shot.

HIT HIGH ONES HARD

Not all short shots are the same, and for this reason they cannot all be handled in the same manner. A ball that is short and bounces up reasonably high—nearly net high or higher—can and usually should be hit hard with some topspin, a forthright rock-em-and-sock-em approach. This is particularly true on the forehand side where a reasonable amount of practice should develop a quite lethal attacking weapon. And if a player develops a big punch like this, he should use it on every possible occasion and should not hesitate to run around setups that are slightly to the backhand side of center. One reliable unanswerable attacking shot is worth more than a whole assortment of partially perfected shots. The only person who wants all the shots is the teaching pro; he has to be able to teach them all. But a player wants simplicity and consistency as contrasted with a wide variety, some part of which is always in slight disrepair.

THE SLICED APPROACH—
A KEY SHOT

Many short balls bounce low and present a difficult problem. If hit hard they will go out because of the sharp angle of elevation needed to clear the net. If hit more gently they cease to be effective approach shots. If aimed lower they hit the net. There is only one real answer: the sliced approach. Made with a sharp crossing motion, using heavy side spin, this shot can be placed accurately and will give a low "kick" bounce that forces the defender to hit up and hopefully bothers him enough so that he is at a disadvantage.

The sliced approach is one of the key shots in tennis. In the preceding section on baseline play the value of slicing and chopping for the defense has already been stressed. And here again we are up against a problem to which the ability to slice is the only *good* answer. The matter is stressed consciously in this book, possibly to the point of overdoing it, precisely because one of the most current beliefs— among those who teach as well as among those who play—is the idea that it is "wrong" to slice. Around the club it is considered dirty: "We don't play that way around *here!*" has actually been said many times, accompanied by a slightly superior and self-righteous manner. Ask any young fellow how he wants to play, and he will say, "I want to hit flat," usually looking at you with a somewhat challenging glare which seems to say, "The ideal only is for me. I shall not compromise. Don't give me any of that impure and low-down cut stuff. My game is going to be free of such corruption."

Ask twenty pros "How do you teach people to play the ball?" It is a good bet at least nineteen and probably twenty will talk about flat, or flat with a little top, or some variation on these two. Try and find *one* that will say "I always incorporate the ability to slice into my program," unless you first bring it to his attention. Most teachers ignore it or consciously avoid it as wrong or inferior technique.

By contrast *watch* the better players at just about any level of excellence except beginners. You will see them block-slice when in trouble, you will see them slice low and high backhands, you will see many *good* players who do not have a topspin or flat backhand at all— all they can do is slice. Watch it another way: what is a spin service except a huge premeditated slice? What is a volley, since good volleys always carry a little backspin? In sum, this much maligned slicing is an ever-present element in the game of tennis wherever it is played.

Leaving out prejudice and ignoring current fashionable thinking, let us be reasonable. Why should we think it is a good, effective, clean-cut, ethical thing to do to spin a ball forward to achieve an objective but reverse ourselves and consider it poor, ineffective, underhanded, and inferior to spin a ball the other way to achieve an objective? The only reasonable approach is to ask the question, "Can spin help us?" and to accept any ways in which its use can assist us to our objective of controlling the ball to the discomfiture of our opponents. As far as the ethical considerations go, the habit of saying, "That isn't fair!" to those who use spin is merely an attempt to legislate off the court something one finds hard to handle. There seems to be no verdict as to side spin, possibly because the self-appointed jurists don't recognize it when it occurs.

Topnotch players use spin in a host of subtle ways: curving services in toward the opponent to cramp him, curving them away to make him stretch, creating a kick bounce to bother him, looping heavily for sharp angles, or to get at his feet. All these tricks and many more are based on spin, and many of the spins are created by slicing.

To revert to our subject, the sliced approach, this is the only equipment for attacking the net that most good players possess on the backhand side. A good many will assert they hit the ball "flat," but this is a very loosely used word: almost always there is backspin on the ball, which means that it has been sliced or cut to a greater or lesser degree. And if it is cut to a greater degree—i.e., considerably—it will be more effective because of the low kick bounce that follows, forcing the defender to hit sharply upward. In practicing this shot it is important to try to get a lot of "heavy spin" on it. Methods for achieving this effect are presented in the section on techniques. (See Chapter 7.)

THE LOOPED ANGLE

Some short shots that pull us in happen to be far to the side quite near the line. While these are a little unusual they do occur. It is difficult to play them straight according to theory because there is very little court to aim at unless one goes back toward the center, and this is not good. One answer to these tantalizers is a very sharp crosscourt angle, to the corner of the service court or sharper, and this is facilitated by using comparatively heavy topspin to get the ball to drop before it reaches the alley. This shot technically resembles the defensive sharply angled passing shot, but here it is used to run an opponent hopelessly far out of court.

It is usually unwise to follow this to net, as the alley is wide open, but if the answer is a floating deep return to the backhand, the attacker should be prepared to advance and volley so as to cancel out the time advantage being sought by the defender in his attempt to recover his position. And if the angle is to what the attacker considers a weak side, he may be well advised to follow it to net in spite of the longer distance he must cover to reach a good

position. This is very much a matter of judgment and the skills of the defender as revealed in the context of the match.

THE DROP SHOT

The greatest change of pace shot in tennis is the drop shot. On all soft surfaces it can be literally devastating if used judiciously and with reasonable deception. If prepared in exactly the same way as other halfcourt shots there is no giveaway, and it thus becomes a constant additional worry to the defender. It is just in this way that the drop shot makes its greatest contribution: if an opponent must constantly watch out for it, then he must constantly stay close to the baseline so as to be within reach. He can never drop back that extra step to give himself more time to cope with more forcing shots. Thus these harder shots tend constantly to be more effective because of the threat of the drop, even though it is used only occasionally.

This is a subtlety all too often ignored by those who sneer at the drop shot, like the fellow who once said he never played a drop shot because there was always a better shot. In a way he was right, but in the total picture he was dead wrong. It is exactly comparable to the defensive necessity for lobbing against a net rusher, no matter how good his overhead, to prevent him from closing in too soon and too far to cut off the pass.

On a slow clay or composition court after a rain, the drop shot can actually become almost a major weapon, and in women's tennis it takes on a formidable significance. Women are seldom able to come in nearly as fast as men, but a ball can be dropped just as short by a girl as by a boy. Often players are not too skillful or knowledgeable about what to do with a drop shot once they reach it. In such cases the drop can be a fundamental means of defeating them. In intermediate tennis this is true far more frequently than most players appreciate and goes unexploited because so few players put any time at all into learning a drop. Like the slice approach, the drop shot tends to be neglected by all but the best, perhaps because it is another one of those cut shots that are generally viewed with contempt by players and ignored by instructors.

HALFCOURT TECHNIQUE NEEDS DRILL

Halfcourt technique is by far the least stressed by almost all teachers. This is natural with beginners, who certainly must learn first to keep the ball in play. But with intermediate players, certainly with all players who exhibit any reasonable athletic talent, the ability to make an acceptable approach with forehand and backhand, and the trick of dropping the ball, should be started as soon as moderate rallying skill has been achieved. The usual process is to leap across the halfcourt problem and start teaching them net play. This is good but the instructor should not neglect the shot that gets them there and should not forget that fiendish little weapon, the drop. These errors of omission are committed all too often by pros, particularly school and college coaches. The usual excuse—they still have not yet mastered the baseline fundamentals—is invalid, for very frequently the school boy has been taught the volley. Their practice habits reveal clearly what has and has not been taught them. They practice at the baseline, advance to the net and volley a bit, serve a few, then play. They are unaware that they have neglected about one-third of the techniques necessary for success. In this they reflect their teachers, and it is an omission we should strive to correct.

The basic reason for this failure to teach halfcourt skills is the fallacious assumption that once you have a baseline forehand and backhand this takes care of all forehand and backhand ground strokes anywhere in the court. It is important to draw serious attention to the sharp differences that distinguish baseline from halfcourt techniques so that more of our numerous very competent teachers will give the midcourt area the attention it deserves and needs, and they will recognize that the racket work is drastically different and requires separate attention.

THE APPROACH VOLLEY— FOR GREATS ONLY

There is one halfcourt shot that is pretty much of a modern development, is for the best players only, and is touched on here only as a matter of interest. This is the approach volley. Made with a stiff wrist but a comparatively full arm swing, it enables a player to move to the net even when the ball returns soon, hard, and deep. Played from behind the service line, it attempts to make a short ball out of a deep drive, and if perfected it can be a successful maneuver on any fast surface. It is a big deep-stroked volley, calculated to force a weak return by its pace, and is used as an approach to the net as its name implies rather than as a winner. It reads easy but requires great skill in actual execution. It is not recommended to any except advanced players on fast surfaces. The touring pros use it on canvas and some amateurs on the grass circuit and hard courts; that is about all. The percentage is against it on clay and on composition and for all except the top players.

QUESTIONS

1. Should setups in the halfcourt area be put away?

2. What are the advantages and disadvantages of the center theory?

3. Is "playing a weakness" as easy as it sounds?

4. Why should we hit straight when we attack?

5. When attacking, why should we cover the alley and risk the crosscourt a little?

6. Why are halfcourt skills even more important for the average player than for the greatest players?

7. How does an attacking forehand drive from the halfcourt area differ from a sound baseline forehand drive?

8. Is the popular conception, that approach shots should always be deep, open to question? If so, why?

9. In attacking, how does one achieve deception?

10. Does a player decide to follow to net before or after he plays the ball? Why?

11. On high forehand setups, should one be cagey?

12. What is the best answer to a low short ball?

13. What is the basis for the idea that cutting the ball is "playing dirty"?

14. Do the best players slice?

15. Are there many "cut shots" in tennis?

16. Why do we hear good players say sometimes, "The answer to an angle is an angle"?

17. Under what conditions is the drop shot effective?

18. How can a drop shot help the rest of one's game?

19. Why do halfcourt skills need special attention?

20. Is the approach volley, or "stroked volley," a basic shot?

CHAPTER 15

Area Three—The Forecourt

WINNING THE POINT

The Moment of Truth

The net position is decisive. A player is there to win the point, not merely to return the ball. That is why the net is the never-ending objective of the best players: it is the only area from which aces are possible on a percentage basis. It has been pointed out that it is foolish to attempt winners from the baseline area, and advisable to attack but not to expect an ace from the halfcourt position. Now the shoe is at last on the other foot: if a player is not decisive at net he is not a good player, for he is missing his opportunities. He should go for a winner or a near winner once he gets in close.

The Power Volley

There are a good many ways to make winners. One is the power volley, made with quite a bit of swing, aimed for a large area such as the back corner, calculated to win by sheer speed and pace. It is the nearest thing to an overhead that can be made with a volley. It is possible only if the ball can be taken well above the net so that it can be aimed in a direct line to the target area. It requires a strong wrist, a very firm grip, a good eye, and excellent coordina-

tion, for a good bit of the pace comes from leaning on the shot with the body weight. It is most effective on fast surfaces where the bounce does not take much pace out of the ball. It closely resembles the approach volley except that being executed from closer in, it is used to kill rather than to force, and there is less swing because less length is desired. All in all it is perhaps the most impressive way to finish off a cripple, and gives one a very satisfying superman feeling of prowess.

However attractive this may appear to be, the other side of the coin is most sobering. Most of us are not supermen and fail when we try to be: the wrist is not quite rigid enough, we lose control a little bit, and the shot hits the fence. Or we are not quite coordinated enough to get our weight well into it: it lacks pace and is easy to reach and return effectively. Or, if we are Easterners, the court is very likely clay or composition, and the surface kills the pace even if we succeed in creating quite a bit. Or we are just a little out of practice and can't quite achieve the deadeye accuracy necessary to control such a hard-hit shot. (One should not forget that speed, power, and length magnify even the smallest error into a huge one, as is demonstrated daily on all golf courses: a golf drive that is sliced even a little may easily go astray by hundreds of feet.) How many players are not subject to any of these shortcomings? Not many, and so we are obliged to restrict this type of kill to the greats: playing pros, grass circuit amateurs, and the better hard court players.

The Small Crisp Volley

This shot is the best kill for the majority of players. It does the job, demands no unusual athletic attributes, is suitable for every surface, and does not require more strength than most players possess. It is the shot for everybody and it lends itself to winning by intelligence rather than by sheer physical talent. Most of us will admit we do not have unusual athletic ability, but we like to feel we are at least moderately endowed with brains. It is all this volley requires and with even a little practice will begin to yield results.

The fundamental difference is that the power volley puts the ball through an opponent by force, while the small volley, made with an absolute minimum (two feet?) of swing, uses the other person's power by blocking and seeks to put the ball in a small space as far as possible (not as hard as possible) from an opponent. You should always feel you could have hit it harder but did not choose to. The idea is to "put it away," and note this phrase makes no mention of speed but refers only to the location of the destination of the ball.

The Stop or Drop Volley

If the idea of putting the ball in a very small space is carried to the extreme, the drop volley becomes the logical conclusion. Combined with a deep approach shot which pushes an opponent back, the stop volley obliges him to run the absolute maximum distance to the next shot by dropping the ball very short to the other side. The drop volley is useful on any surface and can be a major weapon on a slow surface or on grass, which, although considered fast because of the skid bounce, will give a very small bounce off a soft shot. The drop requires no great strength, but it does demand

an unusual ability to use the opposite of strength—namely, restraint. It is a very skillful shot—and is also a backfire shot: if you do it badly the ball is set up. In fact, perhaps the most hopeless shot in tennis is a badly executed stop volley: there you are standing at the net as your opponent winds up to polish off the cripple.

As in the case of the power volley, the drop volley is a more advanced shot and must be perfected if it is to be an asset rather than a liability in actual play. It is probably becoming clear to the reader that the small crisp volley represents the happy medium and should be the first objective of everyone who hopes to play net. After this has been mastered to a reasonable degree a player may wish to work up toward a power volley for high balls by swinging a little more and leaning more, and also to experiment with softening up his regular volley until he acquires the knack of making a dink. We come back again to our fundamental principles: learn first what is within everybody's reach, learn first the average workhorse shot, and only later on try for the more difficult extremes of power and touch. The tendency of youngsters to go for the big one right at the start should be discouraged: the *quickest way* to learn a controlled power volley is to perfect an ordinary volley, then expand it gradually. A player of limited talent will not be attempting what is beyond him; he will get something useful with a minimum period of discouraging frustration and failure.

The Half Volley

Every player gets caught with a ball at his feet now and then, either through his own ineptitude or his opponent's skill. This is a difficult shot. The ball is as low as it possibly can be, the net looms high in front of the ball, necessitating an extreme angle of elevation that rules out any idea of using force. The only recourse is to try to be cagey and skillful, and by using a minimum of swing and no power at all the player can hope to sneak the ball back softly and quite low, thus (hopefully) presenting his opponent with a similar problem rather than a setup. Once in a while it is possible to pull off a half volley drop shot for a winner, but this is a pretty brilliant shot and can by no means be counted on. The real answer is for a player never to permit the opponent to put the ball to his feet; when he fails in this regard he should be happy if he can avoid fatal trouble on the next shot. Fundamentally the opponent has defeated the player's purpose, which was to get to net and hit down on him: now the opponent will be hitting down on the player if he does not make a quite clever shot.

The half volley is above all a restrained shot, requiring touch comparable to the drop volley, and is a shot to be avoided whenever possible by closing in and not letting the ball bounce. If a player is rushing in behind a service and his opponent makes a soft short return, trying to make the player volley or half volley from his shoe tops—he shouldn't do it. Stop, let the ball bounce, play an approach shot, then move on in. Thus the player has foiled his opponent's attempt to make him play at a sharply upward angle to the net. In general if a player half volleys he is in trouble.

The Overhead

This is, of course, the real kill shot in the smashing sense—if the player is quite strong, uses his strength, and wins through power. However, control is still necessary and desirable. Often a well placed moderately paced overhead will be a winner, and this is again the shot everybody should learn. It requires only average skill and average brains and average strength. A beginner should perfect this ordinary shot and work up to the more violent smash later on, if he has the strength to aspire to it. Again, the "big" one is acquired more quickly by steps than all at once, and again the player will find his limitations less painfully than through the idealistic all-or-nothing approach.

QUESTIONS

1. What is the objective in the forecourt?

2. Why is the power volley a tough shot for most?

3. Why is the small crisp volley the shot for everybody?

4. Why is the drop volley difficult and dangerous?

5. What is the quickest road to success in learning all three volleys (power, crisp, drop)?

6. Can one be aggressive with a half volley?

7. Why are half volleys to be avoided?

8. Should a "big overhead" be everyone's objective?

V

Doubles

CHAPTER 16

A Lifetime Sport

Doubles is the better half of tennis. This statement, which will surprise many people, is not made without due consideration. There are a good many reasons to justify such a flat assertion.

EVERYBODY'S GAME

Doubles does not require the running and therefore the physical condition demanded by singles; it can be played with pleasure by young and old, men and women, fit, semifit, and unfit. The recent case of the late King of Sweden, who played doubles until he approached the age of eighty, is a good case in point. He could not possibly have played singles this long. So when we see the much publicized slogan "Tennis—the game for a lifetime" we should know it means doubles, not singles. Of course there are a few players who stress condition as a major preoccupation of their lives, or who do almost nothing but play tournaments, and who therefore can say with truth they play singles to keep in condition. But let us face facts: the majority of tennis players play either for fun (without much regard for condition) or in an attempt to counteract their lack of condition. Leading a busy unphysical existence, they frequently lapse into quite bad

shape and say, "I must get some exercise." So they play tennis. Singles, if played with any determination at all, will just about kill such people. Doubles will give them good exercise, some running and jumping about, some healthy huffing and puffing, but it will not run them to death.

Singles is the proving ground of youth where great condition, speed, determination, and sustained concentration are necessary. You never can say, "Yours, partner" in singles when the ball is far away on the other side of the court; you run like mad and get it. Singles is a real physical battle, and there is nothing tougher or more exacting than good singles. Note how fit every top singles player always appears: never an extra ounce, lean and hard, in beautiful condition like a mile runner. This is what the game demands, and if you don't have it, the game will tear you to pieces if you are any good at all. To fully enjoy singles you should be in such fine condition running is a pleasure, not a chore.

What takes place at any good tennis club on a weekend? Take the Longwood Cricket Club in Brookline, Massachusetts: court after court is filled with white-haired people having a grand time playing doubles; only a few courts are being used for singles, usually by younger people. Singles is for the kids; doubles is truly the game for a lifetime.

177

Doubles is more fun than singles. Doing anything in pairs is almost always more pleasurable than doing it alone. Companionship is added to the benefits of the game itself—the outdoors, the exercise, the satisfaction in making shots. Moreover, just because there are four instead of two players there is a lot more strategy and tactics in doubles than in singles. There are more combinations, shot sequences, and two-man plans. By comparison, singles can be dull both to play and to watch. Most experienced devotees of tennis will agree that they lean toward doubles as the more entertaining game to watch and the more pleasurable to play.

Why then is the game of singles stressed far beyond doubles, particularly in the field of publicity? It is because of the tradition we have in all our sports that the important thing is to find the one best player, the champion. A champion pair is not the same thing at all as *the* champion. Therefore, automatically we stress singles as being the more significant part of tennis: the singles title is given far greater weight than the doubles title in most areas; the Davis Cup is four singles and one doubles; and in any great tournament such as Wimbledon the singles events occupy the center of the stage. Doubles formerly got its just deserts once a year at Longwood when the U.S. title was a separate event with no competition from singles, but this was the exception rather than the rule, and it was not considered as important as the National Singles tournament at Forest Hills.

Doubles is a social game perfectly adapted to giving fun to groups, to effecting a desirable mixing by switching partners, and generally to act as a catalyst at a club or a school or a camp or a public park with large groups. Doubles round robins, whether men's, women's, or mixed, are almost always a success at a club on a weekend. Interclub matches that feature doubles more than singles are the more popular because they are the more enjoyable.

There are many fine competitors whose professional lives make it impossible for them to maintain the training schedule demanded by good singles. They can no longer do their best at singles for purely physical reasons. Yet they have the urge to compete, they are still full of fight—they just can't run all day any longer. Doubles is their game; it keeps them in there, in the thick of the fight, and this is a fine thing for all concerned. Long may it be so.

Stressing Doubles

What is our point of view as tennis instructors, or as students learning the game? Is it not so to guide our students or ourselves that all will get the most out of the game throughout their lives? And from this point of view only a few have the talent to hope for great success in singles, whereas anyone with any ability at all can play doubles with pleasure all his life. While an instructor should have his eye out for the talented person (in the local as well as the grand sense) who can achieve a career in singles, he should make a point of teaching everybody the fundamentals of doubles, the fact that it is the most fun, the most sociable, and the game for all one's life.

And there is an important addition to this argument: doubles requires far more varied and all-round racket work than singles. Volleying is inescapable, a beginning must be made on overhead, return of service must be more accurate to avoid the net player, and a lot more thinking is required than in singles where merely getting the ball back crosscourt is the only objective for quite a while. Position play in relation to the whereabouts of the ball becomes of importance. It is a fact that to some extent playing doubles improves one's singles more than playing singles because of the versatility in technique that the game enforces upon all who learn.

Many players will not go to net in singles, and were it not for doubles would be forever limited to service, forehand baseline drive, backhand baseline drive, and the lob. Such people are commonly referred to as "poopers." Even if offered a setup, they move in, play the setup and retreat to the baseline. This craven tactic is usually less an indictment of the player than of his technique: he is not really afraid—he just doesn't have any skill in the halfcourt or forecourt so he quite sensibly avoids both on every possible occasion. Until he adds to his skills this is actually the smartest play open to him; he senses this and acts accordingly.

If all beginners are introduced to doubles, and are taught to stand at net while their partner is either serving or receiving, they never are permitted to become so technically lopsided as the types described in the preceding paragraph. They learn to be at home at the net right from the start, and this naturally tends to become part of their singles play as well as of their doubles. Moreover, their skill at the net position is roughly equal to the skill of the opposition at the baseline—both are beginners. By contrast, if pupils are taught to become quite proficient in one position (the baseline) before they attempt net play, then when they try net they are beginners going against intermediates—an uneven contest which they lose and abandon as a poor play from their point of view. "I'm better if I stay back," they say, and it is true because of this sharp difference in experience. It is not always easy to convince the young, who live very much in the present, that they should take the long view and keep on going to net in spite of poor current results. It is better to try to avoid such a situation in the first place by starting net play right along with baseline play. Doubles gives real meaning to this technical instruction.

OFFENSIVE DOUBLES

Fighting for the Net

Doubles is primarily a battle for the net position. He who is at net can hit down, while anyone not at net must hit up. As in any kind of fight, the fellow on top, hitting down, usually wins. Therefore, the team that most frequently achieves the net position will, as a rule,

dominate the match. It follows that all our tactics revolve around and relate to this most central fact. It has been pointed out that the objective in singles is the net, but it is far more all-important in doubles. Why? Because there are two opponents—an increase of 100 percent—and an increase in width of court to be covered of only nine feet, or 33 percent. Even in singles we cannot win from the baseline because of the narrowness of the court. But the doubles court, in terms of each player, is only eighteen feet wide (half of thirty-six), so that the idea of winning by placing the ball from side to side is completely hopeless: a player can stand in the middle of his half of the court and he is only nine feet from either edge—or one little hop plus a reach. Clearly then we must put the ball *through* him (as contrasted with "put it away"—i.e., where he isn't), or we must get so much on top of the net that we are able to make a truly acute angle in order to put it so sharply to one side that even with two defenders, each specializing in covering his own area, the ball cannot be reached. To put it through him we must also be up there so we can to some extent play down on the opposition.

Few players, even among those who are somewhat advanced, realize the full implication of this fact. It means fight for the net, not some of the time, or most of the time, but all of the time—on your own service and on the other fellow's service also. It is this latter that is most neglected. Everyone knows he is supposed to win his service in doubles by following it to net—but many are unaware that getting to net on the other fellow's service is the best way to break it. A major task that must be faced by all coaches is to teach that a good doubles player is after the net position in all four games, not just during the two when he and his partner serve. And at any time during any point, if he is not at net and his opponents give him any opening at all, he will seize the chance and move forward. This is sound thinking for the simple reason that the truth of what has been said—it is possible to win only at net—does not alter or weaken because the other fellow is now serving. True, the opposition has the initiative, and the task is thus rendered far more difficult, but the nature of the job to be done has not changed at all.

Move In, Move In, Move In

Good doubles players are always moving forward—as they volley, as they return service, as they serve—just about every time they play the ball except when they make a defensive lob. When they are exchanging volleys with an opponent they are on top of the net after two volleys or sooner. Moving in *as* (not after) they play the ball—exactly as one moves in with a singles approach shot—is one of the main characteristics of accomplished doubles players. They do not play the ball and then run to net. They play the ball—and they *are* at net. Not only is this good tactics and good position play but the forward motion of the weight tends constantly to lend more solid authority to their shots. Above all it shows they appreciate that the core of a doubles battle is the struggle for the dominant net position.

Playing the Center—
Covering the Center

Most shots in doubles—probably well in excess of four-fifths—cross the center half of the net. That is, if we divided the net into quarters, most shots would cross one of the two quarters adjacent to the center strap. The ball very seldom crosses the net above the alley on either side. Why does the ball amost always cross the center? First, because so many exchanges are between server and receiver, who are diagonally opposed to each other. Their partners are at net, so neither will play straight since to play directly to a man at net is the game's most stupid shot. So they play diagonally and fight it out—across the center of the net. Second, any ball that is roughly in the center of the court must (please note the word "must," which here means no other choice is possible) be played across the center of the net or it will go out of court. See Diagram 16–1. Naturally,

since people do not wish to err, they play the ball so it will go in—across the middle of the net. Third, the net is lower in the center. Many players like to play the center with the idea of keeping the ball lower, thus forcing the opponents to hit up or at least limiting their opportunities for hitting down. Fourth, if one is to the side and has a ball to play, it is not

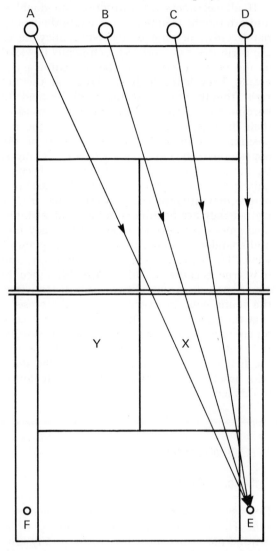

Diagram 16–1. Cover the center unless the ball comes from your alley (D). All other shots can be covered from the center position (X).

natural to play over the high part of the net at the very edge of the court. This is against human nature, which ordinarily tends to play safe. Most of the court is back crosscourt, so unless some special reason appears, such as a wide open alley, a player will tend from natural conservatism to play crosscourt, and this means he plays over the center of the net.

The truth of the foregoing is accentuated when we apply it to individuals rather than teams. Diagram 16–1 shows four places (A to D inclusive) from which the ball may be hit to E. Notice that X, although very close to the center, can reach all of them except the shot from D from his position near the center. In fact, when the ball is at A or B he should be even more to the left to help his partner guard the left half of the net, over which the ball must come. Thus net players should guard the center at all times except when the ball is coming from far over on their side, as from D to E. This is probably a fifth or less of the time since the ball is more frequently in the center than wide. To put it the other way, four-fifths or more of all play in doubles is across the center, so that is where we should be just about all the time. Furthermore, this can be made a tactical certainty by playing shots down the center, leaving the opposition literally no choice and leaving us no worries about where we should be since they must play from B and C.

Serving to the Center

"Serve to the center" is particularly sound advice for the right court but applies also to the left court far more often than many players are inclined to believe. In serving to the right court (forehand), a ball down the center must be returned across the center. The server's partner can pretty much ignore his alley and move over toward the center strap. This acts to reduce considerably the width of net over which the receiver can play without having his shot picked off by the net man. This in turn reduces the server's problem: he has to guard

only a small area as he comes in. By contrast, an angled service pins the server's partner in his alley, which is now directly in front of the receiver's racket (an easy shot), and leaves everything else to the server—whether it be a down-the-center shot, an ordinary return directly at the server, or an angle. It can be summed up by stating that the center service brings the server's partner into the game and makes it possible for him to assume a substantial portion of the burden, while the angled service pretty much eliminates the partner and leaves the server obliged to win his service all alone. Therefore, the standard service to the right court is down the center, and the angle is only used occasionally to keep the opposition honest. See Diagram 16–2.

In the left court another consideration arises which is in opposition to the theoretical preference for the center. This is the desire to play an opponent's backhand, particularly with a twist or a topspin service. Most players tend always to play to the backhand to gain this so-called advantage, but in so doing they are at times wrong. Why? Because everybody knows this is the standard play, and if either of the opposing pair has a good backhand return you can bet they'll have him in the left court to defend this universal trouble spot. Often it would be advantageous from a percentage point of view to play the center, disregarding the fact that it is his forehand, because a surprisingly large number of people have a worse forehand than backhand anyway. Certainly if his backhand turns out to be effective, a thorough testing of his forehand is in order. There is far too much tendency to go at the left court with a closed mind, which fails to give the opposition any credit for intelligent planning in the use of their available resources. This is an unconscious form of arrogance that is often paid for in the coin called defeat.

Serving Wisely

The point has been made that doubles is a battle for the net position and that every shot

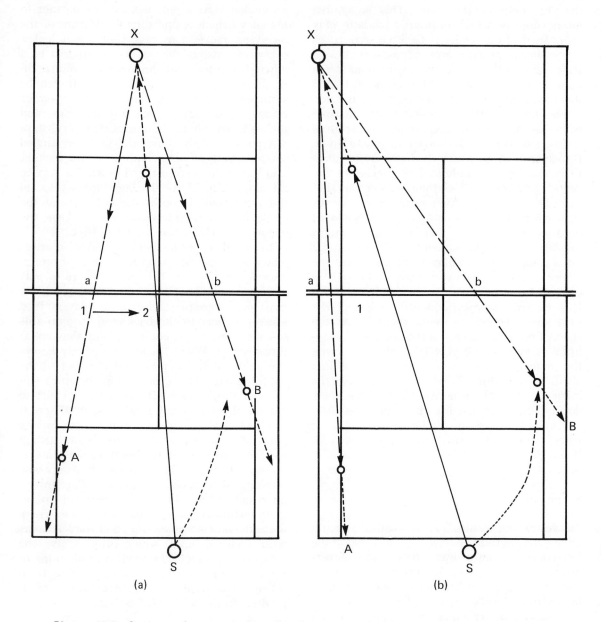

Diagram 16–2. Serving to the center is best. The illustration on the left shows S serving to the center. His partner can move from 1 to 2 without uncovering his alley: he can still cover shot A. X must make shot B accurately to avoid pick-off from 2. Contrast with the illustration on the right, in which the wide service pins the partner at 1, leaving X lots of room over the lowest part of the net to go for the server's feet as he comes in. Note that from a to b is 16 feet (by scale) in Diagram 16–2a, but is 20 feet in Diagram 16–2b. Thus the server must dog-leg as he moves forward in order to cover the extra width.

we make should either be calculated to gain us this position or should capitalize on our having gained it. Our service must serve this concept or we are not serving intelligently. Our opponent, by the rules of the game, may not strike our service until after it bounces. Therefore, if we use a service that does not go extremely fast and carries a heavy spin and takes a big hop, we not only bother our opponent but also give ourselves time to get well in before his shot returns. By contrast, a fast service is no good unless it is an ace or near ace, because if it comes back at all it will return quickly—before we can possibly get in —and it will catch us too far back for an effective first volley. In sum, we probably have not gained the net, so our service failed in its prime purpose. To put it another way, a fast service of course may win, but it also may backfire; a heavy spin service is the most reliable for doubles because it always gives us time to achieve good position.

Getting the First Serve In

To get the first serve in is of *extreme* importance, yet few players do it consistently. Why is it so crucial? The main reason is psychological. On the first service the receiver cannot be sure what sort of a delivery may come at him; we have many choices, and his attitude is necessarily somewhat suspicious and cautious— in a word, defensive. Now is the best time to get the ball *in* and gain that invaluable net position. But if we miss our first serve the shoe at once begins to pinch the other foot: the receiver knows we must get the ball in, we must be careful, we dare not try angles, slams, or any other surprises. So he is free to make plans—aggressive plans—against our now limited possibilities. Often these plans are successful—he gets to net ahead of us or forces an error—and our service is broken on that point. This all adds up to being another cogent reason why a spin service is better, in doubles, than a cannonball: you can get the spin service in all the time.

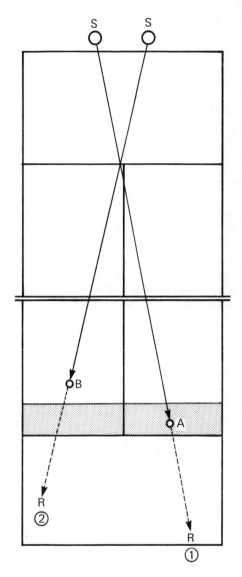

Diagram 16–3. Depth is a serve's greatest asset. The deep service (1) holds the receiver back. The shallow service (2) invites him to move in. Note that in both cases the receiver has taken the same time and distance to judge the ball: A–R exactly equals B–R. If the server is following to net, the ball will return much more quickly from (2)—and he will probably be in trouble. Serve to the last three feet (shaded).

Serving Deep

A deep service forces the receiver to give the server more time to get to net. It is farther back when he plays it, so it takes longer both going and coming. Since the difference of a few feet in position is the distinction between being well positioned and being vulnerable, this matter of depth is reasonably obvious. Experimentation with the height at which one aims in serving and with the amount of lean or rocking motion will soon determine how one can regulate his depth with good consistency.

Thus the server should have four objectives: get the first serve in, spin it, aim deep to gain time to get well in for the first volley, play the center to enable the partner to help as much as possible. It is noted that none of these objectives involve winning, but all seek to gain the advantage that will lead to winning: the net position.

The First Volley

One of the greatest fallacies in doubles is the tendency players have to try for a winner on their first volley. They pull it off just often enough to keep themselves convinced they are on the right track, not realizing that they are losing the percentage all along. A major cause for broken services is missed first volleys. Why is it nonpercentage to go for an ace? Because the server is seldom if ever far enough in to justify trying for an ace. He should volley down the center firmly and crisply and move on in to a more commanding position. He should never try for a winner; and this does not mean hardly ever, it means not even once. Some will surely ask, "What if a very weak return floats back? Shouldn't he kill *this* one?" The answer: he should not kill it; his partner should kill it. The reason the partner is placed at net is precisely so that if a weak ball shows up he takes care of it. That is his job. Therefore, the server should not get to play any shots that are subject to being aced, and the

rule holds: volley solidly to the center and move on in; don't try to win.

This concept of taking more than one shot to win is right in line with our discussion of the dimensions of the court. It is not possible to make winners until you are well into the forecourt, and the first doubles volley is made more in the forward part of the halfcourt area, around the service line. In a sense it is the doubles equivalent of the singles approach shot, and indeed it has the same function: to keep the pressure on an opponent and force him to give us the next shot up at the net where it is possible to be lethal. To state the concept in another way: keep on playing for that net position until you have won it—and don't get any other fancy ideas on the way up. After the net is won you will get your chances to kill—it is then inevitable. Trying to jump the gun means you will be erratic and undependable as a partner and a player. It also indicates either immaturity or conceit: either you don't know how to play the game or you are arrogant enough to believe you can do what experience has indicated cannot be done even by the best.

More about the Center

The best doubles players are practically center maniacs. They serve to the center, volley to the center, close in on the center of the net, smash often down the center. Isn't this an oversimplification? No, it is not. Keeping the ball down the center prevents your opponents from getting ideas and making plans; they *must* return the ball over the center to get it in. So you can close in on the center with the certain knowledge that they must hit the ball to you or lob. Playing down the center tends to draw them together, leaving the angles open if an opportunity for an angle occurs. Playing down the center, like serving down the center, permits your partner to abandon his alley and move across, frequently to pick off the return and put it away. Playing down the center allows you to play aggressively and yet be very steady, for you are aiming the ball as far in as is possible and over the lowest part of the net. It is maximum pressure achieved at minimum risk. How could there be a better policy than that?

It is to be noted that the Australians are, in their doubles, complete center extremists. One player serves, his partner drifts across the center to pick off. One player receives, plays back as low as possible, and his partner drifts across the center to pick off. They are forever cutting across the center just as the opposition is playing the ball. Oh, yes, they get passed down the alley once in a while—but they cut off a half dozen for every one they lose. It is strictly a percentage play and very sound. Of significance also is that this policy tends to force the opposition to try the alley shot that goes over the high part of the net at the edge of the court, inducing, of course, a higher number of errors.

It takes youngsters quite a while to absorb this apparently simple idea. There are so many other possibilities—after all, it is a big court—and it is hard to resist all these fancy ideas. The principle to get across to them is: having ideas is desirable and necessary—after one is all the way up to net. Having ideas and playing anywhere but down the center when one is only part way to the net is nonpercentage. It is not easy to discipline one's self in this manner: to be very conservative and to shun all risk on the first volley, then to unleash one's inspiration, as it were, when on top of the net. But this is what the best players do, and it explains why they make a lot of fine shots and do not make many errors at the same time.

A good teaching trick is to stand a player on the service line, play a string of ordinary drives at him, and ask him to volley angles. Then the instructor moves him in much closer to the net. The instructor plays to him again—to let him see how tough it is to make an angle from halfway in, how easy from far in. Often some object lesson such as this is more productive of results than any amount of theoretical talk (or a book!).

Playing down the center is in doubles like playing crosscourt baseline drives in singles. It is our dependable way of keeping ourselves out of trouble while we try to get our opponents into trouble and while we wait for an opportunity to do something more decisive. Even after we reach the net, if the ball comes over hard and low the answer is to volley it back down the center and keep it going this way until a good chance occurs for a winner.

Avoiding the Edges

A good doubles player seldom plays a ball outside the singles court. If he gets a setup he volleys hard or smashes at someone's feet—an almost sure winner with little risk—or he aims between his opponents down the center. If he has a chance to angle he always angles across the wide part of the court so the ball, in spite of its very sharp angle, *lands* far inside the lines. To put it another way, he makes the angle, not the line. If he drop volleys he tries to drop it very short but not too near a side line. If an opponent at net is crossing frequently and it is necessary to play down his alley to force him to stay where he belongs, the shot is aimed always at the inside alley line, not the outside. If this play is made at the right time —i.e., if it catches him going across—the shot that is four feet in will win as easily as one that plays the outside line, and it will seldom miss. Returns of service are played for the server's feet, not for the outside alley line. Lobs are played high but well inside the side lines. Thus it is not only possible but advisable to shun the edges of the court. Since it is possible to play all the shots with intelligence, imagination, and effective aggression without leaving the singles court, it is nonpercentage to do anything else.

This does not mean the ball should never land in the alley; it means we do not *aim* it there. But in a fast game many a shot goes a good bit to the left or right of where it is aimed, and so we may occasionally get a lucky one in the alley. Or a return of service may go deeper than we aimed it, so it would, on its angled course, reach the alley if not volleyed.

Or if we pass and aim at the inside line we may miss by three or four feet and land only a foot inside the outside line. Always in such cases we should calmly accept our good fortune with a poker face: as Tilden said, "Always make your lucky ones look good." Let everyone think you can hit that outside line every day in the week and twice on Sunday—it will worry them—but aim the next one farther in! All this adds up to the same concept that this book seeks constantly to stress: learn—and teach—that it is possible to play aggressively, daringly, and with imagination and yet still allow for the fact that one is a fallible human being. The big misser is trying to play like a god, and he cannot do it.

Ignoring the Center Service Line

The most common fallacy in players' thinking about their position in doubles is to think and talk in terms of "your side" and "my side" when these terms mean your side of that center white line and my side of it. The first fact to inculcate is that this line means *nothing* except that it shows where a service may and may not land. Look carefully at Diagram 16–4. Note that from X only a difficult and sharp angle can cross even the beginning of the right-hand half of the net, while all easy (and therefore more probable) shots must cross the left half of the net. Thus A and B are well to the left— even B being a trifle to the left of the center.

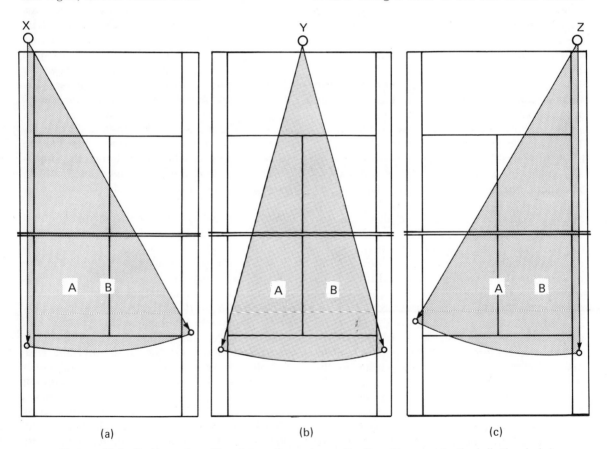

(a)   (b)   (c)

Diagram 16–4. Doubles net position. Ignore the center service line. Stay opposite the ball. The shaded areas show where the ball must come back. Note how drastically good position varies from (a) to (c).

From Z the situation is reversed, and A now finds himself moving to the right so he is actually farther to the right than B was for the return from X. The principle to be learned is that a player's position never relates to any part of the court, line, or area; it relates to the whereabouts of the ball and the part of the net the ball *must* cross to return fairly. The diagrams clearly show that the ball must *always* cross the nearest half of the net: from the left (X), the left half; from the right (Z), the right half; from the center (Y), the center half. Therefore the first fundamental of position play is: *stay opposite the ball.*

This means players should move around a lot in relation to the ball even though they may not be playing it. Thus, if a ball goes to Z, B at once moves to cover his alley and forgets the center; A covers the center and ignores his alley. If the ball goes to X, B at once abandons his alley and moves sharply to the right to guard the center while A guards his alley. The center line is of course ignored, and the concept of "mine" and "yours" comes to mean my or your half of that part of the net over which the ball must be returned.

At this stage it may be pointed out that if we play down the center rather than to X and Z, our opponents must return across the center, and we do not have to keep rushing back and forth to hold our position properly—another reason to be a center fan: our work is both simplified and made easier, and our risks are reduced since sometimes one is hard put to get across the net fast enough when the ball is played sharply from side to side. A further consideration is that if we are obliged to move laterally too drastically, we are more likely to be caught flat by a concealed lob. Thus any discussion of position play always comes back to stressing the center.

However, all this is what we'd like to do but frequently are unable to do if our opponents are any good. They will also be after the center and may often have a man placed there first, so we must play to one side to avoid him. At all such times our position play should stress one half of the net to whatever degree the ball is played to that half.

The concept of "mine" and "yours" can be very inhibiting and can hamper drastically a team's effectiveness at the net. If one player is back and the other up—as on return of service—the net player should be alert to kill *any* cripple anywhere at net. He should not hesitate to rush in front of his partner on such occasions to slam a winner, because he can take the ball when it is most vulnerable—right above the net—and make a sure winner, while his partner often cannot possibly close in fast enough to be this effective. Far from being bad manners to "hog" these, it is failure to do one's job to let a single one of them float back to where they cannot be killed. Crossing in front is reprehensible only if one's partner is right there ready to do his own killing and you rudely deprive him of his big chance. This is doubly bad because it implies a basic distrust on your part, so he probably starts looking for another partner.

Trick Maneuvers and Signals

In advanced doubles, signals are often employed by the serving team. The net player will clench his fist behind his back: this means he will cross, and the server, after a little fake start the correct way, goes to net to arrive at the "wrong" side. If the net player opens his hand it means he will not go across. He may make a fake start and look as though he is crossing but he doesn't. When a player thus abandons his conventional position and crosses all the way in an endeavor to pick off the return it is called a "poach."

Signaling, poaching, and half poaching are not recommended for any except advanced players, since with those less skilled the offensive team usually confuses itself far more than the opposition. A good solid standard game with only an occasional surprise should be the objective for all but the more accomplished.

Crowding the Net—Inviting the Lob

The answer to a team that continually presses to the net is of course the lob; force them back, make them hesitate, penalize their impetuosity. This is actually just what we want our opponents to do: we want them to hit up so we can hit down. While of course this can be carried too far, it is the fundamental tactical principle of the game to strive to create a situation wherein we are top dog and our opponents are the underdog—playing up. They lob, we smash. We have the initiative; we are dominating the match; we are winning or losing points, and they are not.

A very common type of poor doubles player is one who is continually watching for the lob. True, no one ever gets a lob over him, but also he seldom is in close to kill a cripple or to pick off a return. He loses more than he gains. A good doubles player is more afraid of not being well in to net than he is of the lob. He stresses the forward position, invites and risks the lob, and is willing to pay a price in order never to be found lingering back when a chance to cut one off at net occurs. Good doubles is a *very* aggressive game, and the scale of values and percentages favors them who remember Farragut's famous order, "Damn the torpedoes, full speed ahead!"

Do we not all know some players who are quite good at doubles but are too erratic in singles? This is because the bigger court and the necessity for aggression and hitting through people tend to reward the attacker, while in singles—particularly on a slow court—consistency and circumspection pay off. Thus many college teams will have players in their doubles who cannot make the singles line-up. And any coach who estimates his players' doubles value in terms of their singles play is probably making a good many mistakes.

Forming a Good Team

Every player is an individual, and few are completely equipped for doubles either technically or mentally. Therefore the ideal of finding two well-rounded doubles players is unattainable. The attitude of a coach should be to study all his available individuals, hoping to find players who bolster each other. There must be one aggressive player who is eager and able to kill the ball at net. And there must be a touch of conservatism—one of them must remember to keep an eye on the back door (the lob). To put it another way, one must be a playmaker, the other must have the ability to capitalize. One must supply impetuosity, the other must be a steadying influence and be clever to create situations where the first player's aggression can come into play. And they must get along; each must have an appreciation of the fact that the other is filling gaps that would result in defeat if left unplugged.

DEFENSIVE DOUBLES

Attack

While the offense should and does win in doubles, it is not possible to win a match without breaking service. And right here a number of facts should be pointed out which differentiate sharply between average good doubles and "big time" doubles. First, the U.S. and Wimbledon doubles titles are decided on grass—and most of us do not play on grass. Second, just about all the famous players in the Nationals have quite deadly services, so it is hard to make much headway against them. The rest of us do not have such heavy artillery with which to deliver the first blow of each point, and the defensive team has much more of an opportunity to carry out any intelligent plans it may concoct. What follows might well be quite uselessly academic if we were defending against a great service, but since we are not it represents a plan that can and actually has produced results at the level of good college tennis.

The receiving team is usually referred to as the defending team, and the first thing for them to do is to start thinking offensively, not defensively. The job is to break service. This is a positive act and is not to be confused with waiting for the opponents to lose their service. If they are any good they won't lose it—you have to go get it.

The first important consideration is time. The attacker needs time to get to net. If he is allowed this time he will get there, and if any of our discussion of offensive doubles has any meaning, he will usually win the point. The farther back we stand to receive service, the longer it takes the ball to get to us and back to him—and the farther in he gets. The farther in we take the ball, the sooner it gets back—and the less time he has to get far in. So fundamental number one is to play the ball as soon as is humanly possible. It is far more important to get the ball back quickly than to play it impressively with a beautiful stroke. The best doubles players frequently use a no-swing block-and-poke return of service, taking the ball as soon as it has bounced enough for them to get their eye on it—that is, on the rise, before it reaches the top of the bounce. If such a return can be kept low it is often possible to take the net away from the server.

Taking the ball on the rise and aiming short again brings into play the more closed-face halfcourt racket techniques. It also once again exalts the much maligned chops and slices and the extremely abbreviated backswing. All instructors and particularly all team coaches are urged to give this aspect of doubles technique serious attention. Everyone is taught lovely, mellifluous, rhythmic, flowing full-swing ground strokes. How often do people get taught to use a quick, jabby, unbeautiful but time-gaining poke? Just about never, because it is not theoretically attractive. It is not "the best way to hit the ball"—a golfish thought. But it is what good doubles players actually do in order to fight for the net when the other fellow is serving. Once again all readers are urged not to imitate golf, which, since there is no tempo, can demand a perfect swing for every shot. Tempo is the very essence of doubles, and everything must give way to it in the

fight between server and receiver to win the net.

In addition, a return that lands inside the service line is a setup for a singles player while it is most embarrassing to a net-rushing doubles player. Pokes, chips, short loops, angles, and dinks—all these shots are very effective in doubles while the smooth deep singles ground stroke is easy to volley and is as a rule of little use. Once again it is pointed out that doubles fosters a desirable versatility in the racket skills of all who play the game.

A student learning doubles should stand with his toes against the baseline and should step in across the baseline to play the ball. Later as he acquires considerable skill he should stand inside the baseline to begin with, thus demanding of himself the utmost in quickness and reflexes and also putting the utmost pressure on his opponent.

Returning Short Serves

Defensive players should take every inch their opponents give. This advice has a literal meaning. One's position for return of service is based on the defensive assumption that the service will be deep—it will land near or at the service line—and we need time to judge it. However, only the finest players consistently land their services really deep. Most players are inconsistent, aim too low, and often land the ball as much as six or eight feet inside the service line. Thus an alert receiver instantly moves in that six or eight feet. He still has just as much time and distance for judging the ball: he is no closer to it when it bounces than he had originally planned to be in preparing to receive a deep service. But most players look upon a short service as one that gives them plenty of time—extra time. This is true, but they fail to see that if they deny themselves this extra time they also take it away from the server, catch him only halfway in, get him in trouble, and gain the advantage. The important principle to learn is that one must be watching for any shortness in the service, and one must be ready and eager to grab every inch that is offered on every occasion. It ties in with the basic fundamental: move forward toward the net whenever possible, as soon as possible, as much as possible.

It may be added that every foot gained is actually two feet: the ball travels that foot once to get to the receiver and again to get back to the server. Thus a service that lands seven feet inside the line, and is taken six feet nearer the net by the receiver, travels twelve feet less horizontally than one that lands a foot inside. Since we are dealing in small quantities of time, this rather large distance assumes a great significance. It means the receiver actually can break even or win in the race he ordinarily is expected to lose to the server. This is a heaven-sent opportunity to snatch the controlling position away from the server and offers the additional incentive of getting the ball to his feet when he is only halfway in.

A third consideration is that the sooner the receiver plays the ball, the less time his shot will take to get past the server's partner at net. This is of vast importance in good doubles since the server's partner is alert, ready, and willing to cut off and kill anything he can get his racket on. When the service is met six to ten feet inside the baseline his chances are comparatively limited: the ball is by him so quickly he has no time to move. Thus for a variety of reasons—all of them of prime importance—the receiver's first thought is to be ready to move in every inch possible almost to the point where he would be missing the ball for lack of a chance to judge the bounce. This will vary with different opponents; the point is to be always as greedy as circumstances permit in seizing the most forward position possible.

Bluffing

Whenever a server misses his first service the receiver should exert psychological pressure by moving in a step with no attempt at concealment. It is not necessary to be ostentatious,

for then he would know it is an act. Just move in a step and crouch, letting him know by a general attitude that now the receiver is after him. This often worries a server into overplaying or underplaying his second service, thus giving the receiver a free point through a double fault, or an opportunity through a ball that lands short.

Actually this is a good bluff because there are good cards backing the bet. In the preceding section on offensive doubles much was made of getting the first service in to avoid this very predicament: a situation where the server *must* get the ball in and therefore must be careful and cannot do anything different or risky. Now the server has failed to follow this good advice, and the receiver's idea should be to make him suffer the full consequences of his carelessness. In addition to moving in, the receiver should frequently run around the second ball and whale it with his forehand. To do this a receiver must be decisive. Just as the server's racket is about to contact the ball, but too late for him to make any change in the shot, the receiver should take a big jump to the left, committing himself completely and ignoring the possibility of a service to his forehand. If he has any kind of a decent topspin forehand the high bounding service is a setup for a blistering crosscourt return with a lot of spin to dip to the server's feet. The receiver's partner closes on the center to pick off the expected shaky return. It is a great two-shot, two-man play.

A third play against second service is to close aggressively and try for a surprise by popping the ball over the net man's head. If the service is weak and a bit short, one can run around it and hit a hard forehand right down the inside alley line through the server's partner. It should be pointed out that this last suggestion is more to keep them guessing than to make a good play, for, as has been stated, to play a net man is a stupid idea in doubles unless you are hitting down on him. It takes a truly poor service to make this play an intelligent one.

The real point of all these suggestions is that we should think and act offensively whenever our opponent's service—first or second—gives us any opportunity at all to escape our initially defensive role. Very few average doubles players do this, and a majority of players could increase their defensive effectiveness decisively without making any improvements in their actual stroke equipment. It is a matter of how a player thinks when the other fellow serves. It can be summed up by urging everybody to abandon the defensive negative approach that seeks to make it difficult for an opponent to win his serve and to adopt an active positive policy that says, "I am going to take the initiative away from you and I am going to break your service. You aren't going to get a chance to win it."

Position Play on Defense

Where should the receiver's partner stand in doubles? This is a question over which there is continuing argument, often acrimonious. Usually an endless argument means there is more than one answer, and this clearly is such a situation. If the service coming at me is ordinary or weak I want my partner up at net— well up at net, not just inside the service line —so he can capitalize on any favorable situation I create if, as I hope, I make a good return. If the service is very strong and I am pretty sure I can't do much with it, then I want him back near the baseline ready to retrieve and lob along with me.

A good many topnotch players take up the "modified net position": inside the service line but not really up at net. The theory is that if the return by their partner is good they move in, if not they move back. This is a nice theory, but it never gets past the theoretical stage with most ordinary players and has few constructive and many disastrous results. Most of them are not quick enough to react as the theory demands. Thus, if a good chance occurs they are not in there to kill it; they are still too far back and bang it into the net. If a poor situation develops they are too slow to retreat, and the ball is smashed at their feet for a winner.

Thus, they are far enough up to be a target but not far enough to be a killer, so they often lose the point and seldom win it because of their position play. With most players an outright wager on what seems probable is to be preferred to this neither fish nor fowl position

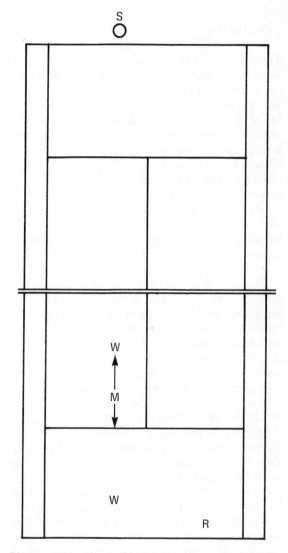

Diagram 16–5. The modified net position (M) and the straight wager positions (W). S=Server. R=Receiver. Only the quickest can start at M and move up or back fast enough. The wager positions are more of a percentage play for average people.

that is conventional. The modified net position, in sum, is no good unless used with skill, speed, and savoir faire. It is not recommended except for the best. See Diagram 16–5.

Using the Lob

The foregoing paragraphs are filled with brave words and good intentions. But the cold facts are unchanged: the other fellow is serving, he has the initiative, he is out to get us into trouble, and he often succeeds. In spite of our best plans and efforts he often makes a good first service and a down the center first volley; he is up at net with his partner, and we are under pressure. In such cases we should lob the second shot—usually over the net man who tends to be closer in than the server. Any other shot merely plays into their hands at net. This lob should be a defensive lob—that is, high—unless one has a good chance and time on the forehand to try a topspin offensive lob.

The reasoning behind this play is simple. We have lost the battle for the net, our opponents have won it, we now have no chance to play offensively, so the risk inherent in any aggressive shot is badly run. So we admit we are on defense and make the most defensive shot there is—a big high deep lob. Another way of saying this is that they have created a situation where we must play up to them and let them hit down on us. The most difficult, exacting, and energy-consuming down-hit shot is an overhead from deep in the court. We must give them a chance—we have no choice—so let it be the meanest and toughest shot we can offer them. If they can put that one away then at least we have forced them to earn the point the hard way as contrasted with an easy volley or smashing a low lob. The next best thing to winning the point is to make it as difficult as possible for the other fellow to win it.

In topnotch tennis most of the players have first-class overheads; they can kill any but the most beautiful lobs. As we watch them put the ball away the lob seems a sorry shot. What good does it do? It does a lot of good, even with these world-class players, as has been pointed out in earlier chapters about tactics in singles. The possibility of the lob holds them back from closing all the way in, and hitting a lot of overheads can be very tiring. Many a match has seen one team wear another down by lobbing. Right at the start it may not seem so effective. Full of energy, they smash with vigor and decision. But keep it up; it is exacting its toll, and they are human. Once they start missing and lose their confidence the whole complexion of their offense changes, and the percentage may well switch to you. In less excellent tennis it is hard to locate a player who can *ever* kill a high deep lob. Lots of us can murder a short low lob; oh, yes, we bounce it out of the park. But a high deep lob —we sweat gumdrops of anxiety, let it land, play it back carefully, work for a better chance. In sum, we admit it stops us, pushes us back, frustrates our offense so we must go to work all over again, hoping for a fatter opportunity. It is not possible to exaggerate the importance of this second line of defense in defensive doubles play—the lob.

It is perhaps necessary to point out here that one should still prefer the offense and should not advocate that receivers back up and lob all the time. We should always seek to be offensive, and only if this attempt fails do we resort to the high defensive lob. The point is to recognize it and admit it when our attempt at offense has failed. Too many—particularly youngsters—persist in a preoccupation with offense. They'll drive hard if they are behind the baseline and their opponents on top of the net. The concept to get across is the principle of the happy mean: a person who does nothing but lob is negative or chicken, a person who never lobs is a pigheaded fool who refuses to face facts.

A sudden change in tactics often will achieve a break before one's opponents succeed in adjusting to it. If the receivers have been standing as far in as possible but the server has been doing well, confer with your partner and suggest, "Let's drop back and lob the return every time this game." This often draws errors and leads to a break. As a permanent policy it is poor. As a one-shot maneuver it has merit. Or to agree with your partner to chip four in a row over the net man—this (that is, the constant repetition) is often an effective surprise and creates a little temporary confusion in the enemy's ranks. It's worth a try.

All these suggestions bring up a great and often unperceived principle of defensive doubles, to wit: when you meet a strong service and the server is winning, you have everything to gain and nothing to lose. Try anything, try everything, have no fear or inhibitions. If whatever you try doesn't work, are you any worse off than you were before? No, you are still losing that service game. In such conditions, conservatism (one definition of which is to cling to the status quo) offers no hope at all. Talk with your partner. Move in and poke low. Stand far back and lob high. Move in and poke over the net man. Try to run around the ball. Hit it hard right at the net man. (The very stupidity of this shot, off a good service, sometimes makes it so surprising that an error results.) If somehow or other you can combine a couple of good plays with a couple of induced errors you have a break. This can happen to anyone's service, and to plot to bring this about can be interesting, challenging, absorbing, and a lot of fun. To get this across to youngsters—that smart and skillful defense is fun, just as a good offense is fun—is a real challenge to a coach or a pro. Since youth always prefers the offense, use that type of language: "We are going to attack their serves, not just defend against them."

Defensive Teamwork

It is important to know your partner's strengths and weaknesses. If he has a fine forehand return of service, then whenever a service goes to his forehand, close in as he hits,

thus anticipating a poor return and being there to kill it. He provokes the setup; you are there to kill it. Likewise, if he has a weakness and they play it, retreat rapidly to the baseline prepared to retrieve and lob; don't obstinately stay at net and eat the next shot. Confer with your partner on problems, such as a net man who is crossing and making trouble for you. Devise a little plan: "You lob your return over him and I'll whack mine right at him—he may be back for another lob." Above all don't hesitate to call out to your partner when information will help him: "Back!" as you lob; "Up!" whenever you feel you are going to make a forcing return; "Take it!" when an overhead in the center is on his forehand, your backhand.

As one gains experience in doubles the concept of "yours" and "mine" comes to have other meanings in addition to the idea of "side." There is the question of the forecourt and the backcourt: if I make a good service and I know you are closing in to kill any and all forecourt cripples that may (we hope) occur, then it is my job as I advance to be prepared to switch quickly over and take any lob that goes over you. I expect you to do the same for me when things are reversed. So the concept ends up with being broad and flexible: if I'm doing the one, you must do the other, whether it is a matter of this or that side, up or back, or any more subtle diagonal combination.

Above all be considerate of your partner. In doubles almost always the wrong man gets the blame: I make a poor return, they whale it through you; you make a short lob, I get the blast; etc. Since you wish to be forgiven your sins it is imperative that you display an equal generosity when the shoe is on the other foot. Even more important is the habit of praising your partner for good work and ignoring his errors. This tends to bring the best out in his game while a critical attitude is usually disheartening. If he makes a really bad error make light of it; this is the best way to help him get rid of it mentally and get off to a fresh start. The golden rule plus an active sense of humor is essential to a real doubles team.

Defensive Pride

Defensive pride has been beautifully exploited by platoon football. To the surprise of many, the defensive players have just as much pride, fun, and pleasure from the game. Really there should be no surprise, for defense presents an equally complex challenge which if met successfully gives an equal sense of accomplishment. The same is true for defensive tennis, whether in singles or in doubles. Each team, each opponent, presents different problems, different strengths and weaknesses, and of course this means any counterattack must vary as it adjusts to these differences. To take pride in never ceasing to work toward finding a way is the core of defensive excellence. To be resilient, to rebound from each temporary defeat for another try with perhaps a new idea or variation of an idea or a basis for action— it is a good service indeed that is so strong it can nullify a continuous imaginative attack of this sort.

False Pride

It is an obvious thing to say—avoid false pride —but there are many who foster false pride within themselves without knowing it. Is it not a common thing to hear a player say, "When I make such a bad shot I *ought* to lose the point"? Right here is a perfect example of unconscious false pride. Our opponents are constantly seeking to get us in trouble. Is it not reasonable to assume that to a considerable degree they will succeed? Is it not the height of unwitting arrogance to demand of one's self that in spite of all the opponent's best efforts one must never make a poor shot? And even if the opposition is not forcing us—as when we serve—is it not pretty cocky to expect to make a fine shot every time? This is asking and expecting a godlike performance—i.e., perfection —and it is a proud man indeed who calmly asserts this is what he proposes to do.

The worst part of false pride—or youthful delusions of grandeur—is that it tends to make

one a quitter. The poor shot followed by the feeling "I ought to lose" means that one tends not to try to pull the point out. Instead one's attitude should be that here is an opportunity to make a terrific goal line stand, to get that ball, lob it high, hang in there. Everybody likes a fighter and will readily forgive him his mistakes since he makes up for them in every way he can. Nobody likes a quitter who more or less ceases to play as soon as things no longer are going his way. It all adds up to: it pays to be a good defensive player. It pays in victories, in respect from others, in self-respect, and in popularity: everybody wants a "tough" partner. Keep it in mind. Last, it pays in satisfaction and fun: you should get as much pleasure from the defensive aspects of the game as you do from the offensive.

AVERAGE DOUBLES

There are thousands of tennis players who are too old and slow or just not quick enough to play first-rate doubles. They cannot get to net behind their serve consistently, and if both of them get up there neither one can cover a lob —it goes for an ace. There has been altogether too much written about how "wrong" it is to play one up and one back, and how parallel doubles is the *only* way for everybody to play. This is just plain unfair to all these good people, and this book intends to stand up for them.

In the first place it is obvious that if one team is capable of the tempo needed for two-up doubles and the other isn't, then it is a mismatch and an unfair contest. No attempt is made here to hold that good one-up and one-back doubles can defeat good two-up doubles. The entire discussion assumes that both teams are in the same league: neither has the speed or stamina needed for first-rate doubles.

Given these limitations in the personnel, the smartest way to play is one up and one back. The net player can play well up because he doesn't have to worry about lobs. The partner in back tries his utmost to force the opponents to put the ball within reach of this net player, the other team of course employs the same tactics, and many a truly dogged and canny contest results. There should be a lot of semi-poaching and now and then a complete poach so as to keep the others guessing. There should be some drop shots to catch the "one back" if he hangs too far back in his worrying about lobs. When a nice chance offers itself, such as a short drive, the back player should make a sortie to the net, trying to force enough with his approach to insure against a good lob. All these calculated risks by both players can make it an interesting and at times exciting game to play and to watch. But the essential point is that it is within the capabilities of the participants instead of being a beautiful theory that they cannot possibly put into execution.

Large numbers of women should play this way, and also many men. It is definitely not a crime to play in the manner best adapted to your talents, even if it wouldn't quite do for the Davis Cup team or the Wightman Cup team. Frequently two players find themselves partners and only one can play net worth a cent. Obviously he should play up and the other should play back. If the opponents try to play two up, lob them. If they hang for the lob— i.e., don't come all the way up—play at their feet. They'll soon be forced to adopt the same system—one up and one back. If one player is a runner and the other a hitter, the runner should play back and the hitter up. Don't hesitate to break every convention. Let the hitter be at net *all* the time, the other player almost never. When the hitter receives serve, he follows his return to net. When his partner receives, the hitter is placed at net to begin with. The partner stays constantly where his mobility can operate to the best advantage—in back. Many a combination of this sort, by thus covering its limitations and pushing its assets to the fore, has made a lot of trouble in the local club tournament and the Sunday round robins.

It is important that players, students, and instructors realize the principle involved here: theoretically first-class doubles assumes the players have all the necessary technical equip-ment plus the athletic talent (speed) plus the stamina to carry out the suggested maneuvers throughout a considerable period of time. *If* you qualify in these respects, then of course you should play parallel doubles—both up together most all the time. If you do not, then don't let big-time conventions control your thinking and prevent an ingenious exploitation of more limited gifts. There is no truer saying than the old one to the effect that there is more than one way to skin a cat. No matter how you do it, stick to the old general's slogan, "I aim to git thar fustest with the mostest." He was a winner.

Last, little children are short and cannot reach lobs or even a high drive. How are they to play doubles except by using the one-up and one-back system? They can start this way and then play two up later when they are older, bigger, and better.

WOMEN'S DOUBLES

There is really no fundamental difference between men's and women's doubles except insofar as strength affects tactics. Since women are not as strong as men they must more often resort to subtlety, and particularly they must make use of a two-shot plan rather than a one-shot blast. The subtlety consists in greater use of the drop volley and angles. If both opponents are well back it is often beyond a woman's strength to put a setup through them. But a drop volley or a short angle may win, and if it doesn't win it pulls one of them in, makes her hit up, and now she is in a vulnerable position and the ball can be played down to her feet for a winner. Thus, while a man can be an effective doubles player without much use of delicate shots, a woman who lacks touch must be a veritable brute or she will not be successful.

Above all women must use their brains. If you cannot blast me off the court—as many men can—you either win by being smart or you lose. Many of the women's matches in the

National Doubles at Longwood are more interesting than the men's matches just because they are more dependent on skill, subtlety, and the use of variety as contrasted with the raw power that tends to dominate the men's matches. A skillful war of maneuver is often more fun to watch than a battle of sheer pressure.

Women can achieve remarkable skill in doubles by emphasizing touch, variety, the clever use of the lob, a devotion to teamwork, percentage tactics, and the exploitation of weaknesses in their opponents. They should concentrate on these opportunities for success. They should avoid trying to hit the ball as hard as the best men unless they are unusually strong. The same goes for most men. In other words, the best any player can do, regardless of sex, is to play as skillfully as possible within the limits of his or her athletic strength and quickness.

MIXED DOUBLES

This is a great game. It already has a large following throughout the land. It is the perfect social game, ideal for mixing, fun, exercise, and play with family and friends. The term "mixed doubles" doesn't mean merely an adult man and an adult woman: it can mean father and daughter against mother and son or any other "mixed" combination. Youngsters love the game, often having a grand time accompanied by quite a bit of noise and chatter. At any level of skill it is· a real fun game. It deserves a lot more promotion than it gets at many tennis installations, and it is hoped that any instructors reading this will give serious consideration to giving it a push wherever they work. Mixed doubles team matches followed by socializing are one good form this game can take. The game is the core around which many other desirable social activities revolve.

There is no difference in the tactics and strategy. The best means both rush the net at every opportunity, while those less talented can play one-up and one-back doubles. Either way it is fun, which is its real meaning.

QUESTIONS

1. Why is doubles "the better half of tennis"?

2. How does playing doubles add to singles skill?

3. What is the basic objective in doubles?

4. Why should one eternally move in when playing doubles?

5. Where do most shots cross the net in doubles?

6. Why are good doubles players preoccupied with the center?

7. Why is it advisable to serve to the center?

8. Should a player try for a winner when serving?

9. Why is it important to get the first ball in?

10. What type of service helps get the first ball in consistently?

11. Is it important to serve deep? Why?

12. What should be the objective on the first volley?

13. If a good service provokes a weak return, what should happen?

14. Do good players use the alleys much in doubles?

15. Does one need to "play the edges" to get winners?

16. Does a player stay on "his side" in doubles?

17. What governs position in doubles?

18. When should a player guard the center?

19. When should a player guard his alley?

20. When should a player "hog" his partner's shots?

21. What is a poach? When is a poach most likely to succeed?

22. Is a lot of tricky signaling a good idea?

23. Should one play doubles cautiously? Why?

24. What are the ingredients of a good doubles team?

25. What should be the first objective of the receiving team?

26. Why is a quick return of service essential?

27. Why should the receiver "crowd" the service as much as possible?

28. What type of backswing should the receiver use?

29. How can the receiver exert psychological pressure on the server?

30. When is it a good idea to "run around the ball" in receiving?

31. What should the receiver's partner be doing? Why?

32. Is it a good idea always to stand in the same place when one's partner is receiving? Discuss.

33. If the receiver's first aggressive defense fails, what is his best move on the second shot?

34. If our opponents have good overheads, should we avoid lobbing?

35. Does conservatism pay against a good service?

36. How can teamwork accentuate strength and cover weakness?

37. How does false pride manifest itself in tennis?

38. When is one-up and one-back doubles legitimate?

39. How can a one-up and one-back team best exploit its talents?

40. Why must women play a brainy game of doubles?

41. Can women play like men?

42. Is good women's doubles as interesting to watch as men's?

43. What are some of the virtues of mixed doubles?

Strategy, Tactics, and Coaching

CHAPTER 17

Strategy and Tactics

DEFINITIONS

Strategy is the overall plan. Tactics is the means employed to implement the strategy. For example: my opponent may be big, strong, a little overweight, and out of condition. My strategy will be to avoid whenever possible any test of sheer strength, and to run him as much as possible. My tactics will be to avoid an exchange of hard drives by pooping (playing soft high shots) a good bit, plus the use of as many angles and drop shots as opportunity permits. Second example: my opponent does not hit hard or attack much but is exceptionally steady at the baseline and likes a long match. My strategy will be to find some way to disturb and break up his endless baseline imperturbability by creating conditions of crisis where he *must* attempt more difficult shots—thus risking error—or lay himself wide open. The tactics would be to go to net when opportunity offers, mingled with quite a few drop shots to force him to attempt that which he is reluctant to do: move in to the net himself. When he does this he cannot merely get the ball back—I'll pass him clean or lob over his head if he makes a mediocre shot. Very frequently with this type of player—the pooper—the drop shot attack is the most effective. Such players are accustomed to being pressed: they move back a bit and lob and lob. But when suction is substituted for pressure they often fall flat on their faces, figuratively speaking (and sometimes almost literally as they rush in and make a poor approach off the drop shot).

KNOW THYSELF

A theoretical discussion of tactics assumes the reader has every shot and can therefore put into practice all possible combinations and all possible plans. This is, of course, the very type of unrealistic theorizing this book wishes to escape. The core of any average player's thinking should be a definite recognition of his own limitations, and a positive appreciation of his own strong points. It has already been pointed out that it is far better to master thoroughly one approach shot than to be fairly good at several. In boxing, a fighter needs only one knockout punch, because he can only knock his man out once. Likewise, a tennis player, given a setup in the halfcourt area, is given only one crack at the ball. What good are a half-dozen shots when you can only play the ball once? While it may with some justification be labeled an oversimplification, there is yet much truth in the assertion that having more than one shot merely complicates a situation in which we are eternally striving for simplicity. Certainly the champions usually boast a greater variety, but here again we ask: are you a champion? Are your students destined to be champions? Do you (or they) have time or the ability to master a variety of shots? The fact is that if each average player could master even *one* halfcourt shot to the point when he could say, "If I can get a chance to do that, I can usually get him," wouldn't it be cause for great joy and celebration, and never mind if the great players can make a few others too? It is not far off the truth to say that variety can easily become the curse of the average tennis player.

So too with tactics, once we come down off the throne occupied by the most gifted players. The average player should try to develop a few tactical moves and stick to them. Take a lefty, for instance. He should stress—endlessly—the opportunity he has to hook his forehand crosscourt to the right-handed player's backhand. He should stress breaking his service out to the backhand. If he masters these two tricks alone, and gets a backhand that will keep the ball going fairly steadily and a defensive lob, he has a game, a plan, tactics: he is effective and hard to beat in his own league. Some simple basic plan like this should be the first objective (to the exclusion of all other tactical objectives) of every aspiring player. Then *if* he has more ability, more time, more desire, of course he should move on to greater variety by adding other skills to his bag of tricks.

The point being made here is that an instructor with an individual or a group should start with an extremely limited plan. Strategy: keep the ball in play. Tactics: hit everything crosscourt. Service: half speed at most, stress getting it in. As a group develops, the individuals in it will learn at different speeds for obvious reasons. The group should therefore be treated like an ungraded primary section in a grammar school: the slower ones are permitted to go slowly, while opportunity to develop further and sooner is offered to the more talented.

THEORETICAL AND PRACTICAL TACTICS

It is great fun to expound and theorize about all the various and subtle plans that may be devised in order to confound our opponents. If one has every shot, and can keep them all under control, it can be almost like chess, there are so many possibilities. From halfcourt we can drop one (pulling him in for the lob or pass), pound the next one into the corner (forcing a weak return to our errorless big volley, stop volley, angle volley, or overhead), hook an angle sharply crosscourt (to pull him far out of court with a view to running him unmercifully), slice a mean skidder down the alley (the kick will confound him, forcing a weak reply), boom it down the center and move in on the center of the net (the center theory), carve a slow but acutely angled slice —well, we have pretty well disposed of him, haven't we? There is nothing to it—on paper, or when we dream.

Why is this so unrealistic? It is because of one tremendously important aspect of a tennis match: the pressure. Every point is precious. Every one we lose is a knife that cuts deep, hurts, and tends to undermine our confidence. We cannot try this, try that. We cannot try anything except those things in which we have confidence, because we don't dare. And to have all these shots so perfected that we have complete confidence—well, there was Houdini, and Tilden, and Toscanini, but those are not my names. Are they yours? In sum, anyone who thinks he is going to do all these beautiful things has delusions of grandeur and isn't going to defeat anybody except himself (and this won't take long).

The instructor must learn to limit himself, to confine himself to a few simple ideas. He must spend more time persuading players to be simple than in explaining all the various possible intricacies. The test should be "Can I play without this shot or this tactic?" If the answer is yes, then forget it for the beginners. By thinking along these lines an instructor will arrive at a clear perception of what the rock-bottom essentials of the game really are and what the most basic tactics really are. The instructor will learn ruthlessly to shut out everything else with a group of beginners until a start has been made on these skills.

With intermediates and advanced players one begins to stress what is desirable as contrasted with what is absolutely essential. Players are taught approach shots, position at net, and an overhead. They are encouraged to go to net whenever a decent opportunity presents itself: that is, a short ball. In this way they move from the rigid limitations of the beginner attitude toward the more varied technique of a well-rounded player.

LIMITED TACTICS

A considerable majority of all schoolboy and college players are inclined to play too impetuously and to defeat themselves. This is not necessarily because they are foolish. It is because they have no conception at all of the true percentages in the game. They do not realize that it is impossible to make a winner from the baseline or the halfcourt and that even at net it frequently requires two volleys, not one, to win. A setup comes to such a player and he thinks, "I should put it away" and so of course he tries to, and makes an error four out of seven times. The subtlety is that three out of seven he actually pulls off the winner, thus convincing himself that he is indeed on the right track. He thinks "I am a little erratic, but my idea is sound" and this is where he is dead wrong, since three out of seven never beat anybody.

To this we must add the fact that from other games boys and girls get the idea of the perfect shot. The home run in baseball, the knockout in boxing, the touchdown pass in football are cases in point. The mistakes that preceded the one great big winner are wiped out in a glorious triumph. Not so in tennis. All your mistakes stay right there on the scoreboard, and count against you. It is as though every incomplete pass scored for your opponent. Young people must be made to realize this and to understand that it is indeed desirable to make winners but only within the limitations set by the necessity for not making errors. This is the percentage concept.

We have stressed the desirability of being positive. Yet here is one place where the conditioning of experience has created a situation where some negatives are in order. We should not try for a winner from the baseline, because it is impossible. We should not try for a winner when we get a setup, because it is impossible. We should force on all good chances and follow to net, and when we are well in, yes, then (and only then) should we try for a winner.

We can sum up by saying that limited tactics (confining one's ideas to the possible) constitute most of the game for all players who are not among the elite who boast the big game and the energy to prosecute it. Therefore, keeping the ball in play and working up to a percentage chance for a winner is most of the game. (By most is meant nine-tenths or more.)

Surely some are now thinking this is overconservative and too preoccupied with defense. Well, clay tennis is primarily a steady percentage game. If you don't like to think of it that way go right ahead—be a Don Quixote and try your luck against the windmill. It may be more dashing, more appealing to our sense of the heroic in athletics, but it doesn't pay to go for winners except on very auspicious occasions. On hard courts and other faster surfaces the emphasis switches more to the attack, but the fundamental limitation of the dimensions of the court cannot be ignored on any court.

Of course, this is one of those gray areas that can (and will) be forever in dispute. Just where you draw the line depends on the individual, the opponent, the context of the match, fatigue, temperament, etc. All these factors can create situations where exceptions to any rule of thumb may perhaps be justifiable. But, as a generalization, the statement that for most tennis players tactics should be nine-tenths or more limited can be solidly defended.

QUESTIONS

1. Define "strategy" and "tactics," showing the difference and giving an example of each.

2. How does knowing yourself relate to tactics?

3. Is great variety desirable for most players?

4. How can theory be kept practical?

5. What are good beginner tactics?

6. Why do most young players defeat themselves?

7. How can young players be taught not to beat themselves?

8. Do you like the concept of "limited tactics"?

CHAPTER 18

Percentage Tennis

THINKING IT THROUGH

"Play the percentages" is an old saying in all sports. No one argues the point, but it is astonishing how few tennis players have any idea what the percentage plays are in various situations. Even teaching pros are at times unaware of percentage thinking when they encounter it. The writer distinctly recalls hearing a very famous teaching (not playing) pro tell how he had followed the playing pro tour for a month and had observed with admiration how these players (at the time Kramer, Gonzalez, etc.) used all the shots except they seldom returned service down the line. He thought they should use this shot more and had even been so bold as to suggest it to the world's best players. Apparently the players had been kind enough not to point out that it is not a percentage play to return service straight; the crosscourt is the better play. If anyone knows the percentages these fellows do; their livelihood depends on this knowledge. Segura once remarked that he *always* made the easiest shot that would accomplish the task. If his opponent were way off court and fell down, he would loft the ball ten feet above the net and land it fifteen feet in for the winner. And Segura literally meant this: *never* take any needless risk whatever.

The concept of percentage is very much neglected by large numbers of coaches and instructors and by almost all but top players. They assume an error is always due to faulty execution. They seldom ask, "Did I miss that because it was too dangerous a shot? Was the risk factor high?" Thus they will try the same shot—the wrong one—literally scores of times and still not learn the error of their ways. They say, "I make too many errors," "I'm not tough enough," "I am too inconsistent." All these statements are true but offer no hope for improvement. They merely assert what is obvious: something is wrong with the way they play. They go out and practice their stroke for hours, yet still make the same errors in the next match.

THREE ASPECTS OF PERCENTAGE PLAY

The Theoretical Aspect

Theoretical percentage play assumes technical excellence. It makes no allowance at all for the fact that each individual is better at some shots than at others. It assumes the player can make with equal ease whatever shot the play demands. It also assumes the opposition has no particular strength or weakness but is evenly equipped to execute whatever is required. While we all know that such a situation never occurs except in the imagination, nevertheless like all ideals it is important to use the concept as a basis for thought and as an objective in our play even if we never quite achieve it.

We have already discussed a plan for the game which includes all parts of the court and all the shots. In capsule form they advise that from the baseline the percentage play is cross-court, from the halfcourt area the straight approach is to be preferred, and from the fore-court the largest effective area—usually cross-court—should be used. It has also been pointed out that the percentages are against winners from the baseline and halfcourt, against win-ners on service (a baseline shot), against win-ners on the first try at a passing shot, against winners on approach shots; therefore on *all* these occasions we should not attempt out-right winners and even if attacking should plan for additional follow-up shots, usually from the net position. How many players—even among quite good ones—realize these percent-ages and play by them? How many coaches understand that in spite of good technique this wisdom or the lack of it can control the out-come because the other fellow has some tech-nique too? How many coaches appreciate that other things being roughly equal, this control of the risk factor will determine the winner in a close doubles match?

There is little question that this is one of the most gravely neglected areas in tennis coach-ing and teaching. People look upon a coach or an instructor as one who can teach the boys and girls how to play the ball. This is a purely technical concept. Actually learning a stroke takes a lot of time and work—hundreds of repetitions—while a percentage tactical con-cept can be acquired in an afternoon. *One* lesson (unless the student is argumentatively stubborn) thus can effect a very considerable improvement in a player's game by eliminating errors and thus increasing consistency and confidence. This should be the first preoccupa-tion of a coach confronted with a squad: let's take what we have and do as well as possible

with it. As we try to reach this goal we can work toward increasing what we have—that is, our technique.

This will not only increase the team's effec-tiveness but also will reveal quite quickly those technical weaknesses that are most damaging: the inability to execute a deep crosscourt from the baseline, the lack of a spin service, no approach shots. The technical work needed will be glaringly exposed by any attempt at percentage play, and almost automatically the player will be forced to put his practice where it will do the most good. A player who cannot make a decent spin service will not be putting a lot of time on a hard flat service, which he has no right to try, by percentage thinking, until he has mastered a spin service. A person whose crosscourts are shaky will not waste time on straight shots. Anyone who cannot return service crosscourt and low in doubles will come to realize he must work on that one before attempting any other return.

The ideal theoretical percentages are a won-derful and necessary basic guide to the work of any effective coach. Almost everything he does —the order of work, emphasis, and long-range objectives—all should spring from a clear pic-ture of where he wants to get in the long run and an equally clear picture of what is step one, two, three, etc., in getting there. With this percentage plan he can be flexible and adjust to each individual on his squad, giving each what he most needs at the particular stage he is at. This sounds too complex and individualistic—a coach cannot give different treatment to each player—but it isn't since there will be groups at various stages. There will develop naturally a group working on spin service, another on crosscourts, another on approaches, others on volley and overhead. It is possible to team them up: the fellow who wants to work on his approach shot will be the right one to practice with the player who wants to practice his passing shot. The server can oppose him who needs a better return of serve, the lob against the overhead, the crosscourt against the crosscourt, etc. Behind all is the concept of percentage play.

The Technical Aspect

The tactical percentage concept deals with when to put the ball where and why. The technical concept deals with the how: how to achieve the tactical objective and at the same time to keep the risk factor at a minimum. It is very important to realize first that technique is the servant of tactics, never the reverse. It is unsound to say, "I like to hit the ball this way so I use these tactics." Always we should say, "Good tactics suggests this shot, and this is the easiest way to make the shot with the least chance for error so I play the ball in this manner."

Knowledge of the use of spin on strokes, shots, and service, a thorough comprehension of the meaning of the word "stroke" as contrasted with "hit," a good grasp of the importance of aiming in arcs rather than straight lines so that we make sure to miss the net as well as aim at the court—these are the basics of technical percentages. They can be summed up in two words: racket work; and a player's mastery of these skills more or less determines the success of his play against others of roughly equal athletic endowment. Leaving out bull sessions and cocktail parties, an extensive knowledge of tactics and percentages is of little use if it cannot be executed on the court. The reason for the title of this book is because of the crucial question: after you know it all, can you *do* it? If you cannot put topspin on the ball then you cannot avoid a considerable risk on all hard drives. If you cannot stroke your service you cannot arc the ball and give yourself margin over the net and in the court. If you cannot slice you cannot deal effectively with low forecourt shots except at great risk. And so forth throughout the entire gamut of the various shots in the various areas of the court.

In spite of the emphasis that was placed on the importance of the tactical percentage picture, it was also pointed out that each idea, such as play crosscourt, can be taught very quickly. By contrast, if a player cannot make a decent crosscourt drive it is quite an undertaking to teach him one. He must learn to prepare

his racket properly, to hit up a little, to spin the ball, and to pivot as he plays so as to turn the ball crosscourt. This takes a lot of dogged patience and drill. It requires at least ten or twenty times as long as is needed for him to grasp the tactical idea. So although technique is a means and not an end, nevertheless it is 90 percent or more of the labor required in building a game. The controlling concept is the theoretical one, yet the title of the book does not lose meaning.

The Competitive Aspect

Once a player has a thorough grasp of the theoretical and technical percentages he should not hesitate to modify them or to take exception, provided there is a persuasive reason that relates to the opponent of the moment. Any definite weakness should be exploited even if it means playing some straight baseline shots or some crosscourt approaches. If an opponent's answer to some specific shot is inadequate, the same maneuver should be repeated more frequently than ordinarily. Examples: if he pushes a drop shot back weakly and lays himself open, pull him in whenever good opportunity offers; if when you angle he plays straight, giving you another beautiful angle—need one say more? If he has a powerful overhead but volleys inconsistently, one would naturally lob only enough to keep him honest.

The element of surprise often justifies departing from a sound rule. First impressions are strong, and it is important that an opponent be denied a clear look at our plan right at the start. It is often wise to break the rules in the first few points. Having thus confused the issue we can revert to the old percentages with considerable success. However, young players sometimes take this advice to mean they should surprise the opponent every time, and they are soon playing the wrong shot so often it has become an unsound policy, not a surprise. It is a good idea to avoid too much talk about exceptions and to stick to proven tactics unless a tangible reason for variation, such as a weakness, presents itself. It is also important to teach the old maxim, "Rules are made to be broken—*after* you know them." Players should be told bluntly to stick to the rule until it is a mental and physical reflex; then and only then should they consider departing from it on auspicious occasions.

There is considerable room for differences in emphasis in carrying out the dictates of percentage play. Let us assume you have a very strong attacking forehand when given a short ball but have no backhand approach. It might then be good tactics for you to attack and go to net whenever you can take one good step inside the baseline for your forehand but not to follow any backhands at all if you can avoid it; just keep the ball going until you get a forehand. This would be playing percentage tennis to the fullest extent your skill permits but not to the extent of attempting what is beyond you. Many a fine player uses what one might call modified percentage play along these lines, either offensively or defensively.

PERCENTAGE PLAYERS FIGHT HARDER

It might almost be said that until one knows percentages one *cannot* fight hard. If a player tries a risky shot and makes an error, where is his fight? The point is over, and he lost it, and there was hardly any fight about it at all. No matter how intrinsically spirited a player may be, he hasn't much fight as a tennis player if he does that very often. A percentage player by keeping the risk factor low even when he attacks gives away very few points and almost never beats himself. One has to beat him or he wins, and he almost always does his best because he doesn't have to be "hot" to put up a creditable showing.

Moreover, the very fact that he has disciplined himself to play according to a set of policies means that he makes the same shot from any given position every time. He has

practiced it and at least to a considerable degree perfected it. He seldom attempts any shot that he is at all unsure of controlling. He almost can't help but be consistent—steadiness and sureness are built into his game.

Last but equally important, a percentage player has thought things through so he knows what he is going to do in all ordinary frequently recurring circumstances. Having a plan like this with no reservations or doubts is perhaps the greatest aid a match player can have. He is completely secure mentally, knows what he is going to do, has practiced it, has confidence in it. Is it not obvious that he can fight harder than one who makes snap judgments: "I guess I'll play this one straight," "What should I do with this one?" etc.? The percentage player not only has a plan—he has a good plan, he knows it, and it makes him feel tough. This solid feeling is just as important to a tennis player in singles or doubles as it is to the offensive and defensive platoons in football.

This of course does not release him from the responsibility of thinking, watching for weaknesses to exploit, or making the most of his pet shots. But as the basis on which to build one's game and as the foundation stone of being a fighter there is nothing comparable to a knowledge of and belief in the percentages.

FROM START TO FINISH— USING PERCENTAGES

The preceding paragraphs have dealt with good players—upper intermediate to advanced —to use popular categories. Many instructors such as club pros and secondary school coaches are dealing with very few of these and a lot of beginners and lower intermediates. They should still deal in and emphasize percentages. Beginners are taught to aim the ball high—three to six feet—above the net, and they are told the "why" too: that we wish to miss the net by the widest margin compatible with getting the ball in. They are taught to aim far in—ten feet or so—and they are told the "why" too: that if we do this then even if the ball goes higher than we aimed it will land in, even if there is a wind it will land in, that to allow a large margin for error at all times is step one in learning the percentages.

Intermediates should be taught to hit everything crosscourt until they get a really fat setup around the service line. Then they should attack but should not aim too close to any lines. They should start practicing approaches more and baseline shots less and should learn a drop shot. Advanced players should drill on what one might call the capitalizing shots: approaches, overheads, accurate touch volleys such as drop volleys—in sum, all the shots which require putting the ball away or forcing, and in particular those shots which demand that a player put the ball in a small space. These are, of course, the most refined and the most difficult.

All players should learn at an early stage to lob *high* when in trouble. It usually does no good to give verbal advice. It is necessary to get them out on the court and make them lob —higher, please; higher, please; now deeper, please—until they *do* lob high and deep.

As each of these shots is taught it is of great importance that the student or player be made to understand exactly why he is being taught this shot to be executed in this manner for this situation. Young people can be very stubborn unless they believe. Moreover, there are so many funny theories going around about tennis—most of them unsound because they are nonpercentage—that the kids are often very hard to convince. A coach at a large university finds this particularly true because the boys come literally from everywhere and thus bring into the group every conceivable

theory, tactical or technical, that one can imagine, plus a few that approach the unimaginable. In addition the boys are at an age when they question all authority, and the tennis coach is the last one who should think he is great enough to be exempt. The final arbiter is reason, and unless an instructor bases his teaching firmly on this rock he will very likely have a squad of doubters, and doubters don't win very much as a rule. There is nothing more absolutely and irrefutably reasonable and logical than sound percentages.

QUESTIONS

1. What are the percentage plays:
   a. From the baseline? (Your opponent is not at net.)
   b. From the halfcourt position? (Your opponent is not at net.)
   c. In trying to pass a net player?
   d. When both opponents are well in at net in doubles and you are back?
   e. In taking up a position at net after an approach?
   f. In placing an overhead hit somewhat from your forehand side?
   g. In returning service against a net rusher?
2. What is the relation of technique to tactics?
3. How do competitive situations modify theoretical percentages?
4. How do percentages relate to "fight"?
5. What are good "beginner" percentages?
6. What is the final arbiter in any dispute about the game?

CHAPTER 19

Coaching

DEFINITION

In this chapter, the word "coach" means to "teach." In these days of athletic scholarships the word is often equated with "recruit." In other words, if a coach can persuade enough fine players to attend a school, the coach is successful, because they will be a winning team. This is usually just not true. As a rule each conference has its regulations that put the member schools on an equal footing. A school that recruits heavily is usually up against other schools that do the same. In high schools it is not possible to recruit: a coach takes the players who live there and that's that. Therefore, the final analysis of coaching skill comes down to what the coach does with the material—at any level of excellence. A poor coach with excellent material will do only fairly well. A good coach will win championships. A poor coach with poor material will achieve nothing. A good coach will achieve respectability with here and there an upset. This is just as true in tennis as it is in team sports like football and basketball. Thus what follows is applicable to all situations and all teams whether made up of recruited stars or run-of-the-mill talent that happens to be at one's school or college.

REASSURING THE WOMEN

Women should be assured that everything in this chapter applies equally to both sexes. The skills, team morale, drilling, tactics, and all other aspects of tennis apply to all players— sex does not alter them in any way. Women's teams are appearing in ever larger numbers throughout the country. It is probably safe to assert that the "explosion in tennis" is more due to increased participation by women than to greater participation by men. Women at schools and colleges need and will profit by competent coaching just as much and in the same manner as men have over an extended period.

THE FUNCTION OF THE COACH

Many years ago President Lowell of Harvard made a remark to the effect that it did not disturb him if Harvard lost an athletic contest, but if Harvard athletes ever ceased to take the field with the intention and expectation of winning, this would be a disaster for Harvard. This remark revealed great insight into the meaning of athletics at educational institutions. Winning every time is not so important, but developing a way of life, an attitude that says, "Anything I do I am going to do well and I mean to succeed at it" is a basic and deeply important educational objective. Without such a fundamental viewpoint it is difficult to the point of being impossible to justify all the money, manpower, and paraphernalia that are poured into intercollegiate athletics. Certainly health is a poor argument; there are many far less expensive ways to keep reasonably fit. Commercial considerations can explain the "gate" sports but have little connection with all the other more numerous unprofitable sports such as tennis. The real guts of the meaning of school athletics is the personal experience of the participants and what it does for them.

The narrow function of a coach is to try to win athletic contests. A broader definition gives him a place in this educational picture of which he is a part. The person who in this larger sense is a coach tries to have all his policies stem from this viewpoint. He attempts to set up a program within which each individual can by personal effort come close to achieving his full potential. This makes possible, in his particular athletic field, the maximum profitable experience during his school career. The next step is to inspire those with natural ability to give it a 100 percent effort insofar as is compatible with other educational values, such as studies.

The appeal of the coach should be based on the axiom, "It is far more fun to do this well, and often to win, than to do it badly, and usually get beaten. It is also more fun for the coaches to succeed, so we are right with you." Once this attitude is established it soon becomes clear that a major *effort* is needed (not to be confused with sacrifice). Those who make the effort, follow it through, and get there have not only succeeded but more important now know what it takes to approach the top in anything they undertake. This is a great contribution to their education: the develop-

ment of the habit of success and an insight into what it takes in struggle and perseverance.

In the course of learning and doing all this they may also be led to learn about themselves. Ask them, "What is fun?" An analysis suggests that the lighter meaning of the word is associated with silly fooling around, kidding, playing for laughs. But the deeper meaning of the word, and the thing all athletes really want, is satisfaction. The football player meets the challenges of cold rain, bumps, and mud, and says later it was "fun." The tennis player runs for two and one-half hours in a long close one that approaches an ordeal (in a sense it is an ordeal) and afterwards says it was "fun." Actually in each case it is the satisfaction of having met a difficult challenge, of having made an effort that was truly great and rugged. This is what "fun" means—real fun—for the athlete. They learn this and its corollaries: that working hard is one of life's true pleasures; the one who gives a lot gets a lot back; the real sucker is the one who is so afraid of being a sucker he won't commit himself to anything. One might say they learn a good bit about how to go at whatever career they choose. And meanwhile they have an outlet for that desire to do great deeds—like an Indian boy's yearning to be a great hunter like his father—which, however corny it may sound, is a characteristic of youth. It is easy to sneer at all this, but it remains a truth.

Thus the function of the coach primarily is to deal understandingly, sympathetically, and constructively with young growing people. He should insofar as is possible provide scope for this development and growth and give it direction and purpose within the limits of his sport. The lesson here is that this educational process is the objective, and victory is its by-product. Any coach who handles his squad in this manner cannot help but get back an effort that in turn cannot help but produce a reasonable share of success against opposition in its own class, not to mention lasting friendships, for young people are as a rule the most, not the least, appreciative.

THE CRUCIAL PRESENT

Many times we hear coaches quoted as saying, "This is a building year." Some coaches would prefer to say that coaching primarily means to build every year, incessantly, to try to keep up with that annual planned catastrophe known as graduation. But to single out one year is to imply that this year's group can't beat anybody until after a season of losing. In short, they are inferior. It also implies that a lot of work that should have been done to fill graduation gaps was not done so there is a hole, or a row of holes, in the team—holes that could have been forecast probably two years and certainly one year ahead, and nothing has yet been done to fill them. This in turn implies criticism of the coaching—and here is the coach himself saying it!

We often hear it said, "Champions are born, not made." This is quite true, and therefore a coach must be lucky to have a great team. But competence *can* be made by the coaching. Therefore the criterion a coach should set for himself is that he should *always* have a good team, and if he is lucky a great team. This is a high standard, but it is not out of reach. Leaving out acts of God such as an injury streak or a flu epidemic, this performance level is attainable by planning and effort.

If this standard is accepted then there is never a "building year" in the sense that victory is out of reach for that season. Every year potentially is a good year, and sometimes we may have a fine year. This approach is of more importance than many appreciate. Athletes are young, and it is a platitude—but true—that youth lives in the present. They want to feel that *this* year they may win, right now, today. And each new group, each year and each match day, wants to have this feeling. In a sense they have a right to it. The coach has many years, but this is *their* year and will not occur again. It is a function of the coach to create a constructive, hopeful, optimistic attitude in the fall—the start of every year—regardless of the current odds in the league they are in.

ENTHUSIASM

Youth brings to you a vast store of enthusiasm, unspoiled by the slings and arrows that have outraged most adults. It is fundamentally important to meet this fervor half way, to come up with an equal spirit that establishes a rapport and a kinship with the squad. Harvard's famous former director of athletics, William J. Bingham, used annually and without fail to remind his assembled coaches that this was the key to youth—enthusiasm. Always this repeated admonition kicked the staff off to a good start; no matter how many times he told us it never failed to help. So, with thanks to Bill Bingham, it is said again here for anyone who may need to have his flagging spirits stirred up a bit. The kids can't live without it, so you'd better dig it up—every single season. It is a must.

ORGANIZATION

At any worthwhile institution academic education comes first and sports second. Therefore a really smooth organization, with people reporting at specified times of the coach's choosing, and a continuous flow that is all planned is a lovely dream that is impossible to achieve. If a player has a lab you've lost him for that day —and that's that. If he has three hour exams and a paper in one week there is little use in pressuring him. It will merely make him unhappy and will also lead him to distrust you since he will feel—rightly—that you have a narrow viewpoint that doesn't take into account other aspects of his career which at times must come to the fore.

There are three constructive approaches a coach can take to this apparently messy situation. First, encourage all players to plan ahead. Point out the busiest time in the tennis schedule, urge them to consider it their duty to keep enough ahead in their work to allow them to concentrate on tennis at certain key times. Some of them will respond to this quite well, others won't, according to their maturity or lack of same and according to their personal natures. But to whatever extent any of them do respond a real gain has been made. Second, find out which players have labs that limit their practice time. Arrange to work with them —technically or in doubles or anything else— on their few free days. By thus giving them some preference you avoid missing them altogether. Third, encourage players to come down in pairs, and keep a written list of things you wish to get done. If Joe and Jim (Sally and Susie) show up early, and you know you want Joe to improve his backhand crosscourt and Jim to work on his spin serve, have Jim serve to Joe's backhand and have Joe return it crosscourt, while you advise and teach first one, then the other. The point is, no matter who shows up at any hour you can keep constantly busy; in fact, you will never come close to catching up to your list. Of course there are often things on your list which are of first importance: Jim is losing matches because he double faults and gets upset. This is a repair job that must be done at the very first opportunity no matter what else has to give way. But in general a very flexible plan of organization is the kind that will best adapt itself to an environment that is genuinely academic.

A different type of organization, which is invisible and confined to the mind of the coach, is far more important and if well done far more fruitful in results. This is the never-ending job of assessing each player, deciding what he needs next (and why) in order to progress, and then managing to get with him to do it. This sounds very obvious, but it isn't. Many players will be convinced when they come to you that they know what is needed. They are often unaware of their real problems. A big selling job, backed by solid reason (the players are sharp), must precede action, because unless you and the player agree on direction, progress is impossible or nearly so. To keep each individual on a good-sized squad coming along as rapidly as time and opportunity permit; to form, keep in mind, and work toward an ideal plan for use of available dou-

bles material; to be mentally at least one and preferably two years ahead in this planning— this is the intangible type of organization that marks a really good coach. Such a coach always has a pretty good team.

PROVIDING OPPORTUNITY AND JUSTICE

This is a real must and requires a lot of thought and planning. A straight challenge system is poor in the opinion of this writer. With a large squad it is better if the coach sets up tournaments within groups. Thus a winner of a few matches can rise above a large number of players without beating them all, which might take him two seasons in a northern college. Near the top, challenges are all right but must be earned: if the number three man is winning and the four is losing, four should be denied the right to play three—he should play down, not up. This sometimes angers a player, but the coach should stick to his guns: he who wins for the team gets more opportunity than he who loses for the team. In all difficult decisions the coach should discuss the problem with the captain and the freshman coach if there is one. If both these think he is wrong then he might well be wise to reconsider. If both agree then he should stick to it even if a violent protest is forthcoming. This matter of who gets chances, when, and against whom is one of a coach's toughest problems unless he prefers, as some do, to let them play challenges without regard for team results. How to run your squad is a very personal matter, and the last thing any writer should do is to try to establish a given system as the one best. The only dogmatic thing that can be said is that opportunity and justice must be provided, and these often require quite a bit of soul searching when the matter isn't black and white but very gray.

The number one player often requires separate treatment. When number one plays a challenge there is everything to lose and noth-

ing to gain. If he or she is in all probability—
on the record—the squad's best player, then it
is sometimes wise to rule that the player cannot be displaced unless beaten twice. Here
again the coach must use judgment more than
a set of rules in the search for justice along
with opportunity. One year may well differ
from another.

INDIVIDUAL ANALYSIS

Quite frequently a player will not accept many
of the less tangible suggestions about percentages, about not being in a hurry to make an
ace, etc. Often in such cases a written analysis
given to the player privately—a full type-writ-
ten page or more discussing this particular
player, showing what he could do, contrasting
it with what he does do, as specifically as
possible—will have a marked effect. He reads
it, takes it with him, looks at it again; perhaps
it sinks in where other approaches failed.
While success is of course not guaranteed, this
method has solved quite a few hard cases. It
should be added that these difficult cases are
more often than not the better players. A poor
player knows he is poor; he is as a rule very
willing to accept advice and criticism and constructive suggestions. A good player knows he
is good and tends to hang pretty stubbornly to
his own ideas of right and wrong. He will not
change easily as a rule. This is the fellow who
is at times a tough nut to crack on percentage
play.

TEAM SPIRIT

This is much more important than many people think who say, "Tennis is an individual
sport; team spirit doesn't mean much." This
is just not so. There have been innumerable
occasions when a team has defeated another
team even though the other team was clearly
superior. Team spirit can have an almost magi-

cal effect of creating a situation where everyone on the team plays "better than he knows
how." When all six men do this at once almost
anything can happen, and the whole becomes
greater than the sum of its parts.

Doubles is the great instrument for forging
team spirit in tennis. It gets the players working together, it provides the second punch if
the first one—the singles—leaves the match
undecided, and above all it is the main hope
the underdog has for overcoming superior personnel. It may almost be said that doubles is
the key to coaching in tennis. Every close
team match is settled by the doubles, so where
are you if you haven't worked on them? And
if a team has indeed worked hard on its doubles and has confidence in them, then it gets
that "we" feeling instead of the "I" feeling.
Once the team wins a close one where the
singles are split 3-3 and all hangs on the doubles, the team feeling tends to grow and solid-
ify, and good morale is almost a certainty for
the rest of the season.

SQUAD SPIRIT AND THE J.V.

Most colleges and schools restrict the budget so
that a big junior varsity schedule is impossible.
Yet it is a fact that some of this year's second
six will be in next year's first six, and this is
true also in doubles. The importance of the
J.V. is so obvious as almost to need no comment, yet some coaches live so much in the
present that they cannot look away from this
year's first six. It is good policy to make a point
of bolstering the morale of the J.V. If they
work hard and push the varsity, the latter will
be on its toes. If they work and progress they
will make a good varsity when they move up.
If they think of themselves as future varsity
players rather than as J.V. players, they develop pride and higher standards for their
personal performances.

The greatest concrete show of concern a
coach can make to his J.V. is to use them
whenever possible. If whenever a sweep in the

singles ices the match the J.V. goes into the doubles they are extremely heartened. Not only do they get to play, but also they get a chance to measure up under match pressure. They know the coach is watching, and they know he is interested in them—this is a real chance to show they are competitors. And of course the coach has an opportunity to spot technical and tactical weaknesses that only pressure reveals. Above all, using the J.V. a lot produces deep squad spirit: *all* the players are for the coach and for the team, not just the top aces.

COACHING IN THE NORTH

Coaching tennis in a northern college or school imposes on the coach and players the severe limitations of an uncooperative climate. It is actually very good training for a coach, because he soon learns that his time is quite limited, so he is forced to devise ways to make the most of what little he has. A ruthless paring away of things that are desirable is necessary until only the bare essentials remain. It is quite common to hear members of northern squads saying, "We ought to do this and that and the other" during the winter, but come spring there is no time to do them unless something even more important is sacrificed. All the moaning and groaning about it is however completely unjustified, because northern teams play other northern teams who operate under similar handicaps. The cold, the wind, the rain are not limited to any one college town; they pretty much blanket the North in April and often even into May. Normally the northern states are in April just about on the line where the warm and cold air are fighting it out. Usually the warm settled weather moves in around May first, and so the northern teams get (sometimes) a whole two or three weeks of decent tennis weather before exams! Some, whose terms end earlier, get less—but few get more. To say the season is short is a masterpiece in understatement.

Now that the worst is known, and it is pretty clear that there are many time-consuming things we cannot do, let us take a more constructive approach: what *can* a tennis coach do in the North? First, he can make the fullest possible use of the fall. The freshmen can be called out, tried out, ranked, and some matches played to test these rankings. Tentative freshmen doubles teams can be formed. A good bit of instruction on the basic fundamentals of percentage tactics can take place, both in singles and in doubles. In this way the freshmen are at once initiated into how the coaches think and teach, and the coaches become somewhat familiar with the new faces and talent.

The fall can be crucially important in curing a weakness such as a poor basic forehand or backhand. It is next to impossible in the spring, with one match following another every couple or three days, to ask a player to make any significant change in his stroke; it upsets him so much he can scarcely play at all. But in the fall, when matches are not being played, it can be done. He can get the new idea and drill and drill until he gets his teeth into the new method so he is ready for the spring matches with an improved technique. This is particularly true of something like a spin service: you have to get him past the point where he doesn't dare try it on second service, or it isn't any good to him. It is pretty true to say that in the North you make your team in the fall and play your matches in the spring.

Another big fall job is to get your doubles in order plus as much insurance as possible. By insurance is meant an extra partner for each good doubles player so that if anyone sprains an ankle or gets the bug the doubles are not totally impaired. If the entire squad is taught the fundamentals of position play and team play it is often possible to create a doubles pool —a group of players all of whom can perform creditably in doubles and therefore can fill in at need. Also it is often true that some of the players who are not so good at singles will be good at doubles. If such players can be uncovered and encouraged they are a real asset: you have fresh strength to put into the fray instead of nothing but singles players who may be tired.

The fall has one intangible but all-important function—it sets the tone. Every aspiring player coming to your school quite naturally has in mind the questions "How do they handle tennis here? Will I get a chance? Will I get help?" There is a good bit of truth in what they say about first impressions; you get them with you or you don't, and if you don't at first it is a tough job later. If the freshmen are led—by deeds not just by words—to believe that your program is dynamic, planned, thoughtful, and really helpful to individuals, an immediate enthusiasm is generated which is the basis of team spirit and team performance. The word goes out—tennis here is good. You have won the first big test—the players are with you. The rest for the most part is merely being industrious.

Often the winter is not a total loss in the North. More and more indoor courts are being built for year-round use. Players can often be given one or two important things to work on, and they may emerge decisively improved in the spring. A striking case of such progress was Ned Weld. As a freshman he had a weak backhand, no spin serve, and no net game. He had ability, scramble, and a good forehand. The first winter he learned a pretty good backhand and a fair spin service. The second winter he perfected the service into a pace-filled topspin and went to net at the drop of a hat. He soon knew where to go, developed savvy, and had some good volleys and approaches going for him. His senior year he was captain. His progress was a real proof that planning plus work can do it, even in New England. This anecdote has real importance in this book because indoor clubs are popping up everywhere like mushrooms. Many a coach and many a green but promising player will have a chance to do the same type of thing in the North of the future. Beyond a doubt the more southerly climates offer the greatest opportunities, but learning tennis in the North is by no means

hopeless and is becoming less so each year. Weld made the effort—others can too.

Limiting Objectives

The main thing in the North is to accept your limitations in time and fit your objectives to what you have, not what you wish you had. Every other northern coach has all the same causes for woe, so the alibis won't hold water. Decide on where you can make the greatest improvements in the shortest time and concentrate on that. In the spring the best bet is usually to stress tactics as contrasted with technique. Technique, which must "sink in," cannot be fooled with much in the spring, while an improvement in a player's thinking usually pays off sooner. The spring is the time for stressing the percentages, in both singles and doubles, for now you are playing matches. Great emphasis should be placed on limited tactics in an effort to achieve some consistency as quickly as possible.

Last, a northern coach must fight to remain constructive in his attitude. Once the cold, or the wind, or the rain gets him down he is out of luck. While he may envy the southern coaches, he is not playing them in his league, and his own league is what counts. Even the southerners, who customarily defeat the northern sections, do not have a soft time at home, because the other teams in their area have equal advantages and are equally formidable. They too have to sweat it out and work for what they get.

COACHING IN THE SOUTH

By "South" is meant the entire southern width of the country from coast to coast—i.e., all areas where a long tennis season obtains. Here much more complete planning is possible. It should be practicable to take any talented player and through drills make him competent in all three areas—baseline, halfcourt, forecourt—and teach him the tactical percentages for each area. Meanwhile competition in squad play and intercollegiate matches should give him the competitive experience without which technique is not too effective. Of course, some players are lazy, some are stubborn, some are unwilling, and the ideal of developing fully all the available talent will never be achieved even in a favorable climate. But southern coaches can and should set their standards high, should make ambitious plans, and should not be content with less than something approaching true excellence (in relation to ability) in their juniors and seniors.

The rapid development of the game and the multiplication of good teams in southern areas show this process is occurring. As junior development programs increase and are supplemented by more and more opportunity at more and more colleges, it is a safe bet that an ever-increasing proportion of youthful talent will be enabled to flourish and get the most from the game. In fact, as athletic authorities tend more and more to promote lifetime participant sports along with the "gate" sports, it is a good probability that this growth will accelerate. All southern areas can be just simply blanketed by the flat statement, "Here is opportunity unlimited."

COACHING SPECIFICS

We all pretty much know what we want the players to do. The objective is clear, but the question of how to get them there is not so simple. If a coach has a mental picture of a systematic development of a well-rounded game he can adapt this to the needs of each player. One such system could be roughly as follows.

I. *Baseline Skills*

1. Drill on deep crosscourts, concentrating on clearing the net by a good margin and on getting depth without risk —i.e., keep the ball away from lines.

2. Drill on deep spin services placed to backhand. Have the players aim higher and higher over the net until they just can't spin it enough to get it in. Note: overdoing this drill can injure the arm.

As soon as a player has mastered this area he will begin to win the rally—note this does not mean win the point—and will get more and more setups from the opposition. This brings him to the halfcourt area.

II. *Halfcourt Skills*

1. The coach should pop the ball to him in midcourt so it sets up nicely, and have him move in, racket high and close faced, and play hard down the line with topspin following to net, with stress on positioning himself well to the right of the center service line.

2. Same setup to backhand; have him play down forehand side and move in using a slice rather than a topspin drive.

3. Same setup to forehand and backhand; have him play a drop shot emphasizing disguise by always getting ready to play a hard shot.

4. The coach should (by chopping) chip little net skimmers that land short and bounce low, and have the player move in and slice them down the line, taking the net position.

5. Set the ball up near the side line; have the player angle sharply crosscourt.

III. *Drills at Net*

1. Make poor, short, low lobs; have the player kill them, emphasizing preparation of racket and feet. As mastery is acquired, improve the lob until the student is playing good overheads. Note: not too much of this, or the arm may get sore.

2. The four volleys (Diagram 19–1)
   a. Forehand crosscourt. From the backhand corner the coach should drive straight; the player then volleys crosscourt with his forehand. Em-

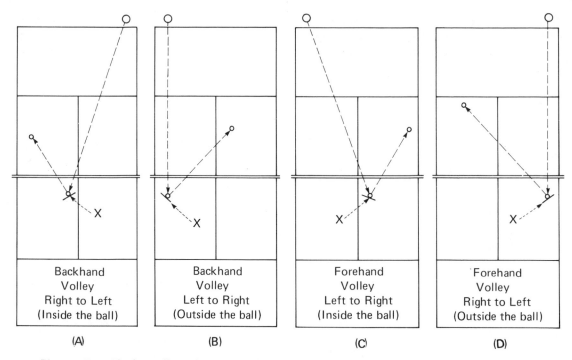

Backhand Volley Right to Left (Inside the ball)	Backhand Volley Left to Right (Outside the ball)	Forehand Volley Left to Right (Inside the ball)	Forehand Volley Right to Left (Outside the ball)
(A)	(B)	(C)	(D)

Diagram 19–1. The four volleys. These are the four most common opportunity situations at net (excluding overhead). Note the 90-degree difference in the presentation of the racket face to the ball in making the contrasting shots (A compared with B, C compared with D). Inability to quickly make these skillful racket preparations accounts for the tendency to volley back to an opponent instead of away from him. Few can do all four without special drilling. Note also that the player closes in decisively. A ball-throwing machine is ideal for drilling these skills.

phasize making a sharp angle without going near a line—land the ball way in. Stress closing in.

b. Backhand the other way. Same positions, coach plays crosscourt, player volleys for open side with backhand. Stress getting inside the ball to make the angle. Stress advancing the racket as near the net as possible even though the ball must be taken later to get inside it.

c. Backhand crosscourt. The coach now places himself in the forehand corner, the player three or four feet to the left of the centerline. The coach drives straight, the player volleys crosscourt with his backhand.

d. Forehand the other way. Same positions, the coach plays crosscourt.

Comment: These are straight technical drills duplicating the situations that occur most frequently in actual play. A coach should **not** hurry. It is usually useless to rush through all four in one day: take one at a time, try to get it right—then repeat, repeat, repeat—fifty or one hundred times. Leave the others for another day.

This drilling process can be refined to any desired degree—to include dropping it, punching it deeper (for going through doubles players), etc. It depends on the development of the player and available time.

An automatic ball thrower can be very useful in these drills.

IV. Composite Drills

Have two players rally crosscourt, trying to keep the ball behind the service line. Whenever a ball lands inside the service line the point is "on," one player attacks, the other defends. Such a drill is fun—they play—and it instills the total pattern of all the skills into the player's mind: what shot to play, when to play it and why, anywhere in the court. It also serves to reveal any department in which a player is weak; the coach makes note and plans further drilling on this individual aspect of the student's game.

V. *Defensive Drills*

1. The lob. The coach makes a forcing shot, the player lobs. Emphasize catching the ball—i.e., let it land on the racket, then a full high-lift follow-through. Make the forcing shot feeble at first, so the player can think and do well, then after he is doing well increase the pressure. End by banging balls at him from the net position so he has very little time; if he can lob these the job is done.
2. The return of service. Combine this with the service drill. Emphasize moving into the ball, short backswing, aggression to cut off any plans by the attacker. Have a specific objective: serve to forehand, hit it back hard down the center; serve to backhand a little short, slice it and take the net; serve and advance to net, have receiver play for feet; serve wide to backhand court, have receiver return sharply crosscourt.
3. Passing shots. Combine with forecourt drills on approaches. Emphasize extra spin, dipping it at the feet, deception, lobbing if attacker closes too far in. Topspin lob practice may be included.

VI. *Doubles Drills*

Four players participate; the coach gives a little talk about one idea, the players try to do it.
1. Serve to center (deep), partner moves across toward center.
2. First volley always down center, close on center.

3. Hit *every* setup for someone's feet—never risk a line.
4. Return of service: crowd it to break it, take the net.
5. How to use the lob, when, and why; now let's try it.
6. Shot sequences: I play low, you close in to kill.

If coaching of this sort is done, pretty soon the players become quite knowledgeable offensively and defensively. As usual the play reveals individual glaring shortcomings—inability to execute the desired shot—and these require individual drilling on technique. But at least now they are using their resources intelligently, and the work needed for further gains almost defines itself.

THE PRINCIPLE OF DRILLING

The foregoing is abbreviated. Each coach must constantly use his judgment, devise new drills for special situations, and lay stress where it is obviously needed. To attempt to enumerate all the possibilities would merely mean to repeat the section on technique. It is enough to say that technique requires a golfer's attitude: any shot he is muffing he drills at the first opportunity. In tennis often someone is needed to set up the ball, and the coach can do it best because he can also spot the fault and specify the cure. A drill of this sort can sometimes transform a worried loser into a confident winner by solving the problem that was nagging him and undermining his confidence.

It is usually not enough to spot an error and mention why it was an error. A coach should watch for a recurring fault, an error that tends to repeat itself and be not a one time but a continual drain on results and morale. One example will suffice. One player seemed to look good but always made just a few too many errors. Observation revealed that most of the errors occurred on approach shots. One long drill on these and the player was a winner in the next team match. It is not possible to do everything; therefore, to pick out what is key and concentrate on it is the job. The simile that likens a person's game to a slice of swiss cheese is always valid: you can't plug all the holes, but you can try to plug the biggest one.

All players should be encouraged to drill themselves. "I'll set up twenty for you, then you set up twenty for me." "I'll set it up, you practice your approach, I'll try to pass you." "I'll practice lobs, you hit overheads." The point is to persuade them to form the habit of improving their games not by vaguely hitting a lot of balls but by having a specific objective in mind that will add to their skills. Afterward they can play, keep up their whole game, and enjoy themselves. If this system of practicing in pairs is used a lot, it actually achieves a huge increase in the effectiveness of the coach: his lessons continue on and on even when he is not there. If he is dealing with considerable numbers, this multiplication of himself is his only hope of coping with the vast amount of work that needs to be done.

Subdivision

Great subdivision is possible in the matter of drills. To volley well one needs four volleys: both ways with the forehand and both ways with the backhand. Each of the four is sharply different. Two of them—the crosscourt—involve getting far around outside the ball. The other two demand that we get far inside the ball. Each needs a separate concentrated drill by the coach. Quite often a player will pick up two or three of these volleys quickly but will have to work very long and hard to get the fourth going at all well. Every player has his easy shots and his hard shots in the learning process.

A further subdivision may be advisable with a player who volleys well but does not close in well. A separate drill on closing in—concentrating on playing the ball at the earliest possible instant and ignoring everything else—can be enormously helpful to one who has this specific weakness. It is mostly a leg drill.

There is little profit in attempting to enumerate every small thing that might arise; it would doubtless require another book to hold them all. But there is indeed one big lesson here. A coach is dealing constantly with muscle knowledge (habit) and thought habits. In each case the most effective method so far devised for creating a desired habit is to repeat the act or the mental reaction a large number of times. This seems to create a groove in the mind—or whatever it is that represents a habit in that thing we call our brain. It does little good to say, "Play like this" unless this is followed by having the player do it a very considerable number of times. Thus one secret of good coaching is the ability to devise a little drill for whatever fault needs correction—and the patience to set up the ball in this particular way or that again and again and again until the player makes the right shot and makes it with good technique as automatically as if he had been born with it. Drill is the key to success; it is the only way to achieve real advances.

Drill should not be confused with practice. Every team practices—that is, goes out on the court and plays every good day. This, of course, is necessary. But the team whose coach constantly inserts this drill for this player and that drill for that player and a few drills (overhead and approaches and doubles tactics) for all players—this team moves ahead faster. If this advantage, small though it is, is gained continually throughout four years with a given group of players it is clear it can easily be a determining factor if their rivals started out anywhere nearly on an even basis. It can almost be said that a team that merely practices tends to stand still: it does no more than polish up the status quo. A team that practices and also drills on new skills or old weaknesses preserves the status quo and also continually builds new strength. Fair players become good, and good become excellent.

A coach who accepts the maxim, "Genius is nine-tenths perspiration," and makes the individual drill the basis of his patient labor—this man will create a snowball that keeps getting bigger as it rolls, not spectacularly and quickly but inevitably and inexorably. He cannot help but get competitive results if he also teaches good tactics. But once again the theme of racket work is stressed, and this is what takes the time—90 percent of it—even if tactics are undoubtedly 50 percent in importance. Perhaps another well-worn quote is appropriate: "Genius is the infinite capacity for taking pains." If we substitute "drilling on racket work" for "taking pains" we have a first-class formula for coaching success.

PERCENTAGES—YESTERDAY, TODAY, AND FOREVER

An eternal preoccupation with percentages is a necessary characteristic of any coach worth his salt. They are not obvious at all to nine out of ten freshmen, and eight out of ten sophomores forget them over the summer. It is a good idea to be dramatic when occasion permits so as to leave a vivid example of percentage thinking in the player's mind. If he takes a first volley (in doubles) at the service line and angles it for an ace, bellow "No!" decisively. He is astonished and will often say, "But coach—that's the best volley I've made this year" or something like that. This is your chance: extol his volley as a great shot but a bad thought. It was too risky from that far back, and one shouldn't have to make the volley of the year to win. Can you do it again? No? Well, then. Etc. And ram home the lesson: judge *all* shots this way—in terms of percentages, not in terms of individual excellence. Of course the other three are listening too. In this way a percentage manner of thinking permeates the squad and there is gradually less "big missing."

In singles, encourage toughness. Point out that most points are lost, not won (a fact). Point out that the pros don't aim for lines—they aim well inside the lines; can you do better? Youth always tends to be reckless and to put pressure on itself by trying the risky shot. This is the greatest battle a coach has

—to make clear to them not only that this is a fact, but why, how, where, and what to do instead, all over the court, in singles and in doubles. It is a big job.

Technique should be related to percentages. You put topspin on a shot, not because it is "right"—that is meaningless—but because that lets you aim well above the net and still be sure of hitting well inside the court. It is the percentage way to stroke the ball from one given spot to another.

A considerable selling job is often needed before the new players are on your side. They think you want them to be a pusher (horrible thought to a young firebrand!), that you are overconservative, that you don't believe in putting the ball away. But keep at it. They will see it in time, and then you have made a tough player out of a reckless misser. Often more improvement is possible this way than by technical instruction, for he who thinks wrong cannot escape doing wrong.

Very frequently the main difference between a tournament-toughened player and another will be completely in the fact that one knows percentages and the other doesn't. This is where coaching can really close the gap. Your player is physically equally talented; he is just plain ignorant when it comes to playing a match, and good guidance can make a dramatic improvement, at times quite quickly. You can't teach a player a backhand in a day, but you can teach him to aim it farther inside the lines in a few moments.

QUESTIONS

1. What is the function of athletics in an educational institution?

2. What is the function of the coach?

3. What does "fun" mean to an athlete?

4. Can champions be "made"?

5. What can a coach hope to achieve with average to poor material?

6. Is enthusiasm important in coaching?

7. What kind of organization works in an individual sport like tennis?

8. What kinds of planning should the coach do?

9. How does individual analysis help?

10. Is team spirit important in individual sports?

11. How important is it to coach doubles?

12. How does the junior varsity fit in?

13. How is a northern coach limited?

14. Is fall practice important in the North?

15. How does fall practice differ from spring practice? Why?

16. How does the favorable climate make coaching different in the South compared with the North?

17. What are some good baseline drills?

18. What are some good halfcourt drills?

19. What four basic drills are needed for volleying?

20. Describe a composite drill.

21. How can you drill defensive situations?

22. What should you drill in doubles?

23. How can the principle of drilling be used to multiply the effectiveness of the coach?

24. Why is knowledge useless without drill?

25. How does "practice" differ from "drilling"?

26. Can you drill percentages?

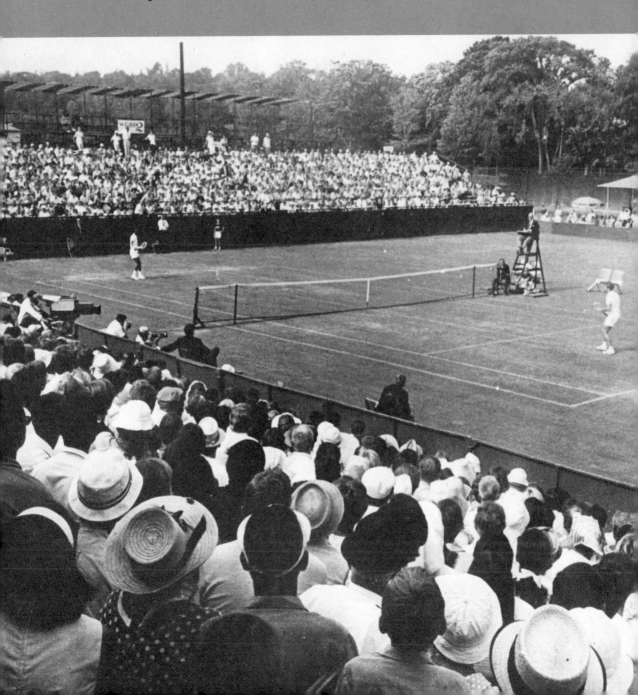

VII
Etiquette and Spectating

CHAPTER 20

Etiquette

SPORTSMANSHIP

"Nice guys lose" is a very popular saying these days. In an attempt to be a good competitor many people think it helps to have bad manners. The reverse is more often true. A bad call wins a point and is on a player's mind for the rest of the match. Did the player gain or lose? Bad conduct such as stalling may upset one's opponent, but it also antagonizes all who behold. Did the staller gain or lose? By contrast, a match is very seldom lost by the one or two close ones handed an opponent when a player wasn't sure they were out. The player's conscience is clear, he can fight his hardest all the way, and the crowd is seldom against him.

The depth of a player's sportsmanship is severely tested when his opponent cheats. Does the player retaliate? Or does he really believe in his ethics so that he calls the shots straight no matter what someone else does on the other side of the net? This is the most difficult thing to do, but it remains the only correct answer to such a situation. It is the code of the game that says, "Call them right," and a player accepts that code when he walks on the court.

This does not mean that a player sits supinely while a crook steals the shirt off his back. In a tournament or any kind of a match a player may stop and refuse to continue with-

out a referee, stating clearly that he thinks the lines are not being called correctly. In a friendly game the player should ignore the cheating, but refuse to play with that person again. He will get the point, for no one knows better than the cheater that he is cheating, and like all thieves he is continually in a sweat about being found out. So making repeated excuses will let him know with certainty why the player's attitude has taken this turn. Being a nice guy by no means equates with being a soft guy. It is quite possible—and desirable—to be as hard as flint in dealing with cheating without any of this "fight fire with fire" stuff that is so often used as an excuse to cheat back. Cheating back destroys the whole strength of one's position. It all adds up to the fact that the only sound policy is never to cheat under any circumstances whatever, because no circumstances whatever are an adequate excuse or justification.

The Davis Cup Final in 1972 in Europe was a great example of the point being made here. Our opponents took every opportunity to behave questionably, had the gallery on their side, and in many cases the officials (linesmen, etc.) made concrete and blatantly partisan decisions in their favor. We can be very proud that the Americans refused to be drawn into similar muddy conduct, and comported themselves impeccably throughout. And what was the result? The conditions were as adverse as is conceivably possible, yet the Americans' fortitude and competitive determination were so hardened by this ill treatment that they just wouldn't lose. It was their opponents who faltered and failed to realize their best hopes. To the surprise of the cynics, the nice guys won, and moreover had the further satisfaction of knowing there was not even the slightest taint attached to their prize, themselves, or their country.

The person who is a good sport always has a lot of friends and admirers, wins as much and usually more than the poor sport, and spreads a little happiness around himself instead of a lot of murky ill-feeling. Tennis is a great game. It should be kept that way. So let this section close with the assurance that nice guys and gals usually win the prize and always get the respect and most of the fun.

MANNERS

It is always necessary to explain to players that a line call is not a subject for argument—you call them on your side, the other fellow on his. They argue shrilly, "I *saw* it!" when it was on the other side of the net, and more time is spent in shrieking at each other—a dismal spectacle—than in actual play. This can be so bad it is funny when four youthful doubles players get to raging at each other over a simple out or in call. It is a good idea to give a talk at group lessons—five or ten minutes is ample—to get the idea across that argument is futile, time wasting, and bad manners.

A few other details can bear mentioning. One player gives a ball to another by bouncing it to him conveniently; it is very rude to hit it any old place, forcing him to chase it. When beginning a rally, the player should hit gently so he can get the rally going; he should not blast the opponent off the court with a hard deep one. The server calls out the score after each point, thus avoiding lengthy arguments and post mortems. The second ball should not

be "quick served" after missing the first; one's opponent has a right to take up a new position if he wishes. Consideration of other players, when developed into a habit, requires no thought or effort, and the absence of the simple courtesies will alienate many people in a short time.

DRESS

Custom in tennis has in the past specified white, and this has set tennis players apart for many years as the most attractively dressed of all athletes. Recently there has been a determined uprising against what appeared to some as a stuffy, autocratic, and snobbish regulation, to be attacked as much (or more) for its aura of dictatorial control as for its lack of merit. The argument has for the most part been emotional. What follows is an attempt at a rational analysis.

It should be clearly established to start with that there is only one attitude that can be justified—namely, that in any formal event, players should be presentable. To argue that a boy should and must have short hair is absurd. To ask that he comb it and control it when representing himself or any institution such as a college or club is reasonable. But even this requirement is so vague and so open to argument that it would seem impossible to formulate an ironclad rule. It appears that good taste cannot be legislated or enforced without subjective dictatorial control, which is one main bone of contention in the current controversy. One is up against the same difficulties—so far apparently insoluble—that confront those who would define and legislate obscenity. It's a fine idea, most of us are for it, but no one seems able to do it! It is probably fair to draw the conclusion that the whole concept is so purely a matter of opinion that no definitive ruling is possible.

The old tradition has much in its favor. White is so cool, so clean looking, that it is always a pleasure to behold a dozen club courts filled with players all in white. This, of course, is a subjective judgment by the author, and is offered with no pretense of further authority. Doubtless it should be modified, to admit there are other cool colors such as pastels, and that a touch of color here and there can be very attractive. But the thesis is offered: tennis has always been a cool game and white is the coolest, so the old standard was well founded even if too rigid in the opinion of many.

It is suggested that we can have freedom and at the same time good taste, and the greatest teacher is example. Let's not be hide bound, but let's keep tennis cool: when you've got a good thing, hang on to it!

Beyond this attitude it is stuffy and unfair to enforce formality. Children love to go barefoot; let them, it is healthy. They like to wear blue jeans, often sawed off at the knees to give a vaguely Huck Finn atmosphere. Let them; there is no harm, and it is a saving to their parents. Whites all the time can be expensive. Moreover, children go from cutting a lawn or sailing or swimming directly to the tennis courts without going home. To insist that they change every time approaches a new high in pointless discipline. This is the old "clothes make the man" approach that died long ago and goes over like a lead balloon these days.

There are, of course, limits. Many are offended if a player goes entirely shirtless. In deference to these it is good at a club or a park to enforce a "shirts on" rule. In general, a reasonable decorum should be enforced and is justifiable. People should be presentable, and what this means at any given tennis center must be played a bit by ear. Geography can make a difference: it can be dangerous to go barefoot in some places, or the courts are too hot, etc. About the only general rules that can be made are that cool colors are de rigueur for matches and reasonable presentability at other times.

QUESTIONS

1. What are your feelings about the controversy over "all white is proper for tennis"?

2. Does having good manners mean one is "soft"?

3. Do nice guys lose?

4. Give a few examples of good versus bad manners: constantly recurring situations on the court.

CHAPTER 21

Watching Tennis

SPECTATOR TECHNIQUE

As thousands of new fans are created by the current tennis explosion, it is clear from the reactions of the gallery that many have little idea of what is going on before their eyes. Not having watched much tennis, they confine their attention to the ball and thereby miss many fine points that have a decisive effect on what occurs. There are actually a good many different ways to watch a match, and spectators, particularly those wishing to learn something for the benefit of their own game, would do well to vary their manner of watching. It is surprising how interesting and enlightening it is to adopt first one approach, then another. What follows describes a few of the spectating tricks that can be very rewarding in perceiving what a player is doing and how he does it. This can apply to technique, tactics, and strategy.

WATCHING THE SERVER EXCLUSIVELY

Keep your eyes on the server even after he has played the ball. If he takes the net, watch how he moves in quickly after serving, then hesitates, crouched, ready to break to either side for the return. Watch where he puts his first volley and the position he takes up in anticipation of the second return, always crouched. Note how he anticipates *forward*, seldom sideways, so as to get on top of the net. Watch his quick reaction when the opponent lobs. You can see just how he does it by *not* watching the ball, just watching him all the way.

WATCHING THE DEFENDER EXCLUSIVELY

Take note of where the defender stands to receive service. If the service is severe, note his abbreviated swing, and how he tries to move his weight into the ball to get solidity into his shot. When he tries a passing shot in the subsequent exchange, watch his racket technique—does he hit it flat and hard, or does he spin it a lot to make a dipping angle shot? How good is he at lobbing the second or third shot? Does he do it? What do you think *he* is thinking? Does he strike our daringly on his return of service, playing for lucky winners, or does he play for the server's feet, trying to get him in trouble rather than try for a winner? What is his plan? How often does he return crosscourt rather than down the line? Is his plan the same off his forehand and backhand, or does he return differently off the two sides? If you keep watching him alone you can often discern a great deal of his thinking in the battle of wits he wages against the attacker. Tennis is a thinking game. Get with it!

CONCENTRATING ON SERVICE

The greatest servers are often confronted by the greatest defenders. Keep mental track of how often the server uses his "bomb," how often he breaks one out wide to the forehand in the right court, how often he serves directly at him, how often he changes the speed and break of the ball by increasing or decreasing the amount of spin, how often he curves one in close to cramp the receiver. All these tricks are comparable to those of a baseball pitcher who mixes up fast balls, hooks, sliders, slow balls, etc. A great server doesn't just hit the ball well. He is a canny thinker who usually manages to keep his opponent guessing a little—off balance both mentally and physically. By concentrating your thinking on the service alone you can achieve considerable perception into what each is doing to the other. This makes it all much more interesting for you.

ADVANTAGES OF WATCHING SLOW SURFACE TENNIS

Composition courts (often called "clay," which they are not) are slower than grass, hard courts, and synthetics. Therefore, the defender has a much better chance to achieve respectability with his return, thus forcing a more lengthy exchange. While the server still has an advantage, it is no longer so decisive as on a fast surface. This makes for much more interesting tennis. Instead of the eternal net player against the baseline defender, we see some baseline rallies, a "battle of the backhands," and shots that are just about totally missing in

fast court tennis, such as the drop shot, now become part of the game. More varied techniques and tactics are demanded of the players. Instead of being able to say, "Here I come —try to stop me," the server now finds the defender can indeed stop him quite frequently if his attack is unvaried and obvious. This makes for much more interesting tennis for the spectator, more thinking by the players, and far more doubt as to whether each player will indeed win his service. And doubt is what makes any contest exciting. A close contest by two average players is far more worth watching than a cut-and-dried performance by a top player winning with ease. *Sports Illustrated* recently wrote that Ivy League football is more interesting and exciting to watch than any other football, pro or amateur. Why? Because the teams are so evenly matched, they use many varied types of offense and defense, and the issue is usually in doubt down to the last few minutes, sometimes the last few seconds. Certainly the teams are not the best, but they are the best to watch. "Clay" tennis creates a comparable situation. One service break is no guarantee of a set; the tide and momentum can turn at any time. This is the formula for good spectating. Power still has its place, but is by no means totally in charge.

WATCHING FOR STYLE ON CLAY

On fast surfaces all good players are forced into one type of offense: follow service to net. The defender is thus confined to limited choices: play for his feet as he comes in, strike out for a winner, bang it right at him, or lob. On clay he has more options. His opponent is not always at net. He can attack one side of his opponent's game and try to break it down. He can use slices to create a kick bounce, hoping to hurt the other fellow's timing. When he gets a short ball he can attack all four corners of his opponent's court, using drop shots (suction) as a variation from hard hitting (pressure). His opponent must bear all this in mind when the crisis occurs. There are many more opportunities for retrieving and angling, and a high deep lob is very difficult to kill. He can be a "counterplayer," using his opponent's power to his own ends. Agility and court covering and steadiness pay greater dividends. Altogether the complete tennis player is the clay player, and spectators have far more opportunity to see all the possibilities of the game on clay than on a fast court, and should again use varied watching techniques to discern what the players are doing and thinking.

WATCHING FOR TECHNIQUE

Here it is very important *not* to watch the ball. Watch one player, watch him prepare his racket and feet, watch his racket leave the ball as well as come to it—watch what he does almost to the total exclusion of the ball. While ordinary spectators are interested in the action and the result of the exchange, the technical analyst is interested only in what the player actually does with himself and his racket.

The most difficult thing to do is to learn to watch the racket *leave* the ball, as has been pointed out. Our natural curiosity causes us to watch the ball to see where it goes. This is fatal to thorough analysis, since the follow-through shows a great deal of what actually happened, to the ball (spin), and to the weight (pace). It takes a little effort of the will to do this, but all instructors are urged to acquire the ability to do this since it is essential to understanding technique and to being a good analyst with one's students.

If an instructor encourages promising players to do a good bit of varied types of spectating, they will often derive much more from a match than the excitement of the contest. They will pick up skills and tricks, both tactical and technical, and it will be a more concrete and lasting contribution to their improvement than the "inspiration" one gets from watching

true professionals do their stuff. Their understanding is deepened and their knowledge is increased, so they both play better and become more adept at adjusting to their opponents, finding a weakness, and finding ways to win.

Students and players should be cautioned not to be bowled over by one or two spectacular shots. "Watch what he does *all* the time." "Notice Billie Jean *always* gets her second service *deep*, so it isn't a winner, but she has the advantage, and wins the percentage." A great player knows his greatest shots always involve some luck and are nonpercentage. The audience seldom does. They see the player, in a hopeless predicament, strike out for a one-in-six possibility—and *make it*. They go home thinking, "That's what the great players do!" when the fact is they never try such shots except when there is everything to gain and nothing to lose, and the point, percentage-wise, is already lost. Watch what they do again and again—their bread and butter game—and it at once becomes clear they are very, very *tough* and take few if any unnecessary risks. This is the message spectating students should take home.

Another point should be stressed with students. They should be advised to spend half their time watching the *receiver*, having their eyes on him when the ball is being served, not on the server. The natural thing to do is to watch the server and follow the ball to the receiver. By this time the receiver's racket is playing the ball; you didn't see at all how he reacted, how his racket got there. Thus, as a rule spectators learn little about defensive tricks. They are *always* watching the offense. Yet receiving is 50 percent of the game, and therefore deserves 50 percent of our attention. Again it takes an effort, but is well worth it.

DOUBLES SPECTATING

Doubles is a team sport. Most of those in the huge new tennis audience think of tennis as an individual sport. Actually doubles is more interesting to watch than singles. Why? Because there are many two-shot plays in which one player creates an opportunity and his partner capitalizes, and there are many planned moves, poaches, half poaches, fake poaches, and even rotation, whereby one team attempts to confuse the other. There is a lot going on: the players *not* playing the ball move a lot, anticipate, cut in, retreat, etc. All tennis spectators should become familiar with doubles and, as in singles, should at times purposely avoid watching the ball and instead concentrate on one player exclusively: the receiver, the receiver's partner, or the server's partner.

It is probably a reasonable prediction that doubles spectating will grow in popularity as the new tennis audience comes to understand and appreciate it, because it is the best game for spectators. Don't be a laggard; be one of the first to get with it, intelligently and knowledgeably. It's worth the effort.

NEW DEVELOPMENTS

Marathon Matches

Until the recent burst of tennis into the "big money" and television, no one worried about how long a tennis match lasted. Marathon matches were common, with some going to truly phenomenal lengths involving sets that reached 22-20 and even higher (the Davis Cup record is something like 39-37!). Matches were discontinued because of darkness and resumed the following day. There was even considerable pleasure in the thought, "How long will this go on? Isn't it amazing!"

Such an unpredictable situation is totally unacceptable for tightly scheduled television coverage and big money events with each round preplanned, tickets sold in advance, and starting times advertised. A conclusion must be reached within a specified time, the next event must start on time, and there must be some way of maintaining the schedule.

Sudden Death

Led by the ingenious proposals of Jimmy Van Alen, the imaginative innovator of VASSS (Van Alen Simplified Scoring System) and creator of the Tennis Hall of Fame at Newport, R.I., various schemes have been tried and are presently being tested in leading events. All are calculated to control the time involved in a match, and all involve a new element: sudden death. This means that when a tie has reached a certain stage, the next point is game point, or set point, or match point, or all three —both ways.

The Tie-Breakers

Most popular, and by now quite generally accepted, is the nine point tie-breaker that can take place in any set at six games all. The players alternate, serving two points each, until one has won five points. If the score reaches four points all, the last server serves once more, but the receiver has choice of court (left or right). The winner of that point wins the set.

There is also a less popular twelve point tie-breaker, in which the old requirement of being two points ahead in order to win still obtains. This is less popular, since the old interminable return to deuce is still in force.

The No-Ad Seven Point Game

A more recent development is the introduction of sudden death into each game, ruling that when the score reaches deuce (three points each), the winner of the seventh point wins the game. Again the receiver has choice of court (left or right). This is being used by the NCAA and many college leagues.

You'll Like It

People accustomed to the old scoring system are often disturbed at first by these "queer" developments. But they make sense in many ways, and make the game more exciting to watch. The gain in managing the time element is so obvious as to need little discussion. If a game can't go beyond seven points, and a set can't go beyond a high of seven-six, then a match is sure to be concluded within a calculable period. This is good for many besides television schedulers. All tournaments, where players often waited hours while the previous round dragged on, can now be planned with assurance that a player scheduled to play at a given hour will actually play at or very near that time. Those who have waited and waited —and waited some more—will be very grateful. College and school matches, often incomplete by dark, will now reach a verdict and avoid such an inconclusive conclusion, unsatisfactory to both parties. Few people realize that a tennis team match has for years been by far the longest athletic event, longer than cross country or anything else. Numberless matches were "incomplete because of darkness," with the dining halls closed, the gym forced to stay open long overtime so the players could shower afterwards, and everybody involved late for anything he or she might have planned. So this control of the total elapsed time is a real improvement for the whole of tennis, not merely television. Scheduling is no longer chaotic or impossible.

Players Gain Too

The main criticism of tennis as a spectator sport has been that the server tends to dominate too easily, that there is not enough doubt, suspense, and tension as to who is going to win each game. Sudden death, particularly the seven point game, changes this. A server who misses a couple and gets to thirty-forty now faces *two* break points, not one, because the "deuce" point is game point both ways. This means the server must be more careful not to get behind early in the game, and must consider fifteen-thirty a very dangerous situa-

tion. The suspense begins immediately if the server gets a point behind. One big service will not extricate him. It takes two, and this is not easy against a determined defender. Thus the receiver now has a better chance of achieving a service break and this improves the game for all.

Spectators Gain Most

Above all the spectators gain. They know when a match will occur and about when it will end. They can plan something afterward. Most important, there will be many more tense situations, and sometimes that real moment of truth when the whole match hangs on *this point*, both ways. True, it is tough on the players, but it is great for the spectators.

There is nothing new in all this. It is not a wild experiment. For many years the game of squash racquets has had this type of sudden death scoring, and intercollegiate and national championships have on quite a few occasions come down to the "last point." The suspense builds to an incredible tension, the final point is played before a totally absorbed gallery, everyone holds his breath, and a great burst of applause occurs at the end, followed by total emotional exhaustion. Can a spectator ask for more?

The game is getting better, the prevalence of first-class players has increased enormously, and the current experimental improvements or something close to them will almost certainly become the accepted style of play. It behooves the spectator to familiarize himself with things like tie-breaker, no-add game, pro set (first to reach eight games with two-game lead wins the match, tie-breaker at eight all), intercollegiate set (first to reach twelve, tie-breaker at twelve all), etc. Marathons are a thing of the past. The modern match is keen, lethal, and decisive—with no way of holding off or delaying the final gut issue. Learn about sudden death: you'll like it.

TEAM TENNIS—A NEW APPROACH

The recent appearance of team tennis introduces a wholly new aspect to spectating. The public wants to participate as well as to behold, as in basketball, hockey, football, and baseball. This means yelling, cheering, "riding the opponent," and all the other forms spectator involvement takes in other sports. This is a great shock to players and old-style spectators alike, accustomed as they are to the decorous, inhibited traditions that decree, "Do not cheer errors," "Do not make noise while the ball is in play," etc. The fact is, whether one likes it or not, the change is here to stay. To tell spectators not to cheer when an opponent makes an error is like asking them not to cheer a fumble recovery by the home team in football.

The public pays for tickets and feels it has a right to be part of the action. Spectators will demand this right (they already have) and it is up to the old-timers and the players to get used to it.

QUESTIONS

1. Why watch the player exclusively instead of the ball?

2. What aspects of the defender's play should the spectator watch?

3. How does clay (composition) court play enhance the spectator's ability to watch and learn?

4. How does team tennis affect spectating?

Index

Special Orientation Chart